D1711981

Modern
Canadian
Verse

Modern
Canadian
Verse

In English and French

A. J. M. Smith

Toronto
Oxford University Press
1967

PUBLICATION OF THIS BOOK WAS ASSISTED BY THE CANADA COUNCIL

Printed and bound in England by
HAZELL WATSON AND VINEY LTD
AYLESBURY, BUCKS

CONTENTS

xvii PREFACE

xix ACKNOWLEDGEMENTS

E. J. PRATT
1883–1964
  1 From *The Cachalot*
  7 From *Towards the Last Spike*
 10 From *Behind the Log*

PAUL MORIN
1889–1963
 12 À ceux de mon pays
 13 Harmonie pour un soir
    d'Italie
 15 Musique des noms
 17 Le plus aimé de mes jardins
    arabes . . .
 18 Perdrix

W. W. E. ROSS
1894–1966
 18 Fish
 19 The Snake Trying
 20 The Creek
 20 On Angels

F. R. SCOTT
b. 1899
 21 Lakeshore
 23 Vision
 24 Cloth of Gold
 25 Bangkok
 26 À l'ange avantgardien
 26 A Lass in Wonderland

CONTENTS

ROBERT FINCH
b. 1900

28 Aria Senza da Capo
28 Turning
29 Room
29 The Collective Portrait

ALAIN GRANDBOIS
b. 1900

30 L'Étoile pourpre
33 Noces
36 Cris

ALFRED DESROCHERS
b. 1901

39 Je suis un fils déchu
41 Hymne au vent du nord
45 'City-Hotel'

ROY DANIELLS
b. 1902

46 Journey

A. J. M. SMITH
b. 1902

48 News of the Phoenix
49 Resurrection Arp
50 Ballade un peu banale
51 Brigadier
53 What the Emanation of
   Casey Jones Said to the
   Medium
54 Watching the Old Man Die

RONALD EVERSON
b. 1903

55 Laprairie Hunger Strike
55 Cold-Weather Love
56 Old Snapshot
56 Letter from Underground

SIMONE ROUTIER
b. 1903

56 Neige et nostalgie
57 Le divin anéantissement

vi

EARLE BIRNEY
b. 1904

59 Bushed
61 Midstream
62 The Bear on the Delhi Road
63 El Greco : *Espolio*
64 Cartagena de Indias
69 Sinalóa

ROBERT CHOQUETTE
b. 1905

71 Vivre et créer
72 From *Suite marine*

FRANÇOIS HERTEL
b. 1905

78 Art poétique
79 Au pays de Québec
81 Le Chante de l'exilé

MALCOLM LOWRY
1909–1957

85 Salmon Drowns Eagle
86 Sestina in a Cantina
88 Xochitepec
89 Christ Walks in This Infernal
District Too

A. M. KLEIN
b. 1909

90 Autobiographical
93 *In re* Solomon Warshawer
99 Political Meeting
101 Monsieur Gaston
102 Montreal

JOHN GLASSCO
b. 1909

104 The Rural Mail
105 The Entailed Farm
107 The Cardinal's Dog
108 Brummell at Calais
109 The Day

CONTENTS

DOROTHY LIVESAY
b. 1909

114 Fantasia
116 The Prophetess
120 The Leader

RALPH GUSTAFSON
b. 1909

121 Armorial
122 Transfigured Night
122 My Love Eats an Apple
123 The Swans of Vadstena
123 In the Yukon

ANNE WILKINSON
1910–1961

124 In June and Gentle Oven
125 Leda in Stratford, Ont.
126 The Red and the Green
127 Lens
129 Adam and God
130 Falconry
131 Variations on a Theme

WILFRED WATSON
b. 1911

134 Invocation
134 Canticle of Darkness
136 The White Bird
137 Emily Carr

SAINT-DENYS GARNEAU
1912–1943

138 Le Jeu
140 Accompagnement
141 Monde irrémédiable désert
142 Poids et mesures
143 From *La Mort grandissante*

GEORGE WOODCOCK
b. 1912

147 Imagine the South
148 The Island

IRVING LAYTON
b. 1912

149 The Birth of Tragedy
150 Berry Picking
151 Cain
153 The Day Aviva Came to Paris
156 A Tall Man Executes a Jig

GEORGE JOHNSTON
b. 1913

160 Music on the Water
161 Noctambule
161 The Bulge
162 O Earth, Turn!

DOUGLAS LE PAN
b. 1914

162 A Country Without a
    Mythology
163 Coureurs de bois
165 An Incident
166 Nimbus

PATRICK ANDERSON
b. 1915

167 From *Poem on Canada*

R. A. D. FORD
b. 1915

174 A Window on the North
175 Back to Dublin
176 Revenge of the Hunted

GEORGE WHALLEY
b. 1915

176 Affair of Honour

RINA LASNIER
b. 1915

178 La Malemer

ANNE HÉBERT
b. 1916

185 La Chambre fermée
187 Le Tombeau des rois
189 Vie de château
189 La Fille maigre
190 Mystère de la parole
192 Ève

CONTENTS

ELDON GRIER
b. 1917
194 'More than Most People'
195 'Sensible is the Label'
196 'I Am Almost Asleep'
196 On the Subject of Waves ...

P. K. PAGE
b. 1917
197 Element
198 Images of Angels
201 Puppets
202 Man with One Small Hand
203 Arras

MIRIAM WADDINGTON
b. 1917
204 Catalpa Tree
205 My Lessons in the Jail
206 The Season's Lovers

MARGARET AVISON
b. 1918
207 Intra-Political
211 Voluptuaries and Others
212 In a Season of
Unemployment
213 A Story
216 The Word
218 For Dr and Mrs Dresser

LOUIS DUDEK
b. 1918
219 García Lorca
221 From *Provincetown*
224 The Marine Aquarium (from *Atlantis*)

ALFRED PURDY
b. 1918
228 Evergreen Cemetery
229 Wilderness Gothic
230 Dead Seal
232 What Do the Birds Think?
234 The Winemaker's Beat-étude

PETER MILLER
b. 1920

236 The Prevention of Stacy
    Miller
237 The Capture of Edwin
    Alonzo Boyd

GILLES HÉNAULT
b. 1920

240 Sémaphore
246 Bestiaire
249 Notre Jeunesse

ÉLOI DE GRANDMONT
b. 1921

251 From *Le Voyage d'Arlequin*
252 Le Chasseur
253 Les Parents exemplaires

RAYMOND SOUSTER
b. 1921

254 May 15th
257 Ladybug
257 The Six-Quart Basket
257 Ties
258 Choosing Coffins

ELI MANDEL
b. 1922

259 Minotaur Poem II
259 Four Songs from the Book of
    Samuel
261 Song

MILTON ACORN
b. 1923

262 I've Tasted My Blood
263 The Fights

PIERRE TROTTIER
b. 1925

264 Femme aux couleurs de mon
    pays
265 Les Malédictions
266 Le Soldat inconnu
267 Le Temps corrigé

FRANCIS SPARSHOTT
b. 1926

268 Entanglement
269 Improperia
270 Paysage choisi

JAMES REANEY
b. 1926

271 The Katzenjammer Kids
272 From *A Suit of Nettles*
274 Le Tombeau de Pierre Falcon
275 To the Avon River Above
Stratford, Canada

PHYLLIS GOTLIEB
b. 1926

277 This One's On Me

DAVID KNIGHT
b. 1926

280 'When the Students Resisted,
a Minor Clash Ensued'
281 The Chief of the West,
Darkling
283 In Memoriam S. L. Akintola,
January 15, 1966
284 The Palms

PHYLLIS WEBB
b. 1927

285 Propositions
286 'The Time of Man'
287 Poetics Against the Angel of
Death

JEAN-PAUL FILION
b. 1927

288 Rien à manger
289 Géographie du labeur
quotidien
290 Feu contre fer

GILLES VIGNEAULT
b. 1928

291 Mon pays
292 Chanson
293 Quelqu'un était ici

PAUL-MARIE LAPOINTE
b. 1929

293 Arbres

ROLAND GIGUÈRE
b. 1929

299 Vivre mieux
300 Mémoire d'ombre
301 La Vie dévisagée
303 Roses et ronces
305 Histoire naturelle

D. G. JONES
b. 1929

307 I Thought There Were Limits
308 The Perishing Bird
310 Soliloquy to Absent Friends
314 Beautiful Creatures Brief as
      These

PETER DALE SCOTT
b. 1929

314 Argenteuil County
317 The Loon's Egg

HENRY BEISSEL
b. 1929

319 From *New Wings for Icarus*

JEAN-GUY PILON
b. 1930

322 L'Étranger d'ici
323 Les Cloîtres de l'été . . .
324 'Je murmure le nom de mon
      pays'

FERNAND OUELLETTE
b. 1930

326 Femme
327 Géologie
328 Langue de l'aile

SYLVAIN GARNEAU
1930–1953

329 Mon École
330 Le Jeu
331 La bonne entente

GATIEN LAPOINTE
b. 1931

332 Au Ras de la terre
333 Le Temps premier
334 From *Ode au Saint-Laurent*

JAY MACPHERSON
b. 1932

340 'Go take the World'
340 The Martyrs
341 Hail Wedded Love!
341 Leviathan
342 The Beauty of Job's
Daughters
342 The Third Eye
343 The Boatman
344 The Ill Wind

ALDEN NOWLAN
b. 1933

344 God Sour the Milk of the
Knacking Wench
345 The Wickedness of Peter
Shannon
346 The Grove Beyond the
Barley
347 Stoney Ridge Dance Hall

JOE ROSENBLATT
b. 1933

348 Metamorpho I
349 Saphire (Metamorpho's
Chick)

JACQUES GODBOUT
b. 1933

350 From *Les Pavés secs*
352 Parce que ton nom
355 Ces Racines

LEONARD COHEN
b. 1934

356 Out of the Land of Heaven
357 The Genius
358 The Only Tourist in Havana
Turns his Thoughts
Homeward

GEORGE BOWERING
b. 1935

360 The Grass
360 Moon Shadow
362 Inside the Tulip
362 Está muy caliente

DARYL HINE
b. 1935

364 The Double-Goer
367 Under the Hill
367 Trompe l'Œil

GEORGE JONAS
b. 1935

369 For the Record
370 Four Stanzas Written in
Anxiety

DAVID WEVILL
b. 1935

371 In Love
372 Snow
373 Spiders
374 Body of a Rook

JOHN ROBERT COLOMBO
b. 1936

376 Ideal Angels
377 How They Made the Golem

MICHÈLE LALONDE
b. 1937

379 Le Silence effrité
380 Le Jour halluciné
381 Combien doux
382 La Fiancée

SUZANNE PARADIS
b. 1937

383 Dépouillements
385 Les Naissances secondes
386 Le Coup de grâce

LIONEL KEARNS
b. 1937

387 Stuntman

CONTENTS

JOHN NEWLOVE
b. 1938   389 The Double-Headed Snake
             390 The Pride

GÉRALD GODIN
b. 1938   397 Pour Maria (1)
             399 Cantouque d'amour

MARGARET ATWOOD
b. 1939   401 The Explorers
             402 The Settlers
             403 Eventual Proteus
             405 Against Still Life
             407 From 'The Circle Game'

WILLIAM HAWKINS
b. 1940   412 The Wall
             413 A New Light
             413 Spring Rain

GWENDOLYN MACEWEN
b. 1941   414 Arcanum One
             415 The Caravan
             416 The Thing is Violent

ANDRÉ MAJOR
b. 1942   416 Verte ma parole
             418 Toute douceur d'une fille

ANDRÉ BROCHU
b. 1942   419 Indicatif présent
             419 Un Enfant du pays
             421 L'Espoir pays sauvé

ROBERT HOGG
b. 1942   422 Little Falls
             423 Poem

MICHAEL ONDAATJE
b. 1943   424 A House Divided

             425 INDEX OF AUTHORS

xvi

PREFACE

This book has grown out of what was to have been a new edition of *The Oxford Book of Canadian Verse*, brought up to date and enlarged by a generous selection of the new poetry of the late fifties and sixties. It soon became clear that an emphasis on the present and the future rather than on historical sequence demanded a new book and a new proportion. The development of Canadian verse since the rise of modernism in the twenties could not be presented as an appendage to the poetry of the nineteenth century. It would be better to let it stand by itself.

And I think it better to let it speak for itself – hence no long and analytical introduction. And no formal or tendentious classifications. The only order imposed on the poems is the conventional one of chronology, and the only pattern is that which is inescapably suggested by the fact that *these* particular poems by *these* particular poets have been chosen. I believe them to be representative of the variety and quality of the best work being done in Canada today. All but a scant half-dozen of the poets are still living; most of them are actively and continuously writing and publishing. The oldest, like Scott or Grandbois or Birney, are writing as well as or better than they ever did, and the youngest, like Newlove or Lalonde or Atwood, give promise of a maturity and cogency that suggest that the next decade in Canadian verse will be as exciting as the last.

There are some assumptions, of course, that every anthologist has to make – assumptions of a limiting or defining sort. This collection aims at variety, and it seeks to be representative – not of the average but of the best. There are qualitative standards of judgement, for which the editor must accept responsibility, relying with what fortitude he can upon nothing more impregnable than his own taste and learning. (Let honesty and good will at least be granted him.) What I have thought of as modern Canadian poetry for the purposes of this anthology is verse of a certain technical distinction that expresses implicitly the special character imposed by geography, climate, history, and society upon an individual poetic temperament. In the last thirty-five years or so the poetry conditioned if not produced by factors of this sort has been modified in a unique way by the technological revolution that is altering the whole world.

Instantaneous communication, electronic and nuclear devices, and the universal half-education supplied by the mass-media have created a very self-conscious world divided into economic and ideological clusters but united by a common fear of possible annihilation. As a result, Canadian poetry in the fifties and sixties has become more like modern poetry in the United States, England, and France, and less like Canadian poetry in the nineteenth century. The distinction that was once valid between a native and a cosmopolitan tradition has grown rapidly less significant. Local, regional, and national influences, whether geographic or social, are ceasing to be of first importance. If no man is an island, neither is any nation an island, even so huge and mainly an empty one as Canada. It is not so much that nationalism has been rejected, of course, as that it has been absorbed. Modern Canadian poetry, I believe this anthology will show, has not left nationalism behind but has transcended it. It has developed a sensibility and a language that are international but not rootless – a biculturalism that joins more than French and English Canada (although some of the younger poets writing in French consider themselves poets of Québec, not of Canada). It joins Canada to the world.

Drummond Point
Lake Memphremagog
Québec
6 MAY *1967*

A.J.M.S.

ACKNOWLEDGEMENTS

Thanks for permission to include copyright poems by the following authors are due to the copyright-holders listed. Sources for the poems are given (whenever possible) in the short bibliographical note that follows each acknowledgement.

ACORN, MILTON : The Ryerson Press.
'I've Tasted My Blood', *Jawbreakers* (Toronto : Contact Press, 1963); 'The Fights', *The Brain's the Target* (Toronto : Ryerson Press, 1960).

ANDERSON, PATRICK : The Ryerson Press.
From 'Poem on Canada', *The White Centre* (Toronto : Ryerson Press, 1946).

ATWOOD, MARGARET : Miss Atwood.
The Circle Game (Toronto : Contact Press, 1966).

AVISON, MARGARET : Miss Avison.
'Intra-Political', 'Voluptuaries and Others', *Winter Sun* (Toronto and London : University of Toronto Press, 1960); 'In a Season of Unemployment', 'A Story', 'The Word', 'For Dr and Mrs Dresser', *The Dumbfounding* (New York : Norton, 1966).

BEISSEL, HENRY : Mr Beissel.
New Wings for Icarus (Toronto : Coach House Press, 1966).

BIRNEY, EARLE : By permission of the Canadian Publishers, McClelland and Stewart Limited, Toronto.
Selected Poems (Toronto : McClelland and Stewart, 1966).

BOWERING, GEORGE : Mr Bowering.
The Man in Yellow Boots (Mexico : Ediciones el Corno Emplumado, 1965).

BROCHU, ANDRÉ : M. Brochu.
Uncollected.

CHOQUETTE, ROBERT : M. Choquette.
Oeuvres Poétiques (Montreal and Paris : Éditions Fides, 1967).

COHEN, LEONARD : By permission of the Canadian Publishers, McClelland and Stewart Limited, Toronto, and the Viking Press Inc., New York.
'Out of the Land of Heaven', 'The Genius', *Spice Box of Earth* (Toronto : McClelland and Stewart, 1961); 'The Only Tourist in Havana Turns his Thoughts Homeward', *Flowers for Hitler* (Toronto : McClelland and Stewart, 1964).

ACKNOWLEDGEMENTS

COLOMBO, JOHN ROBERT: By permission of the Canadian Publishers, McClelland and Stewart Limited, Toronto.
Abracadabra (Toronto: McClelland and Stewart, 1967).

DANIELLS, ROY: Mr Daniells.
Uncollected.

DESROCHERS, ALFRED: La Corporation des Éditions Fides, Montreal.
À l'ombre de l'Orford (Montreal: Éditions Fides, 1929).

DUDEK, LOUIS: Mr Dudek.
'García Lorca', *East of The City* (Toronto: Ryerson Press, 1946); From 'Provincetown', *The Transparent Sea* (Toronto: Contact Press, 1956); 'The Marine Aquarium', *Atlantis* (Montreal: Delta Canada, 1967).

EVERSON, RONALD: Mr Everson.
A Lattice for Momos (Toronto: Contact Press, 1958).

FILION, JEAN-PAUL: M. Filion and Les Éditions de l'Hexagone, Montreal
Du centre de l'eau (Montreal: Éditions de l'Hexagone, 1955).

FINCH, ROBERT: The University of Toronto Press and the Oxford University Press, Canadian Branch.
'Aria Senza da Capo', 'Turning', 'Room', *Acis in Oxford and Other Poems* (Toronto: University of Toronto Press, 1961); 'The Collective Portrait', *Poems* (Toronto: Oxford University Press, 1946).

FORD, R. A. D.: The Ryerson Press.
A Window on the North (Toronto: Ryerson Press, 1956).

GARNEAU, SAINT-DENYS: La Corporation des Éditions Fides, Montreal.
Poésies Complètes (Montreal: Éditions Fides, 1949).

GARNEAU, SYLVAIN
'Mon École', *Objets trouvés* (1951); 'Le Jeu' *Les Trouble-fête* (1952).

GIGUERE, ROLAND: M. Giguere and Les Éditions de l'Hexagone, Montreal.
L'Âge de la parole (Montreal: Éditions de l'Hexagone, 1965).

GLASSCO, JOHN: Mr Glassco and the Oxford University Press, Canadian Branch.
'The Rural Mail', 'The Entailed Farm', 'The Cardinal's Dog', *The Deficit Made Flesh* (Toronto: McClelland and Stewart, 1958); 'Brummell at Calais', 'The Day', *A Point of Sky* (Toronto: Oxford University Press, 1964).

GODBOUT, JACQUES: M. Godbout.
From *Les Pavés secs* (Montreal: Éditions, Beauchemin, 1959); 'Parce que ton nom', 'Ces Racines', *C'est la chaude loi des hommes* (Montreal: Éditions de l'Hexagone, 1960).

GODIN, GÉRALD: M. Godin.
Uncollected.

GOTLIEB, PHYLLIS: By permission of the Canadian Publishers, McClelland and Stewart Limited, Toronto.
Within the Zodiac (Toronto: McClelland and Stewart, 1964).

GRANDBOIS, ALAIN: M. Grandbois & Éditions de l'Hexagone.
Poèmes (Montreal: Éditions de l'Hexagone, 1963).

GRANDMONT, ÉLOI DE: M. de Grandmont.
From *Le Voyage d'Arlequin* (Montreal: Les Cahiers de la fille indienne, 1946); 'Le Chasseur', 'Les Parents exemplaires', *Une Saison en chansons* (Montreal: Éditions, Leméac, 1963).

GRIER, ELDON: Mr Grier.
A Friction of Lights (Toronto: Contact Press, 1963).

GUSTAFSON, RALPH: Mr Gustafson, and by permission of the Canadian Publishers, McClelland and Stewart Limited, Toronto.
'Armorial', 'Transfigured Night', *Rivers Among Rocks* (Toronto: McClelland and Stewart, 1960); 'My Love Eats an Apple', 'The Swans of Vadstena', *Sift in an Hour Glass* (Toronto: McClelland and Stewart, 1966); 'In the Yukon', *Rocky Mountain Poems* (Vancouver: Klanak Press, 1960).

HAWKINS, WILLIAM: Mr Hawkins.
Uncollected.

HÉBERT, ANNE: Les Éditions du Seuil, Paris.
'La Chambre fermée', 'Le Tombeau des rois', 'Vie de château', 'La Fille maigre', *Le Tombeau des rois* (Quebec: Institut Littéraire, 1953); Mystère de la parole', 'Ève', *Poèmes* (Paris: Éditions du Seuil, 1960).

HÉNAULT, GILLES: M. Hénault.
'Sémaphore', 'Notre Jeunesse', *Sémaphore* (Montreal: Éditions de l'Hexagone, 1962); 'Bestiaire', *Voyage aux pays de mémoire* (Montreal: Éditions de l'Hexagone, 1960).

HERTEL, FRANÇOIS: M. Hertel.
'Art poétique', 'Au pays de Québec', *Strophes et catastrophes*, (Paris: Éditions de la Diaspora Française, 1943); 'Le Chante de l'exilé', *Mes Naufrages* (Paris: Éditions de la Diaspora Française, 1951).

ACKNOWLEDGEMENTS

HINE, DARYL : Mr Hine.
 'The Double-Goer', 'Under the Hill', *The Devil's Picture Book* (New York : Abelard Schuman, 1960); 'Trompe l'Œil', *The Wooden Horse* (New York : Atheneum, 1965).

HOGG, ROBERT : Mr Hogg.
 Uncollected.

JOHNSTON, GEORGE : The Oxford University Press, Canadian Branch.
 The Cruising Auk (Toronto : Oxford University Press, 1959).

JONAS, GEORGE : Mr Jonas.
 Uncollected.

JONES, D. G. : The University of Toronto Press and the Oxford University Press, Canadian Branch.
 'I Thought There Were Limits', 'The Perishing Bird', *Phrases from Orpheus* (Toronto : Oxford University Press : 1967); 'Soliloquy to Absent Friends', 'Beautiful Creatures Brief as These', *The Sun is Axeman* (Toronto : University of Toronto Press, 1961).

KEARNS, LIONEL : Mr Kearns.
 Pointing (Toronto : Ryerson Press, 1967).

KLEIN, A. M. : The Ryerson Press and Alfred A. Knopf Inc., New York.
 'Autobiographical', *The Second Scroll* (New York : Alfred A. Knopf, 1951); '*In re* Solomon Warshawer', *Hath Not a Jew* (New York : Ryerson Press, 1940); 'Political Meeting', 'Monsieur Gaston', 'Montreal', *The Rocking Chair and Other Poems* (Toronto : Ryerson Press, 1948).

KNIGHT, DAVID : Mr Knight.
 Uncollected.

LALONDE, MICHÈLE : Mme Duchastel.
 'Le Silence effrité', 'Le Jour halluciné', 'Combien doux', *Geôles* (Montreal : Éditions d'Orphée, 1959); 'La Fiancée', *Songe de la fiancée détruite* (1958).

LAPOINTE, GATIEN : M. Lapointe and Les Éditions du Jour, Montreal.
 'Au Ras de la terre', *Ode au Saint-Laurent* (Montreal : Éditions du Jour, 1963); 'Le Temps premier', *Le Temps premier* (Paris : Grassin, 1962).

LAPOINTE, PAUL-MARIE : M. Lapointe.
 Choix de poèmes. arbres (Montreal : Éditions de l'Hexagone, 1960).

LASNIER, RINA : Mlle Lasnier.
 Mémoire sans jours (Montreal : Éditions de l'Atelier, 1960).

xxii

LAYTON, IRVING: By permission of the Canadian Publishers, McClelland and Stewart Limited, Toronto.
Collected Poems (Toronto: McClelland and Stewart, 1965).

LE PAN, DOUGLAS: Chatto and Windus Limited, London.
'A Country Without a Mythology', *The Wounded Prince and Other Poems* (London: Chatto and Windus, 1948); 'Coureurs de bois', 'An Incident', 'Nimbus', *The Net and the Sword* (London: Chatto and Windus, 1953).

LIVESAY, DOROTHY: Mrs Macnair and The Ryerson Press.
'Fantasia', *Day and Night* (Toronto: Ryerson Press, 1944); 'The Prophetess', 'The Leader', *The Unquiet Bed* (Toronto: Ryerson Press, 1967).

LOWRY, MALCOLM: Dr Birney for the Estate of Malcolm Lowry; copyright © Mrs Margerie Lowry.
'Salmon Drowns Eagle', uncollected; 'Sestina in a Cantina', 'Xochitepec', 'Christ Walks in This Infernal District Too', *Selected Poems of Malcolm Lowry* (San Francisco: City Lights Books, 1962).

MACEWEN, GWENDOLYN: The Ryerson Press.
Breakfast for Barbarians (Toronto: Ryerson Press, 1966).

MACPHERSON, JAY: Miss Macpherson and the Oxford University Press, Canadian Branch.
All poems from *The Boatman* (Toronto: Oxford University Press, 1957), with the exception of 'The Beauty of Job's Daughters', which is uncollected.

MAJOR, ANDRÉ: M. Major
Uncollected.

MANDEL, ELI: Mr Mandell and the Ryerson Press.
'Minotaur Poem', *Trio* (Montreal: Welmar Press, 1954); 'Four Songs from the Book of Samuel', *Black and Secret Man* (Toronto: Ryerson Press, 1964); 'Song', *Fuseli Poems* (Toronto: Contact Press, 1960).

MILLER, PETER: Mr Miller.
Sonata for Frog and Man (Toronto: Contact Press, 1959).

MORIN, PAUL: La Corporation des Éditions Fides, Montreal, and Le Cercle du Livre de France Ltée., Montreal.
'À ceux de mon pays', *Le Paon d'émail* (Paris: Alphonse Lemerre, 1911); 'Harmonie pour un soir d'Italie', 'Le plus aimé de mes jardins arabes', *Poèmes de cendre et d'or* (Montreal: Éditions du Dauphin, 1922); 'Musique des noms', 'Perdrix', *Géronte et son miroir* (Montreal: Le Cercle du Livre de France, 1960).

NEWLOVE, JOHN: Mr Newlove.
Uncollected.

ACKNOWLEDGEMENTS

NOWLAN, ALDEN : Mr Nowlan.
'God Sour the Milk of the Knacking Wench', 'The Wickedness of Peter Shannon', uncollected; 'The Grove Beyond the Barley', 'Stoney Ridge Dance Hall', *The Things Which Are* (Toronto : Contact Press, 1962).

ONDAATJE, MICHAEL : Mr Ondaatje.
Dainty Monsters (Toronto : Coach House Press, 1967).

OUELLETTE, FERNAND : M. Ouellette & Éditions de l'Hexagone.
'Femme', 'Géologie', *Le Soleil sous la mort* (Montreal : Éditions de l'Hexagone, 1965); 'Langue de l'aile', *Séquences de l'aile* (Montreal : Éditions de l'Hexagone 1958).

PAGE, P. K. : Mrs Irwin.
'Element', *As Ten As Twenty* (Toronto : Ryerson Press, 1946); 'Images of Angels', 'Puppets', 'Man with One Small Hand', 'Arras', *The Metal and the Flower* (Toronto : McClelland and Stewart, 1954).

PARADIS, SUSANNE : Mme Hamel.
La Chasse aux autres (Trois Rivières : Éditions du Bien Public, 1961).

PILON, JEAN-GUY : M. Pilon and Éditions Seghers, Paris.
'L'Étranger d'ici', *L'Homme et le jour* (Montreal : Éditions de l'Hexagone, 1957); 'Les Cloîtres de l'été . . .', *Les Cloîtres de l'été* (Montreal : Éditions de l'Hexagone, 1955); 'Je murmure le nom de mon pays', *Pour saluer une ville* (Paris : Éditions Seghers, 1963).

PRATT, E. J. : excerpts reprinted from *Titans, Towards the Last Spike*, and *Behind the Log*, from *Collected Poems of E. J. Pratt: second edition* (1958), by permission of the Estate of E. J. Pratt and the Macmillan Company of Canada Limited.

PURDY, ALFRED : Mr Purdy.
'Evergreen Cemetary', *Poems for All the Annettes* (Toronto : Contact Press, 1962); 'Wilderness Gothic', 'Dead Seal', 'What Do the Birds Think?', 'The Winemaker's Beat-étude', uncollected.

REANEY, JAMES : The author's representative.
'The Katzenjammer Kids', *The Red Heart* (Toronto : McClelland and Stewart, 1949); excerpt from *A Suit of Nettles* (Toronto : Macmillan, 1958) 'Le Tombeau de Pierre Falcon', uncollected; 'To the Avon River Above Stratford, Canada', *Twelve Letters to a Small Town* (Toronto : Ryerson Press, 1962).

ROSENBLATT, JOE : Mr Rosenblatt.
LSD Leacock (Toronto : Coach House Press, 1966).

ROSS, W. W. E. : Mrs Ross.
Uncollected.

ROUTIER, SIMONE : Mme Drouin.
'Neige et nostalgie', *Les Tentations* (Paris : Éditions 'La Caravelle', 1934); 'Le divin anéantissement', *Le long voyage* (Saint-Quentin : Éditions de la Lyre et de la Croix, 1947).

SCOTT, F. R. : Mr Scott.
Selected Poems (Toronto : Oxford University Press, 1966).

SCOTT, PETER DALE : Mr Scott.
Uncollected.

SMITH, A. J. M. : Mr Smith.
Poems: New and Collected (Toronto : Oxford University Press, 1967).

SOUSTER, RAYMOND : Mr Souster, the Oxford University Press, Canadian Branch, and the Ryerson Press.
'May 15th', *As Is* (Toronto : Oxford University Press, 1967); 'Ladybug', 'Ties', 'Choosing Coffins', *The Colour of the Times* (Toronto : Ryerson Press, 1964); 'The Six-Quart Basket', *Place of Meeting* (Toronto : Ryerson Press, 1962).

SPARSHOTT, FRANCIS : The Oxford University Press, Canadian Branch.
A Divided Voice (Toronto : Oxford University Press, 1965).

TROTTIER, PIERRE : M. Trottier and Les Éditions de l'Hexagone, Montreal.
'Femme aux couleurs de mon pays', 'Les Malédictions', 'Le Temps corrigé', *Poèmes de Russie* (Montreal : Éditions de l'Hexagone, 1957); 'Le Soldat inconnu', *Les Belles aux Bois dormant* (Montreal : Éditions de l'Hexagone, 1960).

VIGNEAULT, GILLES : Les Éditions du Vent qui Vire, Montreal.
'Mon pays', *Avec les vieux mots* (Quebec : Éditions de l'Arc, 1965); 'Chanson', *Étraves* (Quebec : Éditions de l'Arc, 1959); 'Quelqu'un était ici', source unknown.

WADDINGTON, MIRIAM : Mrs Waddington and the Ryerson Press.
'Catalpa Tree', *The Second Silence* (Toronto : Ryerson Press, 1955); 'My Lessons in the Jail', 'The Season's Lovers', *The Season's Lovers* (Toronto : Ryerson Press, 1959).

ACKNOWLEDGEMENTS

WATSON, WILFRED : Reprinted with permission of Farrar
    Straus and Giroux, Inc., from *Friday's Child* by Wilfred
    Watson; copyright © 1955 by Wilfred Watson, and
    Faber and Faber Limited, London.
    Friday's Child (London : Faber and Faber, 1955).

WEBB, PHYLLIS : The Ryerson Press.
    The Sea is Also a Garden (Toronto : Ryerson Press, 1962).

WEVILL, DAVID : 'In Love', 'Spiders', 'Body of a Rook', reprinted
    from *Birth of a Shark* by David Wevill by permission of
    the Author, Macmillan & Co., Ltd., London, St Martin's
    Press, New York, and the Macmillan Company of Canada
    Limited. 'Snow' is uncollected.

WHALLEY, GEORGE : Mr Whalley.
    Uncollected.

WILKINSON, ANNE : Reprinted by permission of the Estate of
    Anne Wilkinson and the Macmillan Company of Canada
    Limited.
    Collected Poems (Toronto : Macmillan, 1967).

WOODCOCK, GEORGE : Mr Woodcock and Clarke, Irwin &
    Company Limited.
    Selected Poems (Toronto : Clarke, Irwin, 1967).

There are a few poems whose copyright owners have not been
located after diligent inquiry. The publishers would be grateful
for information enabling them to make suitable acknowledgements in future editions.

From *The Cachalot*

(I)

A thousand years now had his breed
Established the mammalian lead;
The founder (in cetacean lore)
Had followed Leif to Labrador;
The eldest-born tracked all the way
Marco Polo to Cathay;
A third had hounded one whole week
The great Columbus to Bahama;
A fourth outstripped to Mozambique
The flying squadron of da Gama;
A fifth had often crossed the wake
Of Cortez, Cavendish and Drake;
The great grandsire—a veteran rover—
Had entered once the strait of Dover,
In a naval fight, and with his hump
Had stove a bottom of Van Tromp;
The grandsire at Trafalgar swam
At the *Redoubtable* and caught her,
With all the tonnage of his ram,
Deadly between the wind and water;
And his granddam herself was known
As fighter and as navigator,
The mightiest mammal in the zone
From Baffin Bay to the Equator.
From such a line of conjugate sires
Issued his blood, his lumbar fires,
And from such dams imperial-loined
His Taurian timbers had been joined,
And when his time had come to hasten
Forth from his deep sub-mammary basin,

Out on the ocean tracts, his mama
Had, in a North Saghalien gale,
Launched him, a five-ton healthy male,
Between Hong Kong and Yokohama.
Now after ninety moons of days,
Sheltered by the mammoth fin,
He took on adolescent ways
And learned the habits of his kin;
Ransacked the seas and found his mate,
Established his dynastic name,
Reared up his youngsters, and became
The most dynamic vertebrate
(According to his Royal Dame)
From Tonga to the Hudson Strait.
And from the start, by fast degrees,
He won in all hostilities;
Sighted a hammerhead and followed him,
Ripped him from jaw to ventral, swallowed him;
Pursued a shovelnose and mangled him;
Twisted a broadbill's neck and strangled him;
Conquered a rorqual in full sight
Of a score of youthful bulls who spurred
Him to the contest, and the fight
Won him the mastery of the herd.

Another ninety moons and Time
Had cast a marvel from his hand,
Unmatched on either sea or land—
A sperm whale in the pitch of prime.
A hundred feet or thereabout
He measured from the tail to snout,
And every foot of that would run
From fifteen hundred to a ton.
But huge as was his tail or fin,
His bulk of forehead, or his hoists
And slow subsidences of jaw,
He was more wonderful within.
His iron ribs and spinal joists

2

Enclosed the sepulchre of a maw.   E. J.
The bellows of his lungs might sail   PRATT
A herring skiff—such was the gale
Along the wind-pipe; and so large
The lymph-flow of his active liver,
One might believe a fair-sized barge
Could navigate along the river;
And the islands of his pancreas
Were so tremendous that between 'em
A punt would sink; while a cart might pass
His bile-duct to the duodenum
Without a peristaltic quiver.
And cataracts of red blood stormed
His heart, while lower down was formed
That fearful labyrinthine coil
Filled with the musk of ambergris;
And there were reservoirs of oil
And spermaceti; and renal juices
That poured in torrents without cease
Throughout his grand canals and sluices.
And hid in his arterial flow
Were flames and currents set aglow
By the wild pulses of the chase
With fighters of the Saxon race.
A tincture of an iron grain
Had dyed his blood a darker stain;
Upon his coat of toughest rubber
A dozen cicatrices showed
The place as many barbs were stowed,
Twisted and buried in his blubber,
The mute reminders of the hours
Of combat when the irate whale
Unlimbered all his massive powers
Of head-ram and of caudal flail,
Littering the waters with the chips
Of whale-boats and vainglorious ships.

3

(II)

Where Cape Delgado strikes the sea,
A cliff ran outward slantingly
A mile along a tossing edge
Of water towards a coral ledge,
Making a sheer and downward climb
Of twenty fathoms where it ended,
Forming a jutty scaur suspended
Over a cave of murk and slime.
A dull, reptilian silence hung
About the walls, and fungus clung
To knots of rock, and over boles
Of lime and basalt poisonous weed
Grew rampant, covering the holes
Where crayfish and sea-urchins breed.
The upper movement of the seas
Across the reefs could not be heard;
The nether tides but faintly stirred
Sea-nettles and anemones.
A thick festoon of lichens crawled
From crag to crag, and under it
Half-hidden in a noisome pit
Of bones and shells a kraken sprawled.
Moveless, he seemed, as a boulder set
In pitch, and dead within his lair,
Except for a transfixing stare
From lidless eyes of burnished jet,
And a hard spasm now and then
Within his viscous centre, when
His scabrous feelers intertwined
Would stir, vibrate, and then unwind
Their ligatures with easy strength
To tap the gloom, a cable length;
And finding no life that might touch
The mortal radius of their clutch,
Slowly relax, and shorten up

Each tensile tip, each suction cup,
And coil again around the head
Of the mollusc on its miry bed,
Like a litter of pythons settling there
To shutter the Gorgonian stare.

But soon the squid's antennæ caught
A murmur that the waters brought—
No febrile stirring as might spring
From a puny barracuda lunging
At a tuna's leap, some minor thing,
A tarpon or a dolphin plunging—
But a deep consonant that rides
Below the measured beat of tides
With that vast, undulating rhythm
A sounding sperm whale carries with him.
The kraken felt that as the flow
Beat on his lair with plangent power,
It was the challenge of his foe,
The prelude to a fatal hour;
Nor was there given him more than time,
From that first instinct of alarm,
To ground himself in deeper slime,
And raise up each enormous arm
Above him, when, unmeasured, full
On the revolving ramparts, broke
The hideous rupture of a stroke
From the forehead of the bull.
And when they interlocked, that night—
Cetacean and cephalopod—
No Titan with Olympian god
Had ever waged a fiercer fight;
Tail and skull and teeth and maw
Met sinew, cartilage, and claw,
Within those self-engendered tides,
Where the Acherontic flood
Of sepia, mingling with the blood

Out of such chemistry run through by genes,
The food released its fearsome racial products :—
The power to strike a bargain like a foe,
To win an argument upon a burr,
Invest the language with a Bannockburn,
Culloden or the warnings of Lochiel,
Weave loyalties and rivalries in tartans,
Present for the amazement of the world
Kilts and the civilized barbaric Fling,
And pipes which, when they acted on the mash,
Fermented lullabies to *Scots wha hae*.
Their names were like a battle-muster—Angus
(He of the Shops) and Fleming (of the Transit),
Hector (of the *Kicking Horse*), Dawson,
'Cromarty' Ross, and Beatty (Ulster Scot),
Bruce, Allan, Galt and Douglas, and the 'twa'—
Stephen (Craigellachie)[1] and Smith (Strathcona)—
Who would one day climb from their Gaelic
    hide-outs,
Take off their plaids and wrap them round the
    mountains,
And then the everlasting tread of the Macs,
Vanguard, centre and rear, their roving eyes
On summits, rivers, contracts, beaver, ledgers;
Their ears cocked to the skirl of Sir John A.,
The general of the patronymic march.

---

[1] 'Stand Fast, Craigellachie', the war-cry of the Clan
Grant, named after a rock in the Spey Valley, and
used as a cable message from Stephen in London to
the Directors in Montreal.

(II)

[THE PRECAMBRIAN SHIELD]

On the North Shore a reptile lay asleep—
A hybrid that the myths might have conceived,
But not delivered, as progenitor
Of crawling, gliding things upon the earth.
She lay snug in the folds of a huge boa
Whose tail had covered Labrador and swished
Atlantic tides, whose body coiled itself
Around the Hudson Bay, then curled up north
Through Manitoba and Saskatchewan
To Great Slave Lake. In continental reach
The neck went past the Great Bear Lake until
Its head was hidden in the Arctic Seas.
This folded reptile was asleep or dead :
So motionless, she seemed stone dead—just
    seemed :
She was too old for death, too old for life,
For as if jealous of all living forms
She had lain there before bivalves began
To catacomb their shells on western mountains.
Somewhere within this life-death zone she
    sprawled,
Torpid upon a rock-and-mineral mattress.
Ice-ages had passed by and over her,
But these, for all their motion, had but sheared
Her spotty carboniferous hair or made
Her ridges stand out like the spikes of molochs.
Her back grown stronger every million years,
She had shed water by the longer rivers
To Hudson Bay and by the shorter streams
To the great basins to the south, had filled
Them up, would keep them filled until the end
Of Time.
            Was this the thing Van Horne set out
To conquer?

9

From *Behind the Log*

There is a language in a naval log
That rams the grammar down a layman's throat,
Where words unreel in paragraphs, and lines
In chapters. Volumes lie in graphs and codes,
Recording with an algebraic care
The idiom of storms, their lairs and paths;
Or, in the self-same bloodless manner, sorting
The mongrel litters of a battle signal
In victories or defeats or bare survivals,
Flags at half-mast, salutes and guards of honour,
Distinguished crosses, burials at sea.

Our navigators trained their astrolabes
And sextants on the skies in lucky weather,
Or added guesses to dead reckoning,
Hauled up their lead, examined mud or shell
Or gravel on the arming—fifty fathoms,
Now forty, thirty, twenty-five, shallowing
Quickly! *'Engines astern, reefs, keep your lead
Going. Have plenty of water under you.'*
They did not wait till miracles of science
Unstopped the naked ears for supersonics,
Or lifted cataracts from finite vision
To make night and its darkness visible.
How long ago was it since sailors blew
Their sirens at the cliffs while nearing land,
Traversing channels, cocked their ears and waited?
'Where did you hear that echo, mate?'
                                        *'Right off
The starboard quarter, Captain. Took ten seconds.'*
'That's Gull Rock there a mile away. Where now?'
'Two seconds for the echo from port bow.'
'That's Porpoise Head I reckon—Hard a-port!'
With echoes everywhere, stand out to sea.
But when the winds deafened their ears or cloud
And rain blinded their eyes, they were shoved back

Upon their mother wit which either had
To find the exits to the runs and round
The Capes or pile their ships upon the reefs.

And of that lineage are the men today.
They still are calling to the rocks : they get
Their answers in the same hard terms : they call
To steel gliding beneath the sea : they pierce
Horizons for the surface hulls : they ping
The sky for the plane's fuselage : even
The moon acknowledged from her crater sills.
But though the radio bursts and vacuum tubes
And electronic beams were miracles
Of yesterday, dismissing cloud and rain
And darkness as illusions of the sense,
Yet always there to watch the colours, note
The V-break in the beam's straight line, to hear
The echoes, feel the pain, are eyes, ears, nerves :
Always remains the guess within the judgment
To jump the fine perfection of the physics
And smell mortality behind the log.

As weird a game of ping-pong ever played
Was on the sea—the place, off Cape Farewell,
With the back-curtain of the Greenland ice-cap :
Time—'41 autumnal equinox.
The crisis was the imminence of famine
And the cutting of the ganglia and veins
That vitalized the sinews, fed the cells
Of lungs demanding oxygen in air.
The wicks were guttering from want of oil,
And without oil, the bread went with the light,
And without bread, the will could not sustain
The fight, piping its courage to the heart.

Grey predatory fish had pedigreed
With tiger sharks and brought a speed and power
The sharks had never known, for they had been
Committed to the sea under a charter

Born of a mania of mind and will   E. J.
And nurtured by a Messianic slogan.   PRATT
They were not bounded by the parallels.
They found their habitats wherever there
Was open sea and keels to ride upon it.
Off the North Cape they had outsped the narwhals,
The sawfish off the Rios and the Horn.
They did not kill for food : they killed that food
Should not be used as food. They were the true
Expendables—the flower of their type.
They left their mothers for self-immolation,
The penalty the same for being on
Or off the target—for the first to join
Their own combustion to that of the ships,
And for the second, just to go the way
Their victims went—a drunken headlong spiral,
Shunted from an exhausted radius
Down fifteen thousand feet or more of sea,
Engines, propellers, gyros, rudders, dead. . . .

PAUL
MORIN

1889–1963

À ceux de mon pays

Et si je n'ai pas dit la terre maternelle,
        Si je n'ai pas chanté
Les faits d'armes qui sont la couronne éternelle
        De sa grave beauté,

Ce n'est pas que mon cœur ait négligé de rendre
        Hommage à son pays,
Ou que, muet aux voix qu'un autre sait entendre,
        Il ne l'ait pas compris;

Mais la flûte sonore est plus douce à ma bouche
        Que le fier olifant,

12

Et je voulais louer la fleur après la souche,
　　La mère avant l'enfant.

PAUL
MORIN

N'ayant pour seul flambeau qu'une trop neuve
　　lampe,
　　Les héros et les dieux
N'étant bien célébrés que l'argent à la tempe
　　Et les larmes aux yeux,

J'attends d'être mûri par la bonne souffrance
　　Pour, un jour, marier
Les mots canadiens aux rythmes de la France
　　Et l'érable au laurier.

Harmonie pour un soir d'Italie

Nuit de Ravenne ou nuit de Parme,
Je me souviens d'un soir si pur
(Plus diaphane que l'azur
Et plus transparent qu'une larme),

D'un soir si pur, qu'une chanson,
Traversant l'air calme, fut telle
Qu'une harmonieuse dentelle
Faite d'un rire et d'un frisson.

Aux ailes d'une vocalise
La voix adorable monta
Des jardins de la Steccata,
Ce fut d'une tristesse exquise . . .

Ou me trompe-je? Était-ce au chœur
De Notre-Dame-Ravennate
Que jaillissait cette cantate
Vers les sept rubis de son cœur?

Qu'importe? Amoureuse ou brutale,
D'une cellule ou d'un balcon,
Plainte d'ardeur ou d'abandon
Dans la nuit trop sentimentale,

Qu'importe? Une femme chantait
—Jeune ou vieille, nonne ou gredine,
Ariette, hymne, ou cavatine—
Son chaud, voluptueux secret.

PAUL
MORIN

Et, déjouant les portes closes
Qui muraient ma sévère humeur,
Ce cri fit fleurir dans mon cœur
Des larmes, du rire, et des roses.

On aurait dit le tendre vol
D'une colombe paresseuse,
La lente, lointaine berceuse
D'une fontaine en porcelaine,
Ou bien l'âme d'un rossignol
Soupirant au croissant sa peine.

.   .   .

Ce trille de pâtre amoureux,
Fraîche arabesque capriote,
Devrait-il alanguir sa note
Jusque dans mon exil frileux?

Me faudra-t-il entendre, arpège,
Le preste cristal de ta voix
Sous mon banal et morne toit
Qui plie et gémit sous la neige?

Chez l'amant des filles du Rhin,
Ah, pourquoi faut-il que revienne,
Jaune guitare italienne,
Ton mol et sensuel refrain?

Et puisque je me barricade
Avec Parsifal et Klingsor
Dans ma rude ville du Nord . . .
Qu'y viens-tu faire, sérénade?

.   .   .

Nuits douces comme des baisers,
Jardins brûlants comme des lèvres,
Il ne me reste de vos fièvres
Que des regrets inapaisés;

Et je t'ajoute, angoisse vaine,
A mon innombrable désir,
Ô cruel, ô beau souvenir
D'un soir de Parme . . . ou de Ravenne.

PAUL
MORIN

Musique des noms

À RENÉ CHOPIN

Toi, René, vous, Paul Fort, qui chantâtes Racine
Et le nom émouvant de La Ferté-Milon,
Souffrez qu'un vieux poète (aidé par Mnémosyne)
À vos rimes de marbre ajoute un moellon.

Encore un autre, direz-vous, piètre pastiche
De notre superlicoquentieux truqueur . . .
Fi, donc! dans ce pays où tout le monde triche,
Je ne veux qu'évoquer quelques vrais chocs au
        cœur;

Car, bien que de compréhension guillerette,
Je ne puis plus sentir—écoute, Mantouan.—
Les noms stupéfiants d'Ancienne-Lorette,
De Gaduamgoushout et d'Ashuapmouchouan.

The bulls (Saskatchewan?) me met les nerfs en
        boule . . .
Adieu, Lacolle, Hull, Chaudière-Station!
Je te noierai, mémoire, aux eaux de la Bourboule
(Si je ne meurs d'abord à Castor-Jonction).

Jamais un nom français n'a blessé mes oreilles,   PAUL
Excité mon humour ni froissé mon esprit ;   MORIN
Même les plus claquants sont de pures merveilles
—Segonzac, Izernore et Castelnaudary ! —

Et, des plus rudes sons, cette langue bénie
Savait déjà tisser, dans un passé lointain
(Carcassonne ! . . .), la brusque et fantasque
    harmonie
De Locmariaquer et de Romorantin.

Syllabes, ce n'est pas votre cadence noble
Ni votre place dans l'Histoire (Toi, Paris,
Vous, Vendôme, Épernon, Versailles ou Grenoble)
Qui font trembler ma main lorsque je vous écris . . .

Non. C'est l'aérien et féérique vocable,
C'est l'élégance nette et limpide, le mot
Ouvré magiquement et de sens immanquable,
Et qui sent l'églantine et le coquelicot.

Ah ! je donne à qui veut, pour Brive-la-Gaillarde,
Ispahan et Venise, et leurs murmures d'eau
Pour l'azur où s'ébat la grive goguenarde
De Mantes-la-Jolie et d'Azay-le-Rideau.

Islam, amour d'hier, et tes minarets roses,
Je préfère à vos noms Ailly-le-Haut-Clocher,
Les frelons en velours de Fontenay-aux-Roses,
Alise-Sainte-Reine où fleurit le pêcher ;

Mais me plaît, entre tous ces tendres sortilèges,
La carte bleue où Dammarie-emmy-ses-lys,
En un chaste concert de suaves arpèges,
Partage son parfum avec Les Andelys . . .

Le plus aimé de mes jardins arabes …   PAUL
MORIN

Le plus aimé de mes jardins arabes
Est un enclos, sans fontaine et sans fleur,
Où des vieillards, en turban de couleur,
Psalmodiaient de sonores syllabes.

On s'y rendait par un sentier pierreux,
De vieux figuiers y déployaient leurs branches,
Un doux collier d'humbles terrasses blanches
Encadrait cet asile bienheureux.

Avant midi tout n'était que silence,
Les cris des geais seuls traversaient les airs,
Puis des femmes venaient, en voiles clairs,
Y reposer leur bavarde indolence;

On entendait leurs rires assourdis,
Un long murmure arrivait de la rade,
Et quelquefois, rasant la balustrade,
Passait un vol joyeux de pigeons gris.

Au pied d'un mur enguirlandé de lierre
Un fossoyeur à la barbe d'argent
Accomplissait son travail diligent
Avec des bruits de métal et de pierre ..

La double stèle au marbre rose ou noir
Où se fanaient de pauvres broderies,
En recueillant les matinales pluies,
Pour les oiseaux se faisait abreuvoir.

Neige vivante, un essaim de colombes
Tourbillonnait dans l'azur éclatant,
Et, jusqu'au soir d'ambre et d'or, en chantant,
Des enfants nus couraient parmi les tombes.

Perdrix

PAUL
MORIN

Perdrix, les dieux sylvains ne sont pas disparus
Puisque leurs jeux encor sur les menthes humides
Leurs téméraires cris et leurs fuites timides
Animent les halliers où te poursuit l'intrus.

Nymphes, faunes impurs et centaures membrus,
—Que ce soit sur l'Othrys ou dans les
    Laurentides—
Ils habitent tes bois, et leurs flûtes fluides
Scandent de trilles clairs le choc de sabots drus.

Mais, quand le crépuscule éteint sa transparence,
Grotte, source et forêt retombent au silence,
Syrinx ne bruit plus, Aréthuse s'endort . . .

Et toi, sorcière rousse à la griffe trièdre,
Tu redeviens, dans ton palais de feuilles d'or,
La dryade au corps d'ambre enclose au cœur d'un
    cèdre.

W. W. E.
ROSS

1894–1966

Fish

A fish dripping
sparkling drops
of crystal water,
pulled from the lake;
long has it dwelt
in the cool water,
in the cold water
of the lake.

Long has it wandered
to and fro
over the bottom
of the lake
among mysterious
recesses
there in the semi-
light of the water;

W. W. E.
ROSS

now to appear
surprised, aghast,
out of its element
into the day;—
out of the cold
and shining lake
the fish dripping
sparkling water.

The Snake Trying

The snake trying
to escape the pursuing stick,
with sudden curvings of thin
long body. How beautiful

and graceful are his shapes!
He glides through the water away
from the stroke. O let him go
over the water

into the reeds to hide
without hurt. Small and green
he is harmless even to children.
Along the sand

he lay until observed
and chased away, and now
he vanishes in the ripples
among the green slim reeds.

The Creek

W. W. E.
ROSS

The creek, shining,
out of the deep woods
comes with the rippling of
water over the pebbly bottom,

moving between
banks crowded with raspberry
bushes, the ripe red
berries in their short season

to deepen slowly
among tall pines, athletes in
the wind, then the swampy
ground low-lying and damp

where sunlight strikes
glints on the gliding surface
of the clear cold
creek winding towards the shore

of the lake, blue,
not far through reeds and rushes,
where with a plunge, a small
waterfall, it disappears

among the waves
hastening from far to meet
the stranger, the stream issuing
from depths of green unknown.

On Angels

Angels, as well as birds, on silent wing
Proceeding through the upper, open air,
Under the full intense celestial glare,
Perceive the true form of each earthly thing;

Birdlike the eye they deftly, subtly fling
Into the distance. Steadily they stare
Unhindered by the circumambient glare,—
Angels as well as birds can sweetly sing.
They too are known to hover above a nest
Wherein the swathéd soul of man doth lie
Soft-hidden deep in matter as in wool,
And theirs, too, the prerogative of rest,—
To soothe at times in manner wonderful,
With kind and piercing glance of soul and eye.

W. W. E.
ROSS

F. R.
SCOTT

b. 1899

Lakeshore

The lake is sharp along the shore
Trimming the bevelled edge of land
To level curves; the fretted sands
Go slanting down through liquid air
Till stones below shift here and there
Floating upon their broken sky
All netted by the prism wave
And rippled where the currents are.

I stare through windows at this cave
Where fish, like planes, slow-motioned, fly.
Poised in a still of gravity
The narrow minnow, flicking fin,
Hangs in a paler, ochre sun,
His doorways open everywhere.

And I am a tall frond that waves
Its head below its rooted feet

Seeking the light that draws it down
To forest floors beyond its reach
Vivid with gloom and eerie dreams.

F. R.
SCOTT

The water's deepest colonnades
Contract the blood, and to this home
That stirs the dark amphibian
With me the naked swimmers come
Drawn to their prehistoric womb.

They too are liquid as they fall
Like tumbled water loosed above
Until they lie, diagonal,
Within the cool and sheltered grove
Stroked by the fingertips of love.

Silent, our sport is drowned in fact
Too virginal for speech or sound
And each is personal and laned
Along his private aqueduct.

Too soon the tether of the lungs
Is taut and straining, and we rise
Upon our undeveloped wings
Toward the prison of our ground
A secret anguish in our thighs
And mermaids in our memories.

This is our talent, to have grown
Upright in posture, false-erect,
A landed gentry, circumspect,
Tied to a horizontal soil
The floor and ceiling of the soul;
Striving, with cold and fishy care
To make an ocean of the air.

Sometimes, upon a crowded street,
I feel the sudden rain come down
And in the old, magnetic sound
I hear the opening of a gate

That loosens all the seven seas.
Watching the whole creation drown
I muse, alone, on Ararat.

F. R.
SCOTT

Vision

Vision in long filaments flows
Through the needles of my eyes.
I am fastened to the rose
When it takes me by surprise.

I am clothed in what eye sees.
Snail's small motion, mountain's height,
Dress me with their symmetries
In the robing-rooms of sight.

Summer's silk and winter's wool
Change my inner uniform.
Leaves and grass are cavern cool
As the felted snow is warm.

When the clear and sun-drenched day
Makes a mockery of dress
All the fabric falls away.
I am clothed in nakedness.

Stars so distant, stones nearby
Wait, indifferently, in space
Till an all-perceptive eye
Gives to each its form and place.

Mind is a chameleon
Blending with environment;
To the colours it looks on
Is its own appearance bent.

Yet it changes what it holds
In the knowledge of its gaze
And the universe unfolds
As it multiplies its rays.

Tireless eye, so taut and long,   F. R.
Touching flowers and flames with ease,   SCOTT
All your wires vibrate with song
When it is the heart that sees.

Cloth of Gold

The king I saw who walked a cloth of gold,
Who sat upon the throne a child of God,
He was my king when he was most a myth.

Then every man paid homage at his feet.
Some fought his battles and shed ransom blood,
Some slew their rights to magnify his claims.

It was our centuries that cut him down.
Bold kings would totter with the lapse of time.
We pushed them over with our rebel shout.

Yet of this metal are new kingdoms struck.
The unknown kings that filter through the laws
Make baron plans to multiply their fiefs.

We break their shackles but new kings are close.
We smell them in the churches and the schools.
We see their garter on the righteous judge.

And now the corporate kingdoms raise their flags,
Their marriage-contracts stretch their boundaries
And pour their armies into foreign lands.

This clink of gold is echo of a crown.
Father and son are founding dynasties.
Each hailed invention lays a palace stone.

While far across the ploughlands of the East
The single master who is history's dream
Holds up his hand to daze the patient throngs.

It seems the shadow of a king is here
That strides before us to the rising sun,
Some shadow of a king that will not fade.

The tumbled limbs of monarchy are green.   F. R.
A hundred heads survive our mightiest stroke.   SCOTT
These broken dreams, these fragile interludes.

Bangkok

Deep in the brown bosom
Where all the temples rose
I wandered in a land
That I had never owned
With millions all around.

I had been here before
But never to this place
Which seemed so nearly home
Yet was so far away
I was not here at all.

There was a central mound
That took away my breath
So steep it was and round
So sudden by my side
So Asia all beyond.

And when I came inside
I had to walk barefoot
For this was holy ground
Where I was being taught
To worship on a mat.

A great white wind arose
And shakes of temple bells
Descended from the eaves
To make this gold and brown
One continent of love.

And only my own lack
Of love within the core
Sealed up my temple door
Made it too hard to break
And forced me to turn back.

À l'ange avantgardien

F. R.
SCOTT

We must leave the handrails and the Ariadne-
      threads,
The psychiatrists and all the apron strings
And take a whole new country for our own.

Of course we are neurotic; we are everything.
Guilt is the backstage of our innocent play.
To us normal and abnormal are two sides of a
      road.

We shall not fare too well on this journey.
Our food and shelter are not easy to find
In the *salons des réfusés*, the little mags of our
      friends.

But it is you, rebellious angel, you we trust.
Astride the cultures, feet planted in heaven and
      hell,
You guard the making, never what's made and
      paid.

A Lass in Wonderland

I went to bat for the Lady Chatte
      Dressed in my bib and gown.
The judges three glared down at me
      The priests patrolled the town.

My right hand shook as I reached for the book
      And rose to play my part,
For out on the street were the marching feet
      Of the League of the Sacred Heart.

The word 'obscene' was supposed to mean
      'Undue exploitation of sex'.
This wording's fine for your needs and mine
      But it's far too free for Quebec's.

I tried my best, with unusual zest,
　To drive my argument through,
But I soon got stuck on what rhymes with 'muck'
　And that dubious word 'undue'.

So I raised their sights to the Bill of Rights
　And cried : 'Let freedom ring !',
Showed straight from the text that freedom of sex
　Was as clear as anything.

Then I plunged into love, the spell that it wove,
　And its attributes big and bold
Till the legal elect all stood erect
　As my rapturous tale was told.

The judges' sighs and rolling of eyes
　Gave hope that my case was won,
Yet Mellors and Connie still looked pretty funny
　Dancing about in the sun.

What hurt me was not that they did it a lot
　And even ran out in the rain,
'Twas those curious poses with harebells and roses
　And that dangling daisy-chain.

Then too the sales made in the paper-back trade
　Served to aggravate judicial spleen,
For it seems a high price will make any book nice
　While its mass distribution's obscene.

Oh Letters and Law are found in the raw
　And found on the heights sublime,
But D. H. Lawrence would view with abhorrence
　This Jansenist pantomime.

F. R.
SCOTT

ROBERT
FINCH

b. 1900

Aria Senza da Capo

The stork questioned the swan whose moving song
Was more than usually sweet and long :
What's the good news? You'd think you were a
    lark !
I'm going to die, the swan answered the stork.

Turning

This winter's morning, turning the other way
I thought of the wood I had faced the moment
    before,
Crystal arches leaping a crystal floor
Where like brown ghosts of fish the oak-leaves lay.

The view ahead was no view to be spurned,
A plain of whiteness with one raven elm
Lifting the tent of winter on its helm,
The white tent of the sky. Again I turned

And as I turned the sun came out, the sky
Fell down into the wood among the snow
Till snow and sky and sun began to flow
Into an animation like a sea :

Through purple waves brown fishes swam in shoals
Or pondered in blue depths of russet glass,
The trees were azure fountains in a race
To graze the sky or melt into its pools,

And as I looked, remembering the plain
Behind me, the black elm, the white tent,
I marvelled what a single turn had sent
And wondered now whether to turn again.

Room

ROBERT
FINCH

Dear steps may die away,
The cradle lose its king,
Wealth vanish on the wing,
Health dwindle in a day,
Love still has room to sing.

For though love sings in time,
Eternity's its home,
Invisible rooms of room
Through and beyond the hum
Of time's corroding loom.

Thither love's song rings clear
And thence it echoes back
With notes time cannot wake
And words time cannot hear
And strength time cannot take.

The Collective Portrait

Man fools about with self-analysis
Till what he was replaces what he is.
Too slack to start, punished for putting off,
Afraid he knows too much or not enough,
Stunned with remorse and itching with anxiety,
Weary with work and restless with society,
His only consolation is to crawl
Into his heart and cheat it first of all.

He longs to hold the passing moment lest
Another come, yet wishes both were past,
For charmed and sated with himself and others,
Loathing the ones who love him, loving his
    loathers,
His tastes being balked, his longing unfulfilled,
He spills his life, then moans when it is spilled,

Calling the untracked universe confined

ROBERT
FINCH

And building dream ones in his narrow mind.

The farther back his ancestry is thrust
The nearer he derives from Adam's dust.
Though with a gun he makes his fellows skip,
Over himself his senses wield a whip.
Since knowledge less enlightens him than flatters
His heart which in the meantime passion batters,
He takes a try at all but relishes little,
Every ambition won going suddenly brittle.

His strength is weakness, for if you examine
It, his economy's a fear of famine,
His courage is his terror, what may seem
His generosity is self-esteem,
Those waves of reputation hide a reef,
That courtesy is for his own relief,
Precision is precaution not to let
The doctor in, or find himself in debt,

And all his virtues have the same pretence:
Amalgamating vice with innocence.
What modern Hercules can save his life?
Man's many-headed pride requires a knife
Keener than any metal will afford,
Directed by the superhuman Word
Of Virtue's Self, not its similitude,
A son of Adam but the Son of God.

ALAIN
GRANDBOIS

b. 1900

L'Étoile pourpre

C'était l'ombre aux pas de velours
Les étoiles sous le soleil mort
Les hommes et les femmes nus
La Faute n'existait plus

Mais sous les pins obscurs déjà
Au creux des cathédrales détruites
Parmi le chaos des pierres tombales
Parmi la ténèbre et les dernières calcinations
Soudain le cri de l'oiseau
La mort s'agite en haut

ALAIN
GRANDBOIS

La pourpre et l'indigo
Le ciel et l'enfer
Son beau visage entre mes mains
Toutes les caresses insolites
Je l'aimais pour la fin
D'un long chemin perdu

C'étaient les jours bienheureux
Les jours de claire verdure
Et le fol espoir crépusculaire
Des mains nues sur la chair
L'Étoile pourpre
Éclatait dans la nuit

Celle que j'attendais
Celle dont les yeux
Sont peuplés de douceur et de myosotis
Celle d'hier et de demain

Les détours du cri de vérité
La moisson couchée
Au peuplier l'oiseau
Beauté du monde
Tout nous étouffe

Ah vagabonds des espaces
Ceux des planètes interdites
Ah beaux délires délivrés
Le jour se lève avant l'aube

Que les mots porteurs de sang
Continuent de nous fuir
Un secret pour chaque nuit suffit
Je plongeais alors

Jusqu'au fond des âges
Jusqu'au gonflement de la première marée
Jusqu'au délire
De l'Étoile pourpre
Je m'évadais au delà
Du son total
Le grand silence originel
Nourrissait mon épouvante

ALAIN
GRANDBOIS

Mon sang brûlait comme un prodigieux pétrole
Mordant comme un acide extravagant
Aux racines de mes révoltes
Aux lits absurdes de mes fleuves
Et soufflaient soudain
Spirales insensées
Les foudroyantes forges du feu
Et se creusaient soudain
Les cavernes infernales

Rougis les allées
Des vieux parcs solitaires
Balance ta lune de flammes pâles
Au faîte des peupliers frissonnants
Ah je t'aimais de larmes si douces
Ô Toi belle endormie
Au bord bleu du ruisseau

Il y avait aussi
L'étonnant espace minéral des villes
Les couloirs fragiles et déchirés
De son cœur et de mon cœur
Son sourire plus fiévreux chaque jour
Je noyais mes désespoirs
Au sombre élan de son flanc ravagé
Je construisais mes vastes portiques
J'élevais mes hautes colonnes de cristal
J'allais triompher
Mes palais soudain s'écroulaient
Aux brouillards de mes mains

Nul feuillage d'or
Nulle calme paupière
Les cyclônes rugissaient vertigineusement
Les étoiles se rompaient une à une
Toutes les prunelles étaient tuées
Aspirations géantes
Ah Musiques de Minuit
Quelles sources d'extase
Pour vos soifs indéfinies
Chaque instant
Dans la vaine précipitation du temps
Assassinait les ombres du mur fatidique
Requiem sans cesse recommencé

Clameurs clouant le cœur écorché
Dérobant le jour strié de lueurs
Ah visages à jamais fermés
Beau front lisse et glacé de nos mortes

D'autres rivages sans doute
Mon cœur bat-il trop fort
Devant ces mers éteintes
C'est alors que l'oiseau noir crie

ALAIN
GRANDBOIS

Noces

Nous sommes debout
Debout et nus et droits
Coulant à pic tous les deux
Aux profondeurs marines
Sa longue chevelure flottant
Au-dessus de nos têtes
Comme des milliers de serpents frémissants
Nous sommes droits et debout
Liés par nos chevilles nos poignets
Liés par nos bouches confondues
Liés par nos flancs soudés
Scandant chaque battement du cœur

Nous plongeons nous plongeons à pic
Dans les abîmes de la mer
Franchissant chaque palier glauque
Lentement avec la plus grande régularité
Certains poissons déjà tournent
Dans un sillage d'or trouble
De longues algues se courbent
Sous le souffle invisible et vert
Des grandes annonciations

ALAIN
GRANDBOIS

Nous nous enfonçons droits et purs
Dans l'ombre de la pénombre originelle
Des lueurs s'éteignent et jaillissent
Avec la plus grande rapidité
Des communications électriques
Crépitent comme des feux chinois autour de nous
Des secrets définitifs
Nous pénètrent insidieusement
Par ces blessures phosphorescentes
Notre plongée toujours défiant
Les lois des atmosphères
Notre plongée défiant
Le sang rouge du cœur vivant

Nous roulons nous roulons
Elle et moi seuls
Aux lourds songes de la mer
Comme des géants transparents
Sous la grande lueur éternelle

Des fleurs lunaires s'allongent
Gravissant autour de nous
Nous sommes tendus droits
Le pied pointant vers les fonds
Comme celui du plongeur renversé
Déchirant les aurores spectrales
L'absolu nous guette
Comme un loup dévorant

Parfois une proue de galère ALAIN
GRANDBOIS
Avec ses mâts fantômes de bras
Parfois de courts soleils pâles
Soudain déchirent les méduses
Nous plongeons au fond des âges
Nous plongeons au fond d'une mer incalculable
Forgeant rivant davantage
L'implacable destin de nos chaînes

Ah plus de ténèbres
Plus de ténèbres encore
Il y a trop de poulpes pourpres
Trop d'anémones trop crépusculaires
Laissons le jour infernal
Laissons les cycles de haine
Laissons les dieux du glaive
Les voiles d'en-haut sont perdues
Dans l'arrachement des étoiles
Avec les derniers sables
Des rivages désertés
Par les dieux décédés

Rigides et lisses comme deux morts
Ma chair inerte dans son flanc creux
Nos yeux clos comme pour toujours
Ses bras mes bras n'existent plus
Nous descendons comme un plomb
Aux prodigieuses cavernes de la mer
Nous atteindrons bientôt
Les couches d'ombre parfaite
Ah noir et total cristal
Prunelles éternelles
Vain frissonnement des jours
Signes de la terre au ciel
Nous plongeons à la mort du monde
Nous plongeons à la naissance du monde

Cris

ALAIN
GRANDBOIS

J'ai vu soudain ces continents bouleversés
Les mille trompettes des dieux trompés
L'écroulement des murs des villes
L'épouvante d'une pourpre et sombre fumée
J'ai vu les hommes des fantômes effrayants
Et leurs gestes comme les noyades extraordinaires
Marquaient ce déserts implacables
Comme deux mains jointes de femme
Comme les grandes fautes sans pardon
Le sel le fer et la flamme
Sous un ciel d'enfer muré d'acier
Du fond des cratères volcaniques
Crachaient les rouges angoisses
Crachaient les âges décédés
Les désespoirs nous prenaient au cœur d'un bond
Les plages d'or lisse le bleu
Des mers inexprimables et jusqu'au bout du temps
Les planètes immobiles   Ô droites   Ô arrêtées
Le long silence de la mort

Ah je vous vois tous et toutes
Dans les petits cimetières fleuris
Aux épaules des églises paroissiales
Sous le léger gonflement de tertres mal soignés
Vous toi et toi et toi et toi
Vous tous que j'aimais
Avec la véhémence de l'homme muet
Je criais mes cris parmi la nuit profonde
Ah ils parlent d'espoir mais où l'espoir
Ils disent que nous nions Dieu
Alors que nous ne cherchons que Dieu
Que Lui seul Lui
Alors les caravanes des pôles
Dans l'avalanche des glaces vertes
Précipitaient leur monstrueux chaos de gel

Au ventre des belles Amériques
Alors nous dans ce jour même
À deux yeux bien fermés
Ô rêve humilié douceur des servitudes
Nous cherchions les sous-bois de pins
Pour chanter la joie de nos chairs
Ah Dieu dans les hautes mains mouvantes des
    feuillages
Comme nous t'avons cherché
À notre repos nos corps bien clos
Avant le prochain désir comme une
    bourdonnante abeille

Alors les hauts palmiers des tropiques
Balayant les malarias insidieuses
Courbaient des têtes inconquises
Il y avait une petite voile blanche
Sur une coque rouge-vin
Et toutes les mers étaient à nous
Avec leurs tortues monstrueuses
Et les lamproies romaines
Et les baleines du Labrador
Et les îles qui surgissent du corail
Comme une épreuve photographique
Et ces rochers glacés
Aux têtes de la Terre de Feu
Et toute l'immense mer resplendissante
Et les poumons de ses vagues
Nous balançaient comme de jeunes époux
Mer   Ô mer   Ô belle nommée
Quelles victoires pour nos défaites

Alors les forêts pleines comme des souterrains
Où nous marchions en écartant les bras
Nous étouffaient par leur secret
Les souvenirs égarés l'enfance perdue
Ce soleil du matin tendre comme une lune
Ah ces jours imaginaires
Au creux des présences d'herbes

ALAIN
GRANDBOIS

Parmi les barreaux de nos prisons
Elle ne sait peut-être pas pleurer librement
Je réclamais un combat silencieux

ALAIN
GRANDBOIS

De grands arbres d'ancêtres tombaient sur nous
Il y avait des moments solennels
Où nous étions portés par l'ombre
Où nous étions tous tués par les genoux
Notre douleur n'égalait pas
Les instances nourries de larmes involontaires
Les ombres voilaient nos visages
Nos pieds nus saignaient sur l'arête du rocher
Et le nouveau jour nous tendait son piège
Sous les ogives des hauts cèdres

Les forêts dressées mangeaient notre ciel
Ô coulées douces vers les fontaines fraîches
Aux murs d'arbres comme des cloisons définitives
Labyrinthes solennels d'octaves les fronts se
    penchent
Mousses et stalactites vertu des eaux pétrifiées
Sanglants carnages des prochains deuils
Nous étions humbles sans parler de poésie
Nous étions baignés de poésie et nous ne le
    savions pas

Nos corps sauvages s'accordaient dans une pudeur
    insensée
Se frappaient l'un contre l'autre
Comme pour l'assassinat
Quand les délires de la joie venaient
Nous étions émerveillés sous le soleil
Le repos nous transformait
Comme deux morts rigides et secs
Dans les linceuls d'un blanc trop immaculé
Ah souffles des printemps Ah délices des parfums
Fenêtres ouvertes au creux des carrefours des
    villes
On voulait voir une feuille verte

Un oiseau le reflet bleu du lac

ALAIN
GRANDBOIS

Des sapins autour les poumons enfin délivrés

Nous nous prenions la main
Nous avancions dans la vie
Avec cette quarantaine d'années accumulées
Chacun de nous
Veuf deux ou trois fois
De deux ou trois blessures mortelles
Nous avions survécu par miracle
Aux démons des destructions

ALFRED
DES ROCHERS

b. 1901

Je suis un fils déchu

Je suis un fils déchu de race surhumaine,
Race de violents, de forts, de hasardeux,
Et j'ai le mal du pays neuf, que je tiens d'eux,
Quand viennent les jours gris que septembre
    ramène.

Tout le passé brutal de ces coureurs des bois :
Chasseurs, trappeurs, scieurs de long, flotteurs de
    cages,
Marchands aventuriers ou travailleurs à gages,
M'ordonne d'émigrer par en haut pour cinq mois.

Et je rêve d'aller comme allaient les ancêtres;
J'entends pleurer en moi les grands espaces blancs,
Qu'ils parcouraient, nimbés de souffles d'ouragans,
Et j'abhorre comme eux la contrainte des maîtres.

Quand s'abattait sur eux l'orage des fléaux,
Ils maudissaient le val, ils maudissaient la plaine,

39

Ils maudissaient les loups qui les privaient de
    laine.
Leurs malédictions engourdissaient leurs maux.

ALFRED
DES ROCHERS

Mais quand le souvenir de l'épouse lointaine
Secouait brusquement les sites devant eux,
Du revers de leur manche, ils s'essuyaient les yeux
Et leur bouche entonnait : 'À la claire
    fontaine' . . .

Ils l'ont si bien redite aux échos des forêts,
Cette chanson naïve où le rossignol chante,
Sur la plus haute branche, une chanson touchante,
Qu'elle se mêle à mes pensers les plus secrets :

Si je courbe le dos sous d'invisibles charges,
Dans l'âcre brouhaha de départs oppressants,
Et si, devant l'obstacle ou le lien, je sens
Le frisson batailleur qui crispait leurs poings
    larges;

Si d'eux, qui n'ont jamais connu le désespoir,
Qui sont morts en rêvant d'asservir la nature,
Je tiens ce maladif instinct de l'aventure,
Dont je suis quelquefois tout envoûté, le soir;

Par nos ans sans vigueur, je suis comme le hêtre
Dont la sève a tari sans qu'il soit dépouillé,
Et c'est de désirs morts que je suis enfeuillé,
Quand je rêve d'aller comme allait mon ancêtre;

Mais les mots indistincts que profère ma voix
Sont encore : un rosier, une source, un branchage,
Un chêne, un rossignol parmi le clair feuillage,
Et comme au temps de mon aïeul, coureur des
    bois,

Ma joie ou ma douleur chante le paysage.

Hymne au vent du nord

ALFRED
DES ROCHES

Ô Vent du Nord, vent de chez nous, vent de féerie,
Qui va surtout la nuit, pour que la poudrerie,
Quand le soleil, vers d'autres cieux, a pris son vol,
Allonge sa clarté laiteuse à fleur de sol;
Ô monstre de l'azur farouche, dont les râles
Nous émeuvent autant que, dans les cathédrales,
Le cri d'une trompette aux Élévations;
Aigle étourdi d'avoir erré sur les Hudsons,
Parmi les grognements baveux des ours polaires;
Sublime aventurier des espaces stellaires,
Où tu chasses l'odeur du crime pestilent;
Ô toi, dont la clameur effare un continent
Et dont le souffle immense ébranle les étoiles;
Toi qui déchires les forêts comme des toiles;
Vandale et modeleur de sites éblouis
Qui donnent des splendeurs d'astres à mon pays,
Je chanterai ton cœur que nul ne veut
     comprendre.

C'est toi qui de blancheur enveloppes la cendre,
Pour que le souvenir sinistre du charnier
Ne s'avive en notre âme, ô vent calomnié!
Ta force inaccessible ignore les traîtrises:
Tu n'as pas la langueur énervante des brises
Qui nous viennent, avec la fièvre, d'Orient,
Et qui nous voient mourir par elle, en souriant;
Tu n'es pas le cyclone énorme des Tropiques,
Qui mêle à l'eau des puits des vagues
     d'Atlantiques,
Et dont le souffle rauque est issu des volcans;
Comme le siroco, ce bâtard d'ouragans,
Qui vient on ne sait d'où, qui se perd dans l'espace,
Tu n'ensanglantes pas les abords de ta trace;
Tu n'as jamais besoin, comme le vent d'été,
De sentir le tonnerre en laisse à ton côté,
Pour aboyer la foudre, en clamant ta venue.

Ô vent épique, peintre inouï de la nue,
Lorsque tu dois venir, tu jettes sur les cieux,
Au-dessus des sommets du nord vertigineux,
Le signe avant-coureur de ton âme loyale :
Un éblouissement d'aurore boréale.
Et tu nous viens alors. Malheur au voyageur,
Qui n'a pas entendu l'appel avertisseur !

ALFRED
DES ROCHER

Car toi, qui dois passer pour assainir le monde,
Tu ne peux ralentir ta marche une seconde :
Ton bras-cohorte étreint l'infortuné marcheur;
Mais, tandis que le sang se fige dans son cœur,
Tu rétrécis pour lui les plaintes infinies;
Tu répètes sans fin pour lui les symphonies
Qui montent de l'abîme arctique vers les cieux;
Tu places le mirage allègre dans ses yeux :

Il voit le feu de camp où le cèdre s'embrase
Et la mort vient sur lui comme vient une extase.
Demain, sur le verglas scintillant d'un ciel clair,
La gloire d'une étoile envahira sa chair.
Non, tu n'es pas, ô vent du nord, un vent infâme :
Tu vis, et comme nous, tu possèdes une âme.
Comme un parfum de rose au temps du rosier vert,
Tu dispenses l'amour durant les mois d'hiver.

Car il vibre en ta voix un tel frisson de peine,
Que l'esprit faible oublie, en l'écoutant, sa haine,
Et durant ces longs mois où le jour est trop court,
Quand tu chantes, ton chant fait s'élargir l'amour.
Il redit la douleur indistincte des choses
Qui souffrent sous des cieux également moroses.
Nul mieux que toi ne sait l'horreur de rôder seul
Ou séparé de ceux qu'on aime : le linceul
Étendu par la glace entre le ciel et l'onde
Et le suaire épais des neiges sur le monde,
Les cris de désespoir de l'Arctique, l'appel
Poussé par la forêt que torture le gel,
Toute la nostalgie éparse de la terre

Pour le soleil, pour la chaleur, pour la lumière,   ALFRED
DES ROCHERS
Pour l'eau, pour les ébats folâtres des troupeaux,
Et ton désir, jamais assouvi de repos,
Tout cela, dans ton chant soupire et se lamente,
Avec un tel émoi d'espérance démente,
Que nul n'en peut saisir toute la profondeur
Et que notre être faible en frissonne d'horreur.

Sans toi, l'amour disparaîtrait durant ces heures
Où l'hiver nous retient cloîtrés dans les demeures.
Le tête à tête pèse et devient obsédant
S'il ne plane sur lui quelque épouvantement.
Sans toi, l'amant serait bientôt las de l'amante;
Mais quand ta grande voix gronde dans la
      tourmente,
La peur unit les corps, l'effroi chasse l'ennui,
Le cœur sent la pitié chaude descendre en lui,
L'épaule ingénument recherche une autre épaule,
La main transie, avec douceur, se tend et frôle
Une autre main, la chair est un ravissement;
La mère sur son sein réchauffe son enfant,
Et les époux, qu'avaient endurcis les années,
Ont retrouvé soudain leurs caresses fanées.
Le lit triste s'emplit des capiteux parfums
Que répandaient jadis les fleurs des soirs défunts;
Le nuage de l'heure ancienne se dissipe;
Et dans l'étreinte ardente où l'âme participe,
Comme le corps, parfois s'incrée un rédempteur.
Ah ! si l'on te maudit, ô vent libérateur,
Qui chasses loin de nous la minute obsédante,
C'est qu'un désir secret de vengeance nous hante,
Et ce qu'on hait en toi, c'est le pardon qui vient.

Comme un vase imprégné des liqueurs qu'il
      contient,
Ô vent, dont j'aspirai souvent la violence,
Durant les jours fougueux de mon adolescence,
Je sens que, dans mon corps tordu de passions,
Tu te mêles au sang des générations !

Car mes aïeux, au cours de luttes séculaires,
Subirent tant de fois les coups de tes lanières,
Que ta rage puissante en pénétra leurs sens :
Nous sommes devenus frères depuis longtemps !
Car, de les voir toujours debout devant ta face,
Tu compris qu'ils étaient des créateurs de race,
Et par une magie étrange, tu donnas
La vigueur de ton souffle aux muscles de leurs
        bras !

Le double acharnement se poursuit dans mes
        veines,
Et quand je suis courbé sur quelques tâches vaines,
Ô vent, qui te prêtas tant de fois à mes jeux,
Que résonne en mon cœur ton appel orageux,
Je tiens autant de toi que d'eux ma violence,
Ma haine de l'obstacle et ma peur du silence,
Et, malgré tous les ans dont je me sens vieillir,
De préférer encor l'espoir au souvenir !

Hélas ! la ville a mis entre nous deux ses briques
Et je ne comprends plus aussi bien tes cantiques.
Depuis que j'en subis le lâche apaisement.
L'effroi de la douleur s'infiltre lentement,
Chaque jour, dans ma chair de mollesse envahie,
Telle, entre les pavés, la fleur s'emplit de suie.
Je sens des lâchetés qui me rongent les nerfs,
Et ne retrouve plus qu'un charme de vieux airs
À tels mots glorieux qui m'insufflaient des fièvres.
Un sourire sceptique a rétréci mes lèvres,
Et je crains, quelquefois, qu'en m'éveillant,
        demain,
Je ne sente mon cœur devenu trop humain !

Ô vent, emporte-moi vers la grande Aventure.
Je veux boire la force âpre de la Nature,
Loin, par delà l'encerclement des horizons
Que souille la fumée étroite des maisons !
Je veux aller dormir parmi les cîmes blanches,

Bercé par la rumeur de ta voix en courroux,
Et par le hurlement famélique des loups !

ALFRED
DESROCHERS

Le froid et le sommeil qui cloront mes paupières
Me donneront l'aspect immuable des pierres !
Ô rôdeur immortel qui vas depuis le temps,
Je ne subirai plus l'horreur ni les tourments
De l'âme enclose au sein d'un moule périssable;
J'oublierai que ma vie est moins qu'un grain de
    sable
Au sablier des ans chus dans l'Éternité !

Et quand viendront sur moi les vagues de clarté
Que l'aube brusquement roulera sur mon gîte,
Je secouerai l'amas de neige qui m'abrite;
Debout, je humerai l'atmosphère des monts,
Pour que sa force nette emplisse mes poumons,
Et, cambré sur le ciel que l'aurore incendie,
Je laisserai ma voix, comme ta poudrerie,
Descendre sur la plaine en rauques tourbillons,
Envelopper l'essaim maculé des maisons,
Afin que, dominant le bruit de son blasphème,
Je clame au monde veule, ô mon Vent, que je
    t'aime !

'City-Hotel'

'Nous n'irons plus voir nos blondes.'

Le sac au dos, vêtus d'un rouge mackinaw,
Le jarret musculeux étranglé dans la botte,
Les *shantymen* partants s'offrent une ribote
Avant d'aller passer l'hiver à Malvina.

Dans le bar, aux vitraux orange et pimbina,
Un rayon de soleil oblique, qui clignote,
Dore les appui-corps nickelés, où s'accote,
En pleurant, un gaillard que le gin chagrina.

45

Les vieux ont le ton haut et le rire sonore,
Et chantent des refrains grassouillets de folklore;
Mais un nouveau, trouvant ce bruit intimidant,

S'imagine le camp isolé de Van Dyke.
Et sirote un *demi-schooner* en regardant
Les danseuses sourire aux affiches de laque.

ALFRED
DES ROCHERS

ROY
DANIELLS

b. 1902

Journey

In this road that I must take
Three beasts watching from the wood
(Allegory is understood)
A fox, a peacock and a cold snake.

Canada : habitat of fox
Who only here is never hunted
Never shot. Never daunted.
Barking among the barren rocks.

Canada : here no halls of state
No velvet lawn in college close,
But peacocks here proudly unclose
Their tails, scream and defecate.

Canada : where the sly snake
Opens upon you his cold eye
Self-righteously. As you go by
Suddenly fangs are in your neck.

Let me go for I must find
That old stairway to the rock
Where stars tick over like a clock
To lighten me, to clear my mind.

Said the fox, Stay in this wood,
Follow me, I lead, I lead
By speed of turn and turn of speed
None of the hounds have understood.

ROY
DANIELLS

Said the peacock with shrill cry,
I am the cynosure, the pole.
Said the snake, Complete and whole
Wisdom shines in my cold eye.

Let me pass, I must climb
Steps cut in the granite face
If I am to reach that place
Where the stars move out of time.

What is the mountain you must find?
Blomidon or Mont Real?
Remoter Robson? Can you tell
Its name, the mountain in your mind?

A speculative rock apart
From Rockies or the abraded Shield
Or peaks the Appalachians yield.
A mountain not disclosed by art.

Said the fox, Run behind me,
Cross the stream, leap the hedge,
Double, crouch below the ledge.
None of the hounds can ever find me.

Said the peacock, I am I
(And all the little birds answered, Aye)
See my tail like a spread sky
Every feather with purple eye.

Said the snake, Understand
Only I have ancient wisdom
Lore and logic, sense and system.
He struck, his fangs closed in my hand.

I went stumbling through the wood,
The fox's bark defiled the wind,

47

Peacock's dung stank in my mind,
Venom clotted all my blood.

ROY
DANIELLS

Stair to stair, clambering
Till unbroken sky stood tall,
Far below I left them all,
But my mind faltering,

Shaping from the shrunken tree,
Spying in the leaning rocks,
Peacock, snake and veering fox,
Shapes that still I bear with me.

Steeper now new steps ascend
To that ledge that leaves all height;
There must I sustain the light,
There leave breath and blood behind.

A. J. M.
SMITH
b. 1902

News of the Phoenix

They say the Phoenix is dying, some say dead.
Dead without issue is what one message said,
But that has been suppressed, officially denied.

I think myself the man who sent it lied.
In any case, I'm told, he has been shot,
As a precautionary measure, whether he did
    or not.

Resurrection of Arp

A. J. M.
SMITH

On the third day rose Arp
out of the black sleeve of the tomb :
he could see like a cat in the dark,
but the light left him dumb.

He stood up to testify,
and his tongue wouldn't work
in the old groove; he had to try
other tongues, including the Scandinavian.

The saints were all well pleased;
his periods rattled and rolled;
heresies scattered like ninepins;
all the tickets were sold.

When they turned down the gas
everybody could see there was
a halo of tongues of pale fire
licking the grease off his hair,

and a white bird
fluttered away in the rafters;
people heard
the breaking of a mysterious wind (laughter).

He spoke another language
majestic beautiful wild
holy superlative believable
and undefiled

by any comprehensible
syllable
to provoke dissent
or found a schism. . . .

After the gratifyingly large
number of converts had been given receipts
the meeting adjourned to the social hall
for sexual intercourse (dancing) and eats.

A. J. M.
SMITH

Arp talked to the reporters :
on the whole, was glad to have cheated the tomb,
though the angels had been 'extremely courteous',
and death, after all, was only 'another room'.

Ballade un peu banale

The bellow of good Master Bull
    Astoundeth gentil Cow
That standeth in the meadow cool
    Where cuckoo singeth now.

She stoppeth in a moony trance
    Beneath the timeless trees
While ebon-bellied shad-flies dance
    About her milk-white knees.

He snuffeth her from distant field—
    Sly Farmer Pimp approves :
To him the gates and latches yield;
    He smiles upon their loves.

Bull boometh from the briary bush,
    Advanceth, tail aloft—
The meadow grass is long and lush,
    The oozy turf is soft.

He stampeth with his foremost foot,
    His nostrils breathing bale;
Uncouth, unhallowed is his suit;
    The vestal turneth tail.

He feinteth with his ivory horn,
    Bites rump, bites flank, bites nape—
Sweet Saviour of a Virgin born,
    How shall this maid escape!

He chaseth her to pasture wall;
    She maketh stand, poor bird!
He wields his tail like an iron flail.
    Alas! he presseth hard!

.   .   .

I like to think sweet Jesus Christ,
    For His dear Mother's sake,
By some miraculous device,
    Her to Himself did take;

That her preserv'd Virginity
    Flutes holy flats and sharps
In that divine vicinity
    Where Eliot's hippo harps.

A. J. M.
SMITH

Brigadier

A SONG OF FRENCH CANADA

One Sunday morning soft and fine
Two old campaigners let their nags meander;
One was a Sergeant of the Line,
The other a Brigade Commander.
The General spoke with martial roar,
'Nice weather for this time of year!'
    And 'Right you are,' replied Pandore,
    'Right you are, my Brigadier.'

'A Guardsman's is a thankless calling,
Protecting private property,
In summer or when snows are falling,

From malice, rape, or robbery;
While the wife whom I adore
Sleeps alone and knows no cheer.'
    And *'Right you are,' replied Pandore,*
    'Right you are, my Brigadier.'

'I have gathered Glory's laurel
With the rose of Venus twined—
I am Married, and a General;
Yet, by Jesus, I've a mind
To start like Jason for the golden shore
And follow my Star—away from here!'
    'Ah, right you are,' replied Pandore,
    'Right you are, my Brigadier.'

'I remember the good days of my youth
And the old songs that rang
So cheerily. In that time, forsooth,
I had a doting mistress, full of tang . . .
But, ah! the heart—I know not wherefore—
Loves to change its bill of fare.'
    And *'Right you are,' replied Pandore,*
    'Right you are, my Brigadier.'

Now Phoebus neared his journey's end;
Our heroes' shadows fell behind :
Yet still the Sergeant did attend,
And still the General spoke his mind.
'Observe,' he said, 'how more and more
Yon orb ensanguines all the sphere.'
    And *'Right you are,' replied Pandore,*
    'Right you are, my Brigadier.'

They rode in silence for a while :
You only heard the measured tread
Of muffled hoof beats, mile on mile—
But when Aurora, rosy red,
Unbarred her Eastern door,

The faint refrain still charmed the ear,   A. J. M.
    As 'Right you are,' replied Pandore,   SMITH
    'Right you are, my Brigadier.'

What the Emanation of Casey Jones
Said to the Medium

Turn inward on the brain
The flashlight of an I,
While the express train
Time, unflagged, roars by.

Pick out the dirt of stars,
Wipe off the wires of gut,
Uncouple the foetid cars
From the spangled banner of smut.

Then shine, O curdled orb,
Within thy vantage box,
Field that attracts, absorbs
Cats, hairpins, spring greens, clocks,

That twists like vapour, seeps
From tunnel's murky bung
Hole, fogs the vista-dome and creeps
Away, accomplished and undone.

Take note of freedom's prize,
Dissolve and walk the wind,
Ride camels through the eyes
Of moles—the make-up of the mind

Embellishes and protects,
Draws beards between fabulous tits,
Endorses the stranger's checks,
Judges and always acquits.

Turn inward to the brain:
The signal stars are green,
Unheard the ghost train
Time, and Death can not be seen.

Watching the Old Man Die

A. J. M.
SMITH

Watching the old man die
I savoured my own death,
Like a cowardly egotist
Whose every thought and breath
Must turn and twist
Selfward, inescapably.

When he struggled for breath
With a kind of unhinged sigh
I held my own in suspense.
The body cannot lie.
If blood and breath condense
Even the Will cries death.

This I was forced to learn,
Watching the old man die,
Hating his sharpened point
That picked at my watery eye
And jellied my knee joint
Till death was my own concern.

The body cannot lie.
I savoured my own death
And wept for myself not him.
I was forced to admit the truth
It was not his death I found grim
But knowing that I must die.

Laprairie Hunger Strike

Lehmann does well with Largactil;
but the maniac woman won't eat,
she's starving of fear.

Patients are pioneer neighbours
locked in a wood; they help each other
among these iron bedrows.

A scarecrow girl shreds meat
to rub it gently on the woman's lips,
opening rock jaws with kindness.

Dare you come to grips
with a different ending? I see an insane face
of rock world never yielding to love's grace.

Cold-Weather Love

Expanding in the chill,
lake ice elbows itself
and presses down the water.
I hear ice split;
water sprays up in pressure ridges.

Cold squeezes my blood
to run faster.
Remember the rape outside Drumheller
at fifty below?
Canadians are hardy.

Beware of me, my love,
in an eternity of cold;
my death makes me more active.

Old Snapshot

RONALD
EVERSON

I heard an ignorant crow call, 'Life is *now*
now now now now now,'
when I was picnicking with Evelyn, aunt,
fifty years ago.

This instant,
Evelyn and mother (who snapped the photograph)
and I look at the vanished scene. It's pleasure
we feel. We gently laugh,
gathering this one rosebud at our leisure.

Letter from Underground

Like tall men with a battering-plank—the colt
gallops on beetles and dung. He bumps a strand
of pale electric fence. It cuts off land
beyond. The awful jolt
knocks him backward. Shrunken colt on stilts
teeters thin between proud sire and dam.

They know the wires run
endlessly around the pasture. Bright with gilts
of horsedung, underprivileged beetles stroll
flat through muddy land
and under the awful fence and over the world.

SIMONE
ROUTIER

b. 1903

Neige et nostalgie

Neige, tu tombes, tombes et tombes sur le sol
    étonné, puis sensible et résigné,
Sur le sol résigné de mon pays, enjouée et
    volontaire, tu tombes,

De mon pays que j'ai laissé certain printemps
    derrière mes pas,

SIMONE
ROUTIER

Que j'ai laissé sans me retourner pour voir s'il
    était toujours là,

S'il était toujours là robuste et cruel et tumultueux
    et vierge,

Tu tombes, ô neige, profuse, verticale, circulaire,
    neige de mon pays,

Tu tombes obstinée, sur toi-même, inlassablement,

Tu tombes en tourbillon qui aveugle, saccage et
    désempare,

En tourbillon tu tombes distraite et fatale,

Tu tombes sur mon pays là-bas,

Tu tombes et je n'y suis pas.

Le divin anéantissement

Cette assomption de la chair en l'unité de Dieu con-
cerne chacun de nous.—A. D. SERTILLANGES, O.P.

La mer qui berce, chante et endort,

L'Église qui écoute, pardonne et absout.

La mer berçante qui porte la barque et ramène le
    pêcheur,

La mer qui chante et rend la terre au marin,

La mer qui endort l'exilé et dilate le cœur

En mal de plongeurs la mer ne se lasse jamais de
    bercer.

En mal d'âme l'Église ne se lasse jamais de
    prêcher.

Une prière excite une autre prière,

Une lame épaule une autre lame

Et l'écume qui sur la plage

T'apprend la saveur de la mer

A mis des années à t'en préparer le sel.

Entre dans la mer et laisse-toi couper les jambes.

Dans la vague qui porte on n'a que faire des
    chevilles.

Coupe les amarres des attaches charnelles.
L'Église te prend dans ses bras
Et le corps ne peut appartenir à deux étreintes.

SIMONE
ROUTIER

Le coquillage à ton oreille a porté toute la mer.
Le prédicateur t'a conté l'Évangile.
Mais quel infime secret, dans un seul coquillage
L'immense mer a-t-elle pu emprisonner?
Qu'est à l'homme la douceur du plus poignant
    Évangile
En regard de tout l'amour de son Auteur même, en
    lui?

Confonds-toi à la mer : ell se confondra à toi.
Ses trésors, un à un, jour après jour,
D'un coquillage, d'une vague, d'une marée à
    l'autre,
D'une grâce à l'autre tous elle te les confiera dès
    ici-bas.
Ne discute et ne pèche plus sur la plage.
Donne-toi; fais confiance à l'eau.

L'Église n'est point une doctrine, c'est une
    tendresse.
La mer n'est point un abîme, c'est un refuge.
Combien léger ton cœur dans la poitrine de
    l'Église.
Combien libre le poids de ton corps dans l'eau,
Dans l'eau salée de la mer qui porte,
Qui soulève, assainit, dégage et assouplit.

Romps les amarres, jette-toi à Dieu.
Ne supporte plus le soleil qu'à travers l'eau,
La tentation qu'à travers la grâce;
Ne remets plus au sablier du temps le sable,
Bois au sable noyé l'éternité.

Dans la résille d'or que la crête multiple des
    vagues,
A marée basse, forme sur ce sable,

Tends pour toi au fond de la mer,
Laisse-toi prendre, c'est le filet du Divin Pêcheur,
Le filet des troisièmes conversions.

SIMONE
ROUTIER

Seul l'œil t'y peut croire prisonnière,
C'est là que tu conquiers la vraie liberté,
L'exaltante liberté, dans la lumière, des Enfants de
    Dieu.

Abandonne-toi à la mer,
Laisse-la te sculpter à son image,
Te polir de son éternelle patience.

Laisse la grâce t'envelopper, te pénétrer de toutes
    parts
Et tu oublieras les contours de ton corps,
Tu trouveras enfin ceux de ton âme,
Infinie à la mesure de la mer, infinie à la mesure
    de Dieu.

Pour oublier la ville, ne va plus au village,
Pour oublier le village, égare ici tes sandales
Et pour renoncer aux sandales, laisse-toi scier les
    chevilles.
Laisse-moi, dit la mer, t'enlever à la terre,
Laisse-moi t'apprendre le véritable abandon et la
    joie,
Laisse-moi t'apprendre l'extase infinie, mon Divin
    anéantissement.

EARLE
BIRNEY
_____
b. 1904

Bushed

He invented a rainbow but lightning struck it
shattered it into the lake-lap of a mountain
so big his mind slowed when he looked at it

Yet he built a shack on the shore
learned to roast porcupine belly and
wore the quills on his hatband

EARLE
BIRNEY

At first he was out with the dawn
whether it yellowed bright as wood-columbine
or was only a fuzzed moth in a flannel of storm
But he found the mountain was clearly alive
sent messages whizzing down every hot morning
boomed proclamations at noon and spread out
a white guard of goat
before falling asleep on its feet at sundown

When he tried his eyes on the lake   ospreys
would fall like valkyries
choosing the cut-throat
He took then to waiting
till the night smoke rose from the boil of the
        sunset

But the moon carved unknown totems
out of the lakeshore
owls in the beardusky woods derided him
moosehorned cedars circled his swamps and tossed
their antlers up to the stars
Then he knew though the mountain slept, the
        winds
were shaping its peak to an arrowhead
poised

And now he could only
bar himself in and wait
for the great flint to come singing into his heart

Midstream *

EARLE
BIRNEY

AFTER MAO TSE-TUNG

Alone in a cold autumn I stood
where Hsiang-chiang flows north
past the point of Orange-Grove Isle.
The ten thousand hills were crimson,
in crimson tiers the forest.

Up the great hyaline river
struggled a hundred vessels.
Eagles in the vast air poised to strike;
fish in the shallows hovered.
Each living form under the frosty heaven
fought with another for freedom.
I stared from a desolate tower
and asked the immense earth—
who decrees the rise, the fall?

With a hundred friends now, returning
I range back over the rainbow days
the crowded risky years.
O schoolmates, in youth blossoming and tall with
    talents,
we must now in the arrogance of our knowledge
uproot our scented careers.
Fingering mountains only, and rivers,
to hold poetry alive in our minds,
we will use for manure
those bygone dreams of ten-thousand-household
    fiefdoms.
Don't you remember, once it has reached
    midstream
your craft shoots over
as the rapids take flight?

---

* Translated with the aid of Professor Ping-ti Ho of
the University of British Columbia.

The Bear on the Delhi Road

EARLE
BIRNEY

Unreal   tall as a myth
by the road the Himalayan bear
is beating the brilliant air
with his crooked arms
About him two men   bare
spindly as locusts   leap

One pulls on a ring
in the great soft nose   His mate
flicks   flicks with a stick
up at the rolling eyes

They have not led him here
down from the fabulous hills
to this bald alien plain
and the clamorous world   to kill
but simply to teach him to dance

They are peaceful both   these spare
men of Kashmir   and the bear
alive is their living   too
If   far on the Delhi way
around him galvanic they dance
it is merely to wear   wear
from his shaggy body the tranced
wish forever to stay
only an ambling bear
four-footed in berries

It is no more joyous for them
in this hot dust to prance
out of reach of the praying claws
sharpened to paw for ants
in the shadows of deodars
It is not easy to free
myth from reality

or rear this fellow up
to lurch   lurch with them
in the tranced dancing of men

EARLE
BIRNEY

El Greco: Espolio

The carpenter is intent on the pressure of his hand

on the awl   and the trick of pinpointing his
    strength
through the awl to the wood   which is tough
He has no effort to spare for despoilings
or to worry if he'll be cut in on the dice
His skill is vital to the scene   and the safety of
    the state
Anyone can perform the indignities   It's his hard
    arms
and craft that hold the eyes of the convict's
    women
There is the problem of getting the holes exact
(in the middle of this elbowing crowd)
and deep enough to hold the spikes
after they've sunk through those bared feet
and inadequate wrists he knows are waiting
    behind him

He doesn't sense perhaps that one of the hands
is held in a curious gesture over him—
giving   or asking   forgiveness?—
but he'd scarcely take time to be puzzled by poses
Criminals come in all sorts   as anyone knows who
    makes crosses
are as mad or sane as those who decide on their
    killings
Our one at least has been quiet so far
though they say he talked himself into this trouble
a carpenter's son who got notions of preaching

63

Well heres a carpenter's son who'll have carpenter EARLE
    sons   BIRNEY
God willing   and build what's wanted   temples
    or tables
mangers or crosses   and shape them decently
working alone in that firm and profound
    abstraction
which blots out the bawling of rag-snatchers
To construct with hands   knee-weight   braced
    thigh
keeps the back turned from death

But it's too late now for the other carpenter's boy
to return to this peace before the nails are
    hammered

Cartagena de Indias

Ciudad triste, ayer reina de la mar.—HEREDIA.

Each face its own phantom
its own formula of breed and shade
but all the eyes accuse me back and say

> There are only two races here :
> we human citizens
> who are poor but have things to sell
> and you   from outer space
> unseasonable   our one tourist
> but plainly able to buy

This arthritic street
where Drake's men and Cole's ran
swung cutlasses   where wine and sweet blood
snaked in the cobbles' joints
    leaps now in a sennet of taxi horns
    to betray my invasion
All watch my first retreat
to barbizans patched from Morgan's grapeshot
and they rush me

By an altar blackened
where the Indian silver was scratched away
in sanctuary leaning   on lush cool marble
   I am hemmed by a Congo drum-man in jeans
   He bares a brace of Swiss watches
   whispers in husky Texan

Where gems and indigo were sorted
   in shouting arcades
   I am deftly shortchanged
and slink to the trees that lean
and flower tall in the Plaza
   Nine shoeboys wham their boxes
   slap at my newshined feet

Only in the Indio market
mazed on the sodden quais
I am granted uneasy truce
Around the ritual braidings of hair
the magical arrangements of fish
the piled rainbows of rotting fruit
I cast a shadow of silence
   blue-dreaded eyes
   corpse face
   hidalgo clothes
   tall one   tall as a demon
   pass O pass us quickly

Behind me the bright blaze of patois
   leaps again

I step to the beautiful slave-built bridge
and a mestiza girl
   levels Christ's hands at me
   under a dangling goitre

Past the glazed-eyed screamers of *dulces*
swing to a pink lane

where a poxed and slit-eyed savage
   pouts an obscenity
   offering a sister
   as he would spit me
   a dart from a blowpipe

Somewhere there must be another bridge
from my stupid wish
to their human acceptance
but what can I offer—
my tongue half-locked in the cell
of its language—other than pesos
   to these old crones of thirty
   whose young sink in pellagra
   as I clump unmaimed
   in the bright shoes
   that keep me from hookworm
   lockjaw and snakebite

It's written in the cut of my glasses
I've a hotelroom all to myself
with a fan   and a box of Vitamin C
It can be measured
in my unnatural stride
that my life expectation
is more than forty
especially now that I'm close to sixty

older than ever bankrupt Bolívar was
who sits now in a frozen prance
high over the coconut trays
quivering on the heads
   of three gaunt mulatto ladies
   circling in a pavane of commerce
   down upon spotlit me

Out of the heaving womb of independence
Bolívar rode   and over the bloody afterbirth
into coffee and standard oil

from inquisitional baroque
  to armed forces corbusier
He alone has nothing more to sell me

I come routed now   scuffling
through dust in a nameless square
treeless   burning   deserted
come lost and guiltily wakeful
in the hour of siesta
   at last to a message

   to a pair of shoes
   in a circle of baked mud
   worn   out of shape   one on its side
For a second I am shaken by panic
heat? humidity? something has got me
   the shoes are concrete
   and ten feet long

   the sight of a plaque calms
   without telling me much

        En homenaje de la memoria de
            LUIS LOPEZ
         se erigió este monumento
          a los zapatos viejos
       el día 10 de febrero de 1957

Luis Lopez?   Monument to his old shoes?
What???   There was nothing else

Back through the huckster streets
the sad taxi men still awake and horn-happy

   Si señor   Luis Lopez el poeta
   Here is his book
   Unamuno praised it   *si si*
   You have seen *los zapatos*?   Ah?
   But they are us, *señor*

It was about us he wrote
and died   See here this sonnet
always he made hard words
Said we were lazy except to make noise
we only shout to get money
ugly too, backward . . . why not?
It is for a poet to write these things
Also *plena*—how say it?—
plena de rancio desaliño
Full of rancid disarray!
    Si si but look, at the end, when old
he come to say one nice thing
only one ever about us
He say we inspire that love a man has
for his old shoes—*Entonces*
we give him a monument to the shoes

I bought the book   walked back
sat on the curb happier than Wordsworth
gazing away at his daffodils

Discarded queen   I thought   I love you too
Full of rancid disarray
city like any city
full of the stench of human indignity
and disarray of the human proportion
full of the noisy always poor
and the precocious dying
stinking with fear   the stale of ignorance
I love you first for giving birth
to Luis Lopez   suffering him
honouring him at last
in the grand laconic manner
he taught you

—and him I envy
I who am seldom read by my townsmen

Descendants of pirates   grandees   EARLE
BIRNEY
galleyslaves and cannibals
I love the whole starved cheating
poetry-reading lot of you   most of all
for throwing me the shoes of deadman Luis
to walk me back into your brotherhood

Sinalóa

Si, señor, is halligators here, your guidebook say it,
si, jaguar in the montañas, maybe helephants
    quién sabe?
You like, those palm trees in the sunset?
    Certamente very nice,
it happen each night in the guide tourista.
But who the hell eat jaguar, halligator, you heat
    them?
Mira my fren, wat this town need is muy big
    breakwater—
        I like take hax to them jeezly palmas.

So you want buy machete? Por favor, I give you
sousand machete you give me one grand
    bulldozer, hey?
Wat this country is lack, señor, is real good
    goosin,
is need pinehapple shove hup her bottom
(sure, sure, is bella all those water-ayacints)
it need drains for sugarcane in them pittorescos
    swamps—
        and shoot all them anarquista egrets.

Hokay, you like bugambilla, ow you say,
    flower-hung cliffs?
Is how old, the Fort? Is Colhuan, muy viejo,
    before Moses, no?
Is for you, señor, take em away, send us helevator
    for weat.

It like me to see all them fine boxcar stuff full rice,
sugar, flax, all rollin down to those palmstudded
    ports
were Cortez and all that crap (you heat history?)—
        and bugger the pink flamingos.

Amigo, we make you present all them two-weel
    hoxcart,
you send em Québec, were my brudder was learn
to be padre—
we take ditchdiggers, tractors, Massey-Arris yes?
Sinalóa want ten sousand mile irrigation canals,
absolutamente. Is fun all that organ-cactus fence?
Is for the birds, señor; is more better barbwire,
    verdad?—
        and chingar those cute little burros.

Sin argumento, my fren, is a beautiful music,
all them birds. Pero, wy you no like to hear
    combos,
refrigerator trucks? Is wonderful on straight new
    ighway,
jampack with melons, peppers, bananas, tomatoes,
    si, si . . .
Chirrimoyas? Mangos? You like! Is for Indios,
    solamente,
is bruise, no can ship, is no bueno, believe me,
    señor—
        and defecar on those goddam guidebook.

Vivre et créer

Ah! le mal de créer obsède ma jeunesse!
Je voudrais me refaire, afin d'être plus fort
Et meilleur et plus pur, et pour que je renaisse
Et que je vive encor lorsque je serai mort!

Vivre! baigner mon cœur dans l'aurore ineffable!
Chanter la mer profonde et les arbres épais
Jusqu'à ce que la voix de mon corps périssable
Invente un cri d'amour qui ne mourra jamais!

Vivre! vivre! éclater les chaînons de la chaîne!
D'un grand coup d'aile, atteindre au flamboiement
    de Dieu,
Y ravir l'étincelle et faire une œuvre humaine
Qui soit presque divine et pareille au ciel bleu!

Oh! l'infini du ciel m'étreint. Mon cœur avide
Tel l'éponge des mers se gonfle et se remplit.
Mais ma bouche qui s'ouvre est comme un antre
    vide
Où la morne impuissance habite et fait son lit;

Et ma langue se meut comme l'algue marine
Que retient par les pieds le rocher triomphant;
Et quand mon cœur ému se heurte à ma poitrine
Ma langue balbutie un murmure d'enfant.

Eh bien! je boirai tant les souffles d'aventure,
Je ferai tant chanter dans mes jeunes poumons
La respiration de la forte nature,
Que ma voix bondira sur le sommet des monts.

Choses du monde! O clapotis glouton des vagues;
Irascible soleil, étoiles d'argent pur

Aux doigts fins des bouleaux brillant comme des
    bagues;
Vents des plaines, glaciers étincelants d'azur;

Rocs que la mer assiège ainsi que des tourelles;
Frais calice où s'engouffre un oiseau-mouche; ô
    bruit
Métallique et vibrant des brusques sauterelles;
Remous parmi les blés, parfum, saveur du fruit;

Nature aux grands yeux verts, créatrice éternelle
Qui tiens l'humanité dans le creux de ta main,
Ah! que dans ta lumière immense et maternelle
Bondisse immensément mon faible cœur humain!

Prends me jeunesse, Terre ineffable et sauvage,
Aïeule au front sans âge et toujours renaissant!
Verse-moi ta fraîcheur comme un divin breuvage!
Rende le corps de ton fils musculeux et puissant!

Prends-moi, prends-moi, nature aux mamelles
    fécondes!
Chante-moi ta berceuse, et donne la vigueur
A ton petit d'hier qui veut créer des mondes
Et qui tombe à genoux sous le poids de son cœur!

ROBERT
CHOQUETTE

From *Suite marine*

(I) PROLOGUE

Iseut, voici la mer!
                    Du haut de ce rocher
Où le goéland ose et vient s'attacher,
Du haut du vent qui fait valser les grains de sable,
Regarde, Iseut: c'est elle, immense, intarissable,
C'est elle avec l'ampleur qu'ont les gestes de Dieu.

Du haut de ce rocher taillé dans le ciel bleu,
Salut à l'élément père et mère des êtres,

L'eau des cinq océans, le lait primordial !

ROBERT
CHOQUETTE

Source de vie, ô mer, et puissant cordial,
Masse de nuit féconde où les premiers ancêtres
Cherchèrent dans l'effroi leur forme et leur
    couleur;
Paradoxal abîme où l'animal est fleur,
Où la plante respire et dévore la bête,
Où la mort et l'amour et l'amour et la mort
Passent de l'un à l'autre en une vaste fête
Éternelle, salut ! À l'est, au sud, au nord,
Ce qui naissait hier fait place à qui veut naître,
Aux aveugles instincts avides de connaître
L'enchantement d'avoir des yeux. Gloire à la mer
Qui, sous le tendre éclat de ce ciel qui l'azure,
Insatiablement tue et crée à mesure
De quoi nourrir la faim aux mâchoires de fer !
Gloire à la mer et gloire à la vie, et louange,
À la vie implacable où toute forme change
Pour exiger de soi ses élans les plus beaux,
Qui fait de la jeunesse avec les choses mortes,
Qui fait de l'espérance à même des lambeaux,
Si bien que les mangeurs dont les sombres cohortes
Ensanglantent la mer sont d'exaltants tombeaux
Où le sacrifice renaît à l'allégresse !

Mais voici dans la mer le symbole du cœur,
Aux rythmes de fureur, aux rythmes de tendresse,
Gouffre vertigineux sur qui tournent en chœur,
Goélands enroués jusqu'à la frénésie,
Les vigoureux désirs que rien ne rassasie.
Mer, image du cœur, changeant, nouveau toujours,
Cercle d'ombres et de clartés, dont les contours
Flottent dans les vapeurs floconneuses du songe !
Ténèbres de la mer, nuit du cœur, que prolonge
Toujours plus d'ombre encore : abîmes
    tourmentés,
Dieu vous a bien créés d'un seul et même geste,
Sombres replis des mers par des monstres hantés,

Cœur où rampe le goût du meurtre et de l'inceste, ROBERT
CHOQUETTE
Où s'écoutent, pourtant, des voix d'une candeur
Telle que le blasphème expire avant les lèvres;
Mer créatrice de joyaux d'une splendeur
Belle à désespérer les rêves des orfèvres.
Et dans le cœur aussi s'avancent tour à tour
Et reculent, pareils aux puissantes marées,
Le doute et l'espérance, et la haine et l'amour;
Et sur le cœur aussi des barques sont parées,
Et dans la nuit du cœur des carènes sombrées
Pourrissent lentement autour de leur secret.
Ô mer en qui rugit l'effrayant mascaret
Et capable pourtant d'une telle tendresse;
Ô toi l'harmonieuse et toi la charmeresse
Entre toutes, sirène endormeuse à la fois
Et terrible, salut ! C'est grandis par ta voix
Et son écho multiplié qui roule et gronde,
Ô mer, que deux amants, à compter de ce jour,
Vont prêter leur jeunesse aux vieux mots de
    l'amour,
Et qu'une fois encor ces mots créeront le monde
En réglant sur deux cœurs le rhythme universel !
Accueille-nous, Circé : notre amour vient de
    naître !
Notre premier baiser a la saveur du sel !
C'est en face de toi que nous venons connaître,
Dans l'exaltation du cœur mélodieux,
Une félicité qui nous égale aux dieux !

Regarde, Iseut : la mer aussi loin que ton rêve,
Mais, tout près, à nos pieds, la rade et ses oiseaux,
Et ses hommes, ses quais, ses maisons sur la grève,
Et les barques, d'ici qui semblent des berceaux;
Et tout cela, joyeux, grésille d'étincelles,
La grève, les filets, les toits et les nacelles,
Et si nombreux au fil de l'eau, si clairs, si blancs
Si vifs les goélands parmi les goélands,

On croit que c'est la mer, la mer qui bat des ailes !   ROBERT
CHOQUETTE

Iseut, nous descendrons vers ce village étroit,
Ce havre où les pêcheurs, ajustant le suroît,
Mouillent de bleus reflets le clair-obscur des
    portes;
Et nous n'en partirons qu'au mois des feuilles
    mortes,
Qui veut dire jamais, puisque le Temps n'est plus.

Cher village bercé des flux et des reflux,
Cher village inconnu dont le dernier méandre
S'avoue à nos regards en ce jeune matin,
Salut ! joli village où nous allons descendre
Appareiller gaiement la barque du destin.

(II) LA GROTTE DE NEPTUNE

Par un seuil vert et bleu comme une nuit de lune,
On entre dans la grotte, et d'étranges poissons
Dessinés côte à côte ou nageant à la file
Y rôdent sur les murs, y broutent des buissons
Où l'algue se balance à jamais immobile,
Où l'anguille poursuit sa fuite indélébile.
Viens. Imagine ici l'onduleuse maison,
La grotte aux murs de laminaires, où Neptune
Ondoyant et divers recèle sa fortune.
C'est un pays couleur de songe, où l'horizon
Recule en profondeur et donne une âme étrange.
Dans le palais magique où la pénombre effrange
Des rubans de varech vaguement dessinés,
Asseyons-nous, muets d'extase, fascinés.
Que de secrets ! que de trésors ! tant de surprises !
Aux quatre murs, rochers sculptés comme des
    frises,
C'est un foisonnement si riche de couleurs
Que l'œil distingue mal la bête entre les fleurs.

(III) LA SIRÈNE

ROBERT
CHOQUETTE

En ce bleu paradis qu'embaume l'oléandre,
Sur cet îlot désert dont le flanc de corail
Eparpille la mer en miettes de vitrail,
Il semble qu'on ne soit venu que pour surprendre,
Seule, tenant une algue en guise d'éventail
Et sa robe squameuse à la vague enlacée,
La sirène aux cheveux d'ombre glauque et glacée.

(IV) NOCTURNE

Face à face, sans âge et toujours rajeunis,
Deux abîmes : la Mer qui fut jadis fournaise,
La Nuit céruléenne aux arceaux infinis.

Ici règne éternel le temps de la Genèse,
Quand Jéhovah, planant sur les flots esseulés,
Gardait encore en lui le verbe de semence.

L'abîme de douceur, l'autre d'horreur, mêlés
L'un à l'autre, à jamais, en une étreinte immense,
Échangent des mots d'ombre et des mots étoilés.

Je suis l'éternité qui toujours recommence,
Qui ne change jamais et change à tout instant
Et, sans jamais mourir, se recrée elle-même :

La Mer ! Je suis la Nuit, abîme palpitant
Mais éternel à la façon du théorème,
À la façon du cercle, immuable, constant.

Mes astres, entrainés par une loi suprême,
S'équilibrent si bien que j'ai l'illusion
De l'immobilité dans l'âge et dans l'espace.

Je suis la Mer, la mer riche à profusion
De fleurs et d'animaux dont chacun se déplace
D'après l'obscur vouloir de son impulsion.

ROBERT
CHOQUETTE

Je donne forme à la hideur comme à la grâce;
Je risque, en modelant ces animaux, ces fleurs,
Des figures dont Dieu lui-même s'émerveille.

Je suis la Nuit, creuset où fondent les couleurs
Et les reliefs du monde! Et le monde s'éveille
A son rêve, plus haut que la joie et les pleurs.

Je chante, mais mon chant n'est pas fait pour
    l'oreille,
Ô mes doux carillons qui sonnez pour les yeux,
Étoiles de cristal au plus pur du silence!

Je suis la Mer, je suis l'orgue prodigieux
Aux mille voix intarissables, d'où s'élance
Un hymne tel qu'il fait trembler la nef des cieux,

Un chant qui dit l'horreur, la peur, la violence
Nécessaires, le meurtre implacable et joyeux
Au gouffre de la faim que rien ne rassasie.

Je suis la Nuit, la Nuit dont les doigts emperlés
Portent l'étincelante et sombre Poésie!
Je suis la Mer ... Ainsi, l'un à l'autre mêlés,

Abîme de douceur, gouffre de frénésie,
Ils disent des mots d'ombre et des mots étoilés,
Le gouffre de la Mer, glaciale fournaise,

L'abîme de la Nuit aux infinis arceaux,
Tels encore aujourd'hui qu'au temps de la Genèse,
Quand Jéhovah flottait sur la face des eaux.

Art poétique

Je ne veux plus chercher qu'une pure plastique,
Toute facilité me dégoûte à jamais.
Un vers bien fait vaut mieux que la pseudo-
      musique
Des barbouilleurs de mots vautrés dans
      l'à-peu-près.

Que mon vers soit plus dur que les rochers des
      Andes !
Je préfère Malherbe aux poètes du flou.
Que je sois ce berger solitaire des landes
Dont la voix retentit à l'approche du loup !

Mieux vaut un peintre gris qu'une harmonie en
      rose.
Trop facile est la proie acquise d'un regard.
Un peuple adolescent n'est pas mûr pour la prose,
Quand une page vaut, ce n'est que par hasard.

Forgeons des vers d'acier en cet âge atomique,
Fuyons toute paresse et tous les repentirs.
Mieux vaut une pensée, ou volage, ou comique,
Qu'un recommencement de pleurs et de soupirs.

Préférons le fouet au sablier morose
Et sur des fronts de lys marquons le trait du fer.
Sachons que gît la boue au sein de toute rose,
Qu'un Eden somptueux n'est qu'un modeste enfer.

Je te heurte, il le faut, lecteur qui t'ingénies;
Je n'écris ni pour toi, ni pour moi, ni pour rien.
Je n'écris, malheureux d'avoir tant de génie,
Que pour me délivrer du monstre qui me tient.

Je suis cet effrayant rejeton de la Muse,
Cet enfant plus maudit que défunt Lucifer.
Avec ce fol destin, c'est en vain que je ruse,
Je retombe toujours empalé sur ce fer.

Que s'exalte à jamais le don du virtuose,
Que se taise l'angoisse et s'ébauche le cri !
Si mon vers est plus net que la plus rude prose
J'aurai trop bien gagné mon funeste pari.

FRANÇOIS
HERTEL

Au pays de Québec

MÉDITATION PATRIOTIQUE

Ô mon pauvre pays,
Où rien ne change jamais,
Changer pourtant, c'est vivre, ô mon pays !
Et toi, immobile, fixe, tel un œil de verre dans la
    tête de Robot.
Toi, immuable, avec ton estomac gavé de viandes
Et de promesses.
Toi que l'on souille, sur qui l'on bave une sanie
    impure.
Oh ! ce filet glaireux sur ta face de Titan !
Tu n'as donc plus de sursauts.
Quand nos pères, sous la chevelure intacte des
    forêts vierges,
S'en allaient, 'portageant' leurs canots, jouant leur
    chevelure,
Quand nos pères partaient pour ne plus revenir,—
Et leurs veuves prenaient à deux mains, par les
    mancherons, la charrue,—
Quand nos pères n'étaient morts qu'une fois,
Avant l'oubli . . .
Les grands, les très grands n'engendrent point de
    rejetons à leur taille.

Je croule vers le néant. Moi aussi, je suis le fils
  indigne de ceux qui ont écrit une épopée avec
  leur sang.

FRANÇOIS
HERTEL

Ils ne savaient point signer.
Et nous ne pouvons plus même créer avec les
  mots.
Dire que j'ai peut-être du sang de Frontenac dans
  mes veines étroites,
Et que mon front pâle pourrait être la chair de
  Madeleine.
Quand une race est tarie, elle donne des
  politiciens.

Toute cette prose m'assassine. À boire !
C'est une apparition tricolore. Tous les héros,
La robe blanche de Jeanne Mance,
Les habits bleus de la Monongahela,
Et le front pourpre du grand vaincu, Montcalm,
  avec ce coquelicot, là, sur la poitrine . . .
Ils y sont tous, comme au temps de la légende,
Comme au temps de l'Histoire.
De la main, ils font signe : 'Cherche, disent-ils,
  retrouve le filon !'
Et me voici rêvant d'alchimies laborieuses, de
  transfusions
Idéales.
Oh ! laver notre sang maigre dans le leur,
Rouge, riche, du sang de buffle et du sang
  d'orignal,
Du sang qui ne coule pas, qui caille sur la main.
Dans mon rêve confus, c'est tout un fleuve qui se
  bouscule
De ce sang d'une réincarnation possible.
Et c'est une fantasmagorie : le sang de ceux de
  1660, le sang de 1760, le sang
De 1837.
J'en bois, j'en bois. Où suis-je ? À mort !

·   ·   ·

C'était une plaine immense et verte,   FRANÇOIS
Où le soleil buvait les roses.   HERTEL
Et soudain ce fut le cap Éternité.
Rocher indomptable, inviolé et face aux vents,
Aux vents du nord, ces grands oiseaux polaires,
Ceux que d'Iberville a vaincus sur le Pélican;
Aux vents du sud-est qui miaulent comme des
    chats sauvages : les rafales d'Acadie,
Quand le soir tombe sur Port-Royal.
Et le vieux cap les a maudits dans la tempête.
Soudain la forêt s'est dressée. C'était de l'ouest,
    c'étaient des râles,
C'était la voix de Louis Riel.

Et voici qu'une autre voix, que d'autres voix, que
    mille voix m'ont assailli.
Tous à la fois, ils m'ont parlé; les morts m'ont dit :
 'Qu'ils nous chachent au visage,
Qu'ils nous oublient, qu'ils nous maudissent,
 Qu'ils nous renient, qu'ils nous ignorent,
Mais qu'ils tiennent !'
Voilà ce que mes pères ont dit à mes fils !

      .   .   .

Et le poète est descendu du Sinaï.
Il n'a gardé que la substance,
Que le métal coagulé.
 Les temps ne sont pas encore venus.
1939

Le Chant de l'exilé

Mon malheur est trop grand pour tenir en ce
    monde,
Il doit gésir quelque part dans une éternité.
Ma damnation est sur place et mon crime est
    d'être né,

Mais je ne veux pas mourir; j'aime voir le soleil FRANÇOIS
   quelquefois sur la Seine reluire. HERTEL
Mon cœur est transpercé de glaives infinis.
J'ai perdu tout mon sang sur des routes de feu,
La glace est en moi-même à demeure,
Mon enfer est glacial. Je me meurs congelé.
J'ai tout perdu ce qu'on peut perdre en cette vie
Et j'attends sans hâte et sans joie
Le jour où je coulerai comme un clou
À pic, au fond des mers, un soir, sans aucun bruit.
Je ne sais même plus formuler ma formule
Spéciale de damnation terrestre.
J'ai perdu jusqu'au rythme
Qui me permit jadis de chasser mes épouvantes
En cadence.
Je chante sans chanter, je me livre au hasard.
J'ai fini d'être beau, j'ai fini de crâner.
Je fus presque un poète et presque un philosophe.
Je souffrais de trop de presque.
Je fus presque un homme.
Je suis presque un mort.

À moi les sursauts du cadavre
Et les affres de la pourriture apprise
Au contact des vers de la vie !
Que j'aime ceux des tombeaux,
Comme ils sont propres et nets et luisants,
Comme ils font bien ce qu'ils savent faire.
Tandis que les autres, ceux qu'on appelle hommes
   et femmes,
Comme ils vous mordent lâchement au talon
Quand d'être trop absent à cette vie précise
Ils vous soupçonnent,
Quand ils ont enfin compris que vous aviez un
   certain don pour l'inutile,
Un certain amour de l'absolu,
Une certaine soif de l'infini,
Ce qu'ils s'acharnent sur vous désemparé et petit

82

D'avoir tâché d'être grand.

FRANÇOIS
HERTEL

On est frileux toute sa vie et malade,
On est un nourrisson sans mamelle accueillante,
On est un enfant douloureux, abandonné
Sur le Nil de la destinée,
Quand on a cru qu'il fallait jouer le jeu,
Se donner au monde, être bon, croire aux êtres,
Quand on n'a appris, pendant trente années,
Avec application, malgré ses poussées de haine et
    ses goûts de mépris,
Qu'on n'a appris qu'à aimer.
Alors on s'est mis à cette tâche d'aimer,
Un peu au hasard, sans discernement.
On a aimé tous ceux qui se sont trouvés sur la
    route.
On voyait là un devoir, une grande tâche,
Une grandeur.
Puis, on se sentait bon : ça faisait chaud au cœur.
On a aimé des enfants qui, devenus des hommes,
    vous ont renié,
On a aimé des hommes qui, devenus des vieillards,
    vous ont haï pour votre jeunesse
    miraculeusement sauvée.
On a aimé des femmes qui vous ont méprisé parce
    que vous les aviez traitées comme des reines.
On a aimé des vieillards, qui ont eu le temps
    encore de vous vomir dans les râles de leur
    agonie,
Parce que vous persistiez à demeurer jeune
    odieusement.
On a aimé Dieu avec désespoir, avec horreur,
    parce qu'aimer Dieu, c'est renoncer un peu à
    soi,
Et on a senti un jour Dieu se retirer pour ne
    jamais revenir peut-être.
On a été humble jusqu'à l'orgueil de s'anéantir,
On a été chaste jusqu'à cesser de se sentir un
    homme,

On a été pitoyable jusqu'à s'ôter le pain de la
    bouche pour le jeter aux pourceaux,
On a été just jusqu'à être loyal avec ses ennemis.
On a été un idiot sublime.

Et voici qu'un bon matin on se réveille, porc
    parmi les porcs,
Avec tous ces instincts qu'on déplorait chez les
    autres
Et qu'on a cru refoulés en soi,
Avec tous ces instincts luisants comme des fauves
    léchés,
Déchaînés et dévorants.
On s'était cru béni, on n'était que plus sûrement
    maudit que les autres.
Et ce qu'on a vu surtout, ce sont les regards de
    joie de tous,
Des enfants, des hommes, des femmes et des
    vieillards,
De tous ceux en somme qu'on avait aimés,
Pour lesquels on s'était débité
Comme une bûche à brûler dans l'âtre de toutes
    les bienfaisances,
Et qui sont heureux de se rendre compte qu'un
    homme n'est qu'un homme,
Et qu'ils n'ont pas à rougir plus souvent qu'à leur
    tour.

Croulons enfin, colonne,
Mur, écroulons-nous.
Cessons d'être l'opprobre de nos frères,
Et de leur faire honte d'avoir été bon.
Devenons ce tigre impardonné,
Soyons le fouet impitoyable emporté par une
    main sans but
Vers des itinéraires sans pardons.
Claquez donc, fouet de ma vengeance,
Et meurtrissez-moi, haire de ma haine !

Cette humanité tant de foi maudite,
Maudissons-la encore un peu pour la forme
Et pour que Dieu n'ait pas été le seul à se
   repentir de la naissance de l'homme!

FRANÇOIS
HERTEL

MALCOLM
LOWRY

1909–1957

Salmon Drowns Eagle

The golden eagle swooped out of the sky
And flew back with a salmon in her claws,
Well-caught herself, till she could light near by
On her own rock. Meantime she heard loud caws.
So freighted, she could not fly fast nor far;
Nor, by God, could she let that salmon go.
Hoarse scavengers approached over the bar,
The one thing that fierce eagle hated : crow.
Now there was her rock, to stamp her prey loose,
And crows grabbing chunks of wild flesh away.
There is no argument with crows, nor truce,
The eagle said, heading across the bay!
The sea is wide, black and tempestuous,
But let me disintegrate to a hook
Before I share with the incestuous
Daughters of some ineligible rook!
Oh, she'd have made the land easy enough,
But the fish was heavy and pulled her down.
When she lit on the bay to rest, that tough
Salmon turned and threshed in a way not shown
In the books. Twisting over and over,
Pulling the eagle under the water,
Till she would fly off, angry; moreover,
She was tired out. The salmon fought her :
And next time she lit pulled her down under.

85

She never came up again. . . . It appears,   MALCOLM
In the mundial popular thunder,   LOWRY
Any moral to this dins in drowned ears.

Sestina in a Cantina

SCENE : *A waterfront tavern in Vera Cruz at daybreak.*

LEGION
Watching this dawn's mnemonic of old dawning :
Jonquil-coloured, delicate, some in prison,
Green dawns of drinking tenderer than sunset,
But clean and delicate like dawns of ocean
Flooding the heart with pale light in which horrors
Stampede like plump wolves in distorting mirrors.

Oh, we have seen ourselves in many mirrors;
Confusing all our sunsets with the dawning,
Investing every tongue and leaf with horrors,
And every stranger overtones for prison,
And seeing mainly in the nauseous ocean
The last shot of our life before the sunset.

ST LUKE (*a ship's doctor*)
How long since you have really seen a sunset?
The mind has many slanting lying mirrors,
The mind is like that sparkling greenhouse ocean
Glass-deceptive in the Bengal dawning;
The mind has ways of keeping us in prison,
The better there to supervise its horrors.

SIR PHILIP SIDNEY
Why do you not, sir, organize your horrors
And shoot them one day, preferably at sunset,
That we may wake up next day not in prison,
No more deceived by lies and many mirrors,
And go down to the cold beach at dawning
To lave away the past in colder ocean?

ST LUKE
MALCOLM
LOWRY
No longer is there freedom on the ocean.
And even if there were, he likes his horrors,
And if he shot them would do so at dawning
That he might have acquired some more by sunset,
Breaking them in by that time before mirrors
To thoughts of spending many nights in prison.

LEGION
The fungus-coloured sky of dawns in prison,
The fate that broods on every pictured ocean,
The fatal conversations before mirrors,
The fiends and all the spindly breeds of horrors,
Have shattered by their beauty every sunset
And rendered quite intolerable old dawning.

The oxen standing motionless at dawning—
Outside our tavern now, outside our prison—
Red through the wagon wheels, jalousies like
    sunset,
Swinging now in a sky as calm as ocean,
Where Venus hangs her obscene horn of horrors
For us now swaying in a hall of mirrors—

Such horrid beauty maddened all my mirrors,
Has burst in heart's eye sanity of dawning,
No chamber in my house brimful of horrors
But does not whisper of some dreadful prison,
Worse than all ships dithering through the ocean
Tottering like drunkards, arms upraised at sunset.

RICHARD III (a barman)
Vain derelict all avid for the sunset!
Shine out fair sun till you have bought new
    mirrors
That you may see your shadow pass the ocean,
And sunken no more pass our way at dawning,
But lie on the cold stone sea floor of some prison,
A chunk of sodden driftwood gnawed by horrors.

LEGION   MALCOLM
At first I never looked on them as horrors;   LOWRY
But one day I was drinking hard near sunset,
And suddenly saw the world as a giant prison,
Ruled by tossing moose-heads, with hand mirrors,
And heard the voice of the idiot speak at dawning,
And since that time have dwelt beside the ocean.

EL UNIVERSAL (*early edition*)
Did no one speak of love beside the ocean,
Have you not felt, even among your horrors,
Granting them, there was such a thing as dawning,
A dawning for man whose star seems now at
    sunset,
Like million-sheeted scarlet dusty mirrors,
But one day must be led out of his prison?

LEGION
I see myself as all mankind in prison,
With hands outstretched to lanterns by the ocean;
I see myself as all mankind in mirrors,
Babbling of love while at his back rise horrors
Ready to suck the blood out of the sunset
And amputate the godhead of the dawning.

THE SWINE
And now the dawning drives us from our prison
Into the dawn like sunset, into the ocean,
Bereaving him of horrors, but leaving him his
    mirrors. . . .

Xochitepec

Those animals that follow us in dream
Are swallowed by the dawn, but what of those
Which hunt us, snuff, stalk us out in life, close
In upon it, belly-down, haunt our scheme

Of building, with shapes of delirium,   MALCOLM LOWRY
Symbols of death, heraldic, and shadows,
Glowering? — Just before we left Tlalpám
Our cats lay quivering under the maguey;
A meaning had slunk, and now died, with them.
The boy slung them half stiff down the ravine,
Which now we entered, and whose name is hell.
But still our last night had its animal :
The puppy, in the cabaret, obscene,
Looping-the-loop and soiling all the floor,
And fastening itself to that horror
Of our last night : while the very last day
As I sat bowed, frozen over mescal,
They dragged two kicking fawns through the hotel
And slit their throats, behind the barroom
    door. . . .

Christ Walks in This Infernal District Too

Beneath the Malebolge lies Hastings Street,
The province of the pimp upon his beat,
Where each in his little world of drugs or crime
Moves helplessly or, hopeful, begs a dime
Wherewith to purchase half a pint of piss—
Although he will be cheated, even in this.
I hope, although I doubt it, God knows
This place where chancres blossom like the rose,
For on each face is such a hard despair
That nothing like a grief could enter there.
And on this scene from all excuse exempt
The mountains gaze in absolute contempt,
Yet this is also Canada, my friend,
Yours to absolve of ruin, or make an end.

Autobiographical

(I)

Out of the ghetto streets where a Jewboy
Dreamed pavement into pleasant bible-land,
Out of the Yiddish slums where childhood met
The friendly beard, the loutish Sabbath-goy,
Or followed, proud, the Torah-escorting band
Out of the jargoning city I regret
Rise memories, like sparrows rising from
The gutter-scattered oats,
Like sadness sweet of synagogal hum,
Like Hebrew violins
Sobbing delight upon their eastern notes.

(II)

Again they ring their little bells, those doors
Deemed by the tender-year'd, magnificent:
Old Ashkenazi's cellar, sharp with spice;
The widow's double-parloured candy-stores
And nuggets sweet bought for one sweaty cent;
The warm, fresh-smelling bakery, its pies,
Its cakes, its navel'd bellies of black bread;
The lintels candy-poled
Of barber-shop, bright-bottled, green, blue, red;
And fruit-stall piled, exotic,
And the big synagogue door, with letters of gold.

(III)

Again my kindergarten home is full—
Saturday night—with kin and compatriot:
My brothers playing Russian card-games; my
Mirroring sisters looking beautiful

Humming the evening's imminent fox-trot;
My uncle Mayer, of blessed memory,
Still murmuring Maariv, counting holy words;
And the two strangers, come
Fiery from Volhynia's murderous hordes—
The cards and humming stop.
And I too swear revenge for that pogrom.

(IV)
Occasions dear : the four-legged aleph named
And angel pennies dropping on my book;
The rabbi patting a coming scholar-head;
My mother, blessing candles, Sabbath-flamed,
Queenly in her Warsovian perruque;
My father pickabacking me to bed
To tell tall tales about the Baal Shem Tov,
Letting me curl his beard.
O memory of unsurpassing love,
Love leading a brave child
Through childhood's ogred corridors, unfear'd.

(V)
The week in the country at my brother's (May
He own fat cattle in the fields of heaven !)
Its picking of strawberries from grassy ditch,
Its odour of dogrose and of yellowing hay,—
Dusty, adventurous, sunny days, all seven !—
Still follow me, still warm me, still are rich
With the cow-tinkling peace of pastureland.
The meadow'd memory
Is sodded with its clover, and is spanned
By that same pillow'd sky
A boy on his back one day watched enviously.

(VI)
And paved again the street; the shouting boys
Oblivious of mothers on the stoops
Playing the robust robbers and police,

The corn-cob battle,—all high-spirited noise
Competitive among the lot-drawn groups.
Another day, of shaken apple-trees
In the rich suburbs, and a furious dog
And guilty boys in flight;
Hazelnut games, and games in the synagogue,
The burrs, the Haman rattle,
The Torah-dance on Simchas-Torah night.

(VII)
Immortal days of the picture-calendar
Dear to me always with the virgin joy
Of the first flowing of senses five
Discovering birds, or textures, or a star,
Or tastes sweet, sour, acid, those that cloy,
And perfumes. Never was I more alive.
All days thereafter are a dying-off,
A wandering away
From home and the familiar. The years doff
Their innocence.
No other day is ever like that day.

(VIII)
I am no old man fatuously intent
On memoirs, but in memory I seek
The strength and vividness of nonage days,
Not tranquil recollection of event.
It is a fabled city that I seek;
It stands in space's vapours and Time's haze;
Thence comes my sadness in remembered joy
Constrictive of the throat;
Thence do I hear, as heard by a Jewboy,
The Hebrew violins,
Delighting in the sobbed oriental note.

In re *Solomon Warshawer*

A. M.
KLEIN

On Wodin's day, sixth of December, thirty-nine,
I, Friedrich Vercingetorix, attached
to the VIIth Eavesdroppers-behind-the-Line,
did cover my beat, when, suddenly, the crowd I
    watched
surrounded, in a cobbled lane one can't pass
    through,
a bearded man, in rags, disguised, a Jew.

In the said crowd there were a number of Poles.
Mainly, however, there were Germans there :
blood-brothers of our Reich, true Aryan souls,
breathing at last—in Warsaw—Nordic air.

These were the words the Jew was shouting :
I took them down verbatim :

Whom have I hurt? Against whose silk have I
    brushed?
On which of your women looked too long?
I tell you I have done no wrong!
Send home your children, lifting hardened dung,
And let your curs be hushed!
For I am but beard and breathlessness, and chased
    enough.
Leave me in peace, and let me go my way.

At this the good folk laughed. The Jew continued
    to say
he was no thief; he was a man for hire;
worked for his bread, artist or artisan;
a scribe if you wished; a vendor; even buyer;
work of all kinds, and anything at all :
paint a mural, scour a latrine,

indite an ode, repair an old machine,
anything, to repeat,
anything at all,
so that he might eat
and have his pallet in his abandoned stall.

Asked for his papers, he made a great to-do
of going through the holes in his rags, whence he
    withdrew
a Hebrew pamphlet and a signet ring,
herewith produced, Exhibits 1 and 2.

I said : No documents in a civilized tongue?
He replied :

Produce, O Lord, my wretched fingerprint!
Bring forth, O angel in the heavenly court,
My dossier, full, detailed, both fact and hint,
Felony, misdemeanour, tort!

I refused to be impressed by talk of that sort.

From further cross-examination, it appeared,
immediate history : a beggar in Berlin;
chased, as a vagrant, from the streets of Prague;
kept, as a leper, in forced quarantine;
shunned as the pest, avoided like the plague;
then had escaped, mysteriously come
by devious routes and stolen frontiers to
the *nalewkas* of Warsaw's sheenydom.

Pressed to reveal his true identity,
he lied :
One of the anthropophagi was he,
or, if we wished, a denizen of Mars,
the ghost of *my* father, Conscience—aye,
the anatomy of Reason, naked, and with scars;
even became insulting, said he was
Aesop the slave among the animals . . .
Sir Incognito . . . Rabbi Alias . . .

The eldest elder of Zion ... said we knew A. M.
KLEIN
his numerous varied oriental shapes,
even as we ought to know his present guise—
the man in the jungle, and beset by apes.
It was at this point the s.s. man arrived.
The Jew was interrupted. When he was revived,
he deposed as follows :

At low estate, a beggar, and in flight,
Still do I wear my pride like purple. I
Do fear you, yes, but founder not from fright.
Already I breathe your unfuturity.
For you are not the first whom I have met—
O I have known them all,
The dwarf dictators, the diminutive dukes,
The heads of straw, the hearts of gall,
Th' imperial plumes of eagles covering rooks!

It is not necessary to name names,
But it may serve anon,
Now to evoke from darkness some dark frames,
Evoke
Armada'd Spain, that gilded jettison;
And Russia's last descended Romanov,
Descending a dark staircase
To a dank cellar at Ekaterinoslov;
Evoke
The peacock moulted from the Persian loom ...
Babylon tumbled from its terraces ...
Decrescent and debased Mizraim, remembered
    only
By that one star that sentries Pharaoh's tomb ...
Evoke
O Greece! O broken marble! ...
And disinterred unresurrected Rome ...

They would have harried me extinct, these
    thrones!

Set me, archaic, in their heraldries,   A. M.
Blazon antique! . . . For they were Powers . . .   KLEIN
    Once!
But I, though still exilian, rest extant,
And on my cicatrices tally off
Their undone dynasties!
Shall I dread you—who overlived all these?

Here impudence was duly rebuked, and the Jew
confronted with Exhibit 2.

Yes, but that signet ring! . . . Freiherr, that seal
Once flashed the pleasure majestical!
For I, who in tatters stand investitured,
Who, to these knightly men, am dislodged pawn,
Abdicate and abjured,
I was, I am, the Emperor Solomon!
O, to and fro upon the face of the earth,
I wandered, crying: Ani Shlomo, but—
But no one believed my birth.

For he now governs in my place and stead,
He who did fling me from Jerusalem
Four hundred parasangs!
Who stole the crown from off my head!
Who robed him in my robes! Beneath whose hem
The feet of the cock extend, the tail of the demon
    hangs!
Asmodeus!

Mistake me not; I am no virtuous saint;
Only a man, and like all men, not god-like . . .
From birth beset by his own heart's constraint,
Its brimstone pride, the cinders of its greed,
(Brazier behind the ribs that will not faint!)
Beset, inflamed, besooted, charred, indeed,—
Only a man, and like all men, not god-like,
Damned by desire—
But I at least fought down that bellows'd greed,

Tried to put out the sulphurs of that fire! ...   A. M.
At least craved wisdom, how to snuff the blaze,   KLEIN
Sought knowledge, to unravel good from evil,
Sought guidance from the Author of my Days.

The understanding heart, and its enthymemes,
Being granted me, I learned from beast . . . bird
    . . . man;
Would know; and eavesdropped nest . . . and
    house . . . and lair.
The wild beasts spoke to me, told me their dreams,
Which, always biped, towards the human ran . . .
O, how that flesh did long to doff its fur! . . .
The fluttering birds, the twittering birds of the air:
'Would you cast off from your feet,' they said,
    'earth's mass,
That weighted globe of brass,
And soar into your own?
With azure fill your heart! . . . Be hollow of bone!'
And from my self, and from the breed of Adam,
I fathom'd that heart's depths, how it may sink
Down to the deep and ink of genesis,
And lie there, that once could the heavens explore,
A sponge and pulse of hunger on the
    ocean-floor . . .
Saw also, and praised, for then knew possible,
The heart's saltations! . . .
That always—vanitatum vanitas!—
That always after back to grossness fell.
Thus taught, thus prompted, upward I essay'd,—
Some not mean triumphs scored,
Spread truth, spread song, spread justice, which
    prevailed,
Builded that famous footstool for the Lord,—
Yet human, human among mortals, failed!
Was thwarted the greater yearning, the jubilee
Wherein the race might at the last be hailed
Transcendent of its own humanity!

For I, Ooheleth, King in Jerusalem,
Ecclesiast of the troubled apothegm,
Concluding the matter, must affirm mankind
Still undivined.
However, though worsted, I had wrestled, but
*   he—*

Our royal Jew, now questioned *in camera*,
was not, this time, molested. It was thought
some enemy intelligence might come through
from his distractions, some inkling of the plot
now being pursued by his ten losing tribes.
Therefore the record, as ordered, here gives the
   whole Jew,—
for which the subscribing officer subscribes
apology.

But he, unspeakable prince of malice!
Usurper of my throne, pretender to the Lord's!
Wicked, demoniac, lycanthropous,
Goad of the succubi, horrific hordes!
Master of the worm, pernicious, that cleaves
*   rocks,*
The beast that talks,
Asmodeus!—

Who has not felt his statutes? . . . His scientists,
Mastering for him the lethal mysteries;
His surgeons of doctrine, cutting, like vile cysts
From off the heart, all pities and sympathies;
His judges, trembling over their decrees,
Lest insufficient injustice displease;
And his psychiaters, guarding against relapse,
For fear the beast, within the man, collapse.

His statecraft, and its modes and offices?
Here motive is appetite; and oestric hate
The force that freaks and fathers all device.
All love's venereal; or excess; or bait.

Ambush all policy, and artifice;
And all reward conferred, all honour
Hierarchical to the degrees of Hate.

A. M.
KLEIN

Upon his lych-throne, robed in bloodied purple,
Listening to those harmonies where the sigh
Exhaling greets the groan, the groan is pitched to
    the cry,
Asmodeus sits;
And I—

At this point the s.s. men departed.
The Jew was not revived. He was carried and
    carted,
and to his present gaoler brought;
awaiting higher pleasure.

                    And further deponent saith not.

Political Meeting

FOR CAMILLIEN HOUDE

On the school platform, draping the folding seats,
they wait the chairman's praise and glass of water.
Upon the wall the agonized **Y** initials their faith.

Here all are laic; the skirted brothers have gone.
Still, their equivocal absence is felt, like a breeze
that gives curtains the sounds of surplices.

The hall is yellow with light, and jocular;
suddenly someone lets loose upon the air
the ritual bird which the crowd in snares of
    singing

catches and plucks, throat, wings, and little limbs.
Fall the feathers of sound, like *alouette's*.
The chairman, now, is charming, full of asides and
    wit,

building his orators, and chipping off
the heckling gargoyles popping in the hall.
(Outside, in the dark, the street is body-tall,

flowered with faces intent on the scarecrow thing
that shouts to thousands the echoing
of their own wishes.) The Orator has risen !

Worshipped and loved, their favourite visitor,
a country uncle with sunflower seeds in his
     pockets,
full of wonderful moods, tricks, imitative talk,

he is their idol : like themselves, not handsome,
not snobbish, not of the *Grande Allée! Un homme!*
Intimate, informal, he makes bear's compliments

to the ladies; is gallant; and grins;
goes for the balloon, his opposition, with pins;
jokes also on himself, speaks of himself

in the third person, slings slang, and winks with
     folklore;
and knows now that he has them, kith and kin.
Calmly, therefore, he begins to speak of war,

praises the virtue of being *Canadien,*
of being at peace, of faith, of family,
and suddenly his other voice : *Where are your
     sons?*

He is tearful, choking tears; but not he
would blame the clever English; in their place
he'd do the same; maybe.

Where *are* your sons ?
                    The whole street wears one face,
shadowed and grim; and in the darkness rises
the body-odour of race.

Monsieur Gaston

A. M.
KLEIN

You remember the big Gaston, for whom everyone
   predicted a bad end?—
Gaston, the neighbour's gossip and his mother's
   cross?
You remember him *vaurien*, always out of a job,
with just enough clinking coinage
for pool, bright neckties, and blondes,—
the scented Gaston in the poolroom lolling
in meadows of green baize?
In clover now. Through politics. Monsieur
   Gaston.

They say the Minister of a certain department
   docs not move
without him; and they say, to make it innocent,—
chauffeur.
But everyone understands. Why wherever our
   Gaston smiles
a nightclub rises and the neons flash.
To his slightest whisper
the bottled rye, like a fawning pet-dog, gurgles.
The burlesque queen will not undress
unless Monsieur Gaston says yes.
And the Madame will shake her head behind the
   curtain-rods
unless he nods.

A changed man, Gaston; almost a civil servant,
keeps records, appointments, women; speaks
   tough English;
is very much respected.
You should hear with what greetings his
   distinguished approach is greeted;
you should see the gifts he gets,
with compliments for his season.

Montreal

A. M.
KLEIN

(I)

O city metropole, isle riverain!
Your ancient pavages and sainted routes
Traverse my spirit's conjured avenues!
Splendour erablic of your promenades
Foliates there, and there your maisonry
Of pendent balcon and escalier'd march,
Unique midst English habitat,
Is vivid Normandy!

(II)

You populate the pupils of my eyes:
Thus, does the Indian, plumèd, furtivate
Still through your painted autumns, Ville-Marie!
Though palisades have passed, though calumet
With tabac of your peace enfumes the air,
Still do I spy the phantom, aquiline,
Genuflect, moccasin'd, behind
His statue in the square!

(III)

Thus, costumed images before me pass,
Haunting your archives architectural:
Coureur de bois, in posts where pelts were
    portaged;
Seigneur within his candled manoir; Scot
Ambulant through his bank, pillar'd and vast.
Within your chapels, voyaged mariners
Still pray, and personage departed,
All present from your past!

(IV)

Grand port of navigations, multiple
The lexicons uncargo'd at your quays,
Sonnant though strange to me; but chiefest, I,

Auditor of your music, cherish the
Joined double-melodied vocabulaire
Where English vocable and roll Ecossic,
Mollified by the parle of French
Bilinguefact your air!

A. M.
KLEIN

(v)
Such your suaver voice, hushed Hochelaga!
But for me also sound your potencies,
Fortissimos of sirens fluvial,
Bruit of manufactory, and thunder
From foundry issuant, all puissant tone
Implenishing your hebdomad; and then
Sanct silence, and your argent belfries
Clamant in orison!

(VI)
You are a part of me, O all your quartiers—
And of dire pauvrete and of richesse—
To finished time my homage loyal claim:
You are locale of infancy, milieu
Vital of institutes that formed my fate;
And you above the city, scintillant,
Mount Royal, are my spirit's mother,
Almative, poitrinate!

(VII)
Never do I sojourn in alien place
But I do languish for your scenes and sounds,
City of reverie, nostalgic isle,
Pendant most brilliant on Laurentian cord!
The coigns of your boulevards—my signiory—
Your suburbs are my exile's verdure fresh,
Your parks, your fountain'd parks—
Pasture of memory!

City, O city, you are vision'd as
A parchemin roll of saecular exploit
Inked with the script of eterne souvenir!
You are in sound, chanson and instrument!
Mental, you rest forever edified
With tower and dome; and in these beating valves,
Here in these beating valves, you will
For all my mortal time reside!

JOHN
GLASSCO

b. 1909

The Rural Mail

These are the green paths trodden by patience.
I hang on the valley's lip, a bird's eye viewing
All that opposes to makers and masters of nations
Only its fierce mistrust of the word,—
To the smashed records for gobbling and spewing,
Cows that exist in a slow-motion world.

For here is man on man's estate of nature,
Farmer on farm, the savage civilized
Into the image of his God the weather—
Only another anarchist, foiled highflyer
Whose years have grown as a minute in his eyes,
And his grin reveals a vision of barbed wire:

Here birth evokes pleasure and a reflective pity,
Marriage or mating, much of the voyeur,
Sickness, an interest and some hope of booty,
And death strikes like an absurdly barked
    command,
Confounding with its *Easy*, its *As you were*,
His stiff-kneed generation unused to bend.

I sense his hours marked by my two-wheeled cart JOHN
Descending the stony hill : as I stop by his box GLASSCO
The ring of tin as the *Knowlton News* goes in
Is a day's knell,—and the countryside contracts
For an instant to the head of a pin;
Or he comes with a money-order, or to chat.

Getting good money, and money is always good,
We keep the high standards in the front parlour
Like a wedding-cake or a motto carved in wood,
The falling-out of enemies makes no friends.
'Far as I'm concerned, the war can go on forever!'
A man can *make* a dollar, with hens.

Scraping the crumbling roadbed of this strife
With rotten fenceposts and old mortgages
(No way of living, but a mode of life),
How sift from death and waste three grains of
   duty,
O thoughts that start from scratch and end in a
   dream
Of graveyards minding their own business?

But the heart accepts it all, this honest air
Lapped in green valleys where accidents will
   happen!
Where the bull, the buzz-saw and the balky mare
Are the chosen fingers of God for a farmer's sins,
Like the axe for his woods, and his calves and
   chicks and children
Destined for slaughter in the course of things.

The Entailed Farm

A footpath would have been enough.
This muddy mile of side-road has no purpose
Save as it serves for others to link up
Crossroads marked on the map with a nameless
   cross

By way of these choked and heartless fields of
    paintbrush
And the mute, sealed house,

JOHN
GLASSCO

Where the spring's tooth, stripping shingles,
    scaling
Beam and clapboard, probes for the rot below
Porch and pediment and blind bow-window,
And the wooden trunk with the coloured
    cardboard lining
Lies where it fell when the wall of the flying wing
Fell down ten years ago;

Where the stone wall is a haven for snake and
    squirrel,
The steepled dovecote for phoebe and
    willow-wren,
And the falling field-gates, trigged by an earthen
    swell,
Open on a wild where nothing is raised or penned,
On rusty acres of witch-grass and wild sorrel
Where the field-birds cry and contend.

You, tourist, salesman, family out for a picnic,
Who saw the bearded man that walked like a
    bear,
His pair of water-pails slung from a wooden
    neckyoke,
Slipping in by the woodshed,—Come away,
That naked door is proof against all knocking!
Standing and knocking there,

You might as well expect time's gate to open
On the living past, the garden bloom again,
The house stand upright, hay-barn's swayback
    coping
Stiffen, and see as in a fretted frame
Men in the meadow and a small boy whooping
The red oxen down that orchard lane,

Or revive the slow strong greed of the coffined
  farmer JOHN
GLASSCO
Who cleared, stumped, fenced, rotating sinew and
  sweat,
Beating the ploughshare into an honest dollar,
Who living and dying planned to cheat time's
  night
Through the same white-bearded boy,—who is
  hiding somewhere
Now, till you're out of sight,

And have left him alone : alone with the grief or
  anger
Or whatever it is that flickers but will not die
In the dull brain of the victim turned avenger,
At war with a shadow, in flight from passers-by,
From us,—who are free from all but the hint of
  attainder,
Who can meet a stranger's eye

With a good face, can answer a question, give a
  reason,
For whom the world's fields and fences stand up
  plain,
Nor dazzle in sunlight or crumble behind the rain :
From us, with our hearts but lightly tinged with
  poison,
Who composed our quarrel early and in good
  season
Buried the hatchet in our father's brain.

The Cardinal's Dog

MUSÉE D'AUTUN

The unknown Master of Moulins
Painted the Nativity : we see
The stable, the stupid ox and Mary,
Simpering Joseph on his knees

And the Cardinal Rolin on his knees too,
His red robe centred by a rat-faced dog.

They all look at each other : Joseph at Mary,
Mary (her face is blue) at the child,
The Cardinal looks, if anywhere, at the ox;
But the child looks at the little dog,
And the dog at nothing, simply being
   well-behaved :
He is the one who feels and knows.

Pensive little dog (you that I love
Being only flesh and blood) you see
The reason for all this, the dying need
Of the worshipful, the master : so
We are all one, have seen the birth of God

Either through eyes of friend or master,
In a book, a song, a landscape or a child,
For a breath of time are immortal, tuned
To the chord and certainties of animal hope.
And the picture *teaches us*—as Balzac would say—
To trust anything on earth more than man.

Brummell at Calais

A foolish useless man who had done nothing
All his life long but keep himself clean,
Locked in the glittering armour of a pose
Made up of impudence, chastity and reserve—
How does his memory still survive his world?

The portraits show us only a tilted nose,
Lips full blown, a cravat and curly wig,
And a pair of posturing eyes,
Infinitely vulnerable, deeply innocent,
Their malice harmless as a child's :

And he has returned to childhood now, his stature
That of the Butterfly whose *Funeral*

He sang (his only song) for one of his
Dear duchesses, Frances or Georgiana,
In the intolerable metre of Tom Moore—

JOHN
GLASSCO

To a childhood of sweet biscuits and curaçao;
Hair-oil and tweezers make him forget his debts,
The angle of his hat remains the same,
His little boots pick their way over the
     cobblestones,
But where is he going as well as going mad?

Nowhere: his glory is already upon him,
The fading Regency man who will leave behind
More than the ankle-buttoning pantaloon!
For see, even now in the long implacable twilight,
The triumph of his veritable art,

An art of being, nothing but being, the grace
Of perfect self-assertion based on nothing,
As in our vanity's cause against the void
He strikes his elegant blow, the solemn report of
     those
Who have done nothing and will never die.

The Day

The day when it will not matter
The day no longer depending on another day
When time shall have run out
When nothing will matter

(When the cloudy prime movers
Love, hope, ambition
Will have ceased to move in the light of the fact
Of the final day, when the reason for them is gone)

On that day
We shall rise on our elbows and glare around us,
     looking
For the abolished future

In that moment of supreme consciousness   JOHN
Of unmedicinable dismay   GLASSCO
Of absolute loneliness
Of a removal from time
A severance from substance,
When the soul, naked at last, panting in its
    anguish,
Will look for its non-existent home
A place, only another place
To fill the place of the abolished future
To replace an impossible city,
Groping in the weightless void
Of the day no longer leading to another day.

The day too when we shall know
That we were only milestones on the way of those
    we loved
That they only climbed on our loving shoulders
To attain a paradisal view
Of something whose vision we seemed to be
    hindering
Some marvellous city
To which we were only a bridge
Our love a swaying but necessary means;
And that the tears to be shed for our passing
Will be succeeded by a kind of rainbow
Arching between the horizons of our lifeless head
    and feet—
So that our desires shall be forgiven
Our ambition excused
Our existence justified
In the light of a dumb, invisible, absurd future
Which is no longer our concern.

  Here is the man in space
  The stripped, the naked man
  Lying upon the air
  The sport of time and space
  The disinherited man

Released to wander in air
For an agonizing space
In a region void of man
In a place of beating air

JOHN
GLASSCO

Will this be the time for mercy, for the sustaining
    wings
Of the multitudinous cherubs, the winged loves
To fan his temples? Will the prayers of those
Who have adored him all his life assist him then?
Will any pure ingenuous secular piety
Lighten the strokes falling down and down
On his eyes and shoulders on that terrible day,
Or will he still seek in his failing mind for the
    impossible city?

—My soul, recall those midnights in September
When the sleepy autumn winds blew, warm and
    amorous,
Up from the lamplit river and over us,
Thou and I—whom we must at times remember!
When walking through the night we beheld in
    visions
Of the sleeping city our spirit's firm repose,
Luxurious, perfect, like those flowers that close
On the bees they have first made drunken with
    fabulous visions—
Thou who keep'st yet the divine stain of my tears
Psyche, not subject to the enervate years,
Canst thou alone now escape those terrible
    guardians
To roam again that ecstatic city of delights,
Madder than those who pass her superb nights
Dancing to the insane music of her accordions?

(II)

This poor man, this dying one
This breathing horror

Oppressed and insulted
Filthy and hopeless
The mask of humanity
Mock of consciousness
Where is his city
What is he doing?
—All that he is,
His struggle and suffering
Is part of ourselves
Exists for us only,
This is the last gift
Of his life's meaning
All that he sought
In the marvellous city
Relinquished and offered
To us the survivors
        As it will be
Ours to pass on
To those who have taken
Our hearts in their keeping
To those who in turn
Will give from their bounty,
Out of their horror
Their own desolation,
The infinitesimal
Glimpse of a beautiful blessed falsehood
And out of their charity
Pray to the cherubs
To fan our temples.

Give yourself only to love, your whole life long
Give your body, your brain, your heart to
    whoever may choose you
Out of the multitudinous forms and faces of being
Surrender as you would to the first great wave of
    ocean

To the first bird threading the light blue air of
    April
All that surging and singing, lay your cheek
    against it
Open your lips to desire and the liquor of its
    adoration
Consider only the human music taking its way to
    silence
Forget the stones and scents and sounds of the
    fabulous city
Here in the heart of another blooms a miraculous
    home
Hide your proud head, renounce your ridiculous
    freedom
Content you to be the singing prisoner of love.

JOHN
GLASSCO

So on that day
That final day
Removed from time
Dependent on nothing
When nothing will matter,
You will escape
Like a mouse in the darkness
The dream be ended
The city forgotten
The shadow will touch you
Engross you wholly
Softly, securely
And soon, soon
The day of others
Freed of your sickness,
Their own little day
Serene, new born
The day of their freedom
Dawn quietly without you.

DOROTHY
LIVESAY

b. 1909

Fantasia

FOR HELENA COLEMAN

And I have learned how diving's done
How breathing air, cool wafted trees
Clouds massed above the man-made tower
How these
Can live no more in eye and ear:
And mind be dumb
To all save Undine and her comb.

Imagination's underworld! where child goes down
Light as a feather. Water pressure
Hardly holds him, diving's easy
As the flight of bird in air
Or bomber drumming to his lair.

Child goes down, and laughingly
(He's not wanted yet, you see)
Catches fishes in his hand
Burrows toe in sifting sand
Seizes all the weeds about
To make a small sub-rosa boat

Then up he bobs, as easily
As any blown balloon
To greet the bosky, brooding sky
And hunger for the sun.

.   .   .

And child grown taller, clothed in man's
Long limbs, and shaggy hair, his chin outthrust
Searches for years the rounded world
Climbs to its peaks, falls to its valleys green

Striding the trim and trailing towns   DOROTHY
LIVESAY
Fingering the fond arteries
Possessing things, and casting them
Cloakwise to earth for sleeping time. . . .

Sometime the lust wanderer
Will sleep, will pause; will dream of plunging deep
Below it all, where he will need
No clock companion, thorn in flesh, no contact
   man
To urge him from the ground.
For flying's easy, if you do it diving
And diving is the self unmoored
Ranging and roving—man alone.

                    .   .   .

And I have learned how diving's done
Wherefore the many, many
Chose the watery stair
Down, down Virginia
With your fêted hair
Following after Shelley

Or wordcarvers I knew
(Bouchette; and Raymond, you)—
Here is the fascination
Of the salty stare :
And death is here.
Death courteous and calm, glass-smooth
His argument so suave, so water-worn
A weighted stone.
And death's deliberation, his
Most certain waiting-room
His patience with the patient, who will be
His for infinity. . . .

So no astounded peerers
On the surface craft
No dragging nets, no cranes

No gnarled and toughened rope
Not any prayer nor pulley man-devised
Will shake the undersea
Or be
More than a brief torpedo, children's arrow
More than a gaudy top outspun
Its schedule done. . . .

.   .   .

Wise to have learned : how diving's done
How breathing air, cool wafted trees
Clouds massed above the man-made tower
How these
Can live no more in eye and ear :
And mind be dumb
To all save Undine and her comb. . . .

The Prophetess

When the rains began
trees shuddered, and were green
the earth heaved :
fingers of grass pierced the crust
lilies exploded, anemones
blew into being
in the fields mushrooms swelled
like women loaded with child.

You were with child then, Regina
and like the others
set out to gather mushrooms
when the hard hills were softening to green
and the wild fig trees offered shade again
Walking slowly, surely,
eyes to earth
sensitive only
to the earth
you moved off the path

circling round hills
into green shadow —
umbrella trees —
no one saw you.

DOROTHY
LIVESAY

No one saw you.
No one knew what had happened.
Mulenga, your husband, wondered:
he reported you 'lost' to the Boma
but no one went searching.

One day
two days
three — was it three days?
on that day the women returning from hoeing
saw you walking through the gardens
to the village.

        Mulenga! Mulenga!
        Our sister is back, Lenchina!

At first you sat silent, rapt
the child ripe within you
stirring; and you sat on the ground
beside a small flame, stirring the millet.
        Call the elders, you said
And Mulenga brought them
his friends and relatives
(but not the Chief —
it was not to be
the Chief's business).
They sat in a circle
You began slowly to speak.

        Before you, my people
        I come as one naked, buried.
        For I who am living now
        was dead
        and I who died once
        died three times —

Pulled from the well of darkness
by the words clanging
clanging in my head
I reached for the rim of light
only to totter
and fall again

DOROTHY
LIVESAY

And again I was drawn
drawn by the hair
up into the grey
half-morning:

And how I struggled
to hold on fast
to listen, to stare
till the waters fell away
and I was hauled out safe
into dry air.

Look at me, look at me!
I am as one naked, buried
for I who am living now
was dead, three times.

You spoke, and the people answered and
    questioned
cried out and marvelled.

Not a white man's God I saw
lifting me up from death, each time
holding me steady;
not the white man hammered with nails
on a wooden cross;
but a Lord incredibly shining
a sheath of light . . .

and my eyes trembled at the brightness.

Then he came speaking my language

Lenchina, Lenchina, you cannot die :   DOROTHY
LIVESAY
your time is not yet come
and there is work to do.

And he pressed the Book against my
    forehead
and he taught me the songs I must sing.

Ai   Ai   How the people cry out now
as the fire flickers
as the night falls sudden and definite
darkening the faces.
Not by a white man's God
need we be saved
but by the resurrection of a woman
an African mother
Ai   Ai

The drums beat
tentative   questioning
the drums come out of hiding
now strong ones, bold ones
the drums beat louder and louder
for you, Lenchina
standing by the fire now
short and stumpy
rooted as a tree
a tree singing the new hosannah
        Lumpa in the highest . . .

                lumpa   the drums beat
                lumpa   lumpa
                lumpa   lumpa   lumpa

The Leader

DOROTHY
LIVESAY

(I)

But the Copperbelt night is a snake
strangling the drums
squeezing the air
from throats, from lungs;
under its arching coils
a child's cry shrills
in the beerhall's roar
a cauldron boils.

The Copperbelt day is saved
by a strike of thunder
the man on the anthill
crying out 'Kwatcha!'
Wilder than rain pelt
or the beat of sunlight
children shout freedom
waving green branches

(II)

Heaven lets down a rope
whereon I swing
the clapper of a bell
on sounding sky

And all below
they cluster with uplifted faces
black on white
and sway like flowers
to my wild clanging

Whether sun burns me
or moon rivets with steely eye
I shall ring on
till flowers are black mouths
and the stones bleed my song.

RALPH
GUSTAFSON
b. 1909

Armorial

I lay down with my love and there was song
Breaking, like the lilies I once saw
Lovely around King Richard, murdered
Most foully and all his grace at Pomfret,
The roses of England stolen; our love
Was like gules emblazoned at Canterbury
Most kingly in windows and leopards
Passant on bars of gold. This
Was our heraldry.

Our love was larks and sprang from meadows
Far from kingdoms, which regal grew
With rod and bloodred weed and rush
Where water ran; this was our love,
The place where she chose, I could not but come,
A field without myth or rhetoric.
She lay down with love and my hand
Was gold with dust of lily. This
Was our province.

There was song in that kingly country
But I saw there, stuck like a porcupine
On Bosworth Field the arrows through him,
That regal and most royal other
Richard, runt and twitch in a ditch,
His hand wristdeep in lily where
Henry Tudor rolled him, the gules
Of England draining on his shirt.
My love wept.

Transfigured Night

RALPH
GUSTAFSON

Data, data, data
Sang the stars.
I looked up. The turning
Sky was crossed by bars

Of music, great progressions
Knowledge sings,
Tails of metal rockets,
Beating lights and wings

Of words. Products sang
And science soared.
I clenched my eyes the host
Of wonders was so choired.

Look, my love, I cried.
The heavens blaze.
The anthems rise. My love,
The stars! The stars, I cried.

My Love Eats an Apple

She bites into the red skin
Of the white hard apple in bed
And there is joy in heaven
Like innocence and whitefalls
Of snow and waters dancing up
In among green trees perched with more
Apples in tight skin
Hard as a bite and containing
Seven-eighths applesap deadpan.
I try to distil this knowledgeable joy
In crunching heaven.
God sits up there amongst
His shamefully nude nudgers,
Praising sin,

The juice of the plucked   RALPH
Happy apple   GUSTAFSON
In great psalms and paeans
Dripping down His testamentary beard.

The Swans of Vadstena

Alone she feeds the white swans.
And could I know
Her thoughts were not Leda
Enfolded in that thrashing white?

My love encloses her in a strength
Of singing white and the gold beak
Of my violence holds her.
How should she not know?

Where I stand apart, she leans
On the grass by the white swans
As they come to her on the surface
Of the water. Where they move perfectly,

She turns from the violence
To my violence, taken in the white
Tumult, unbelieving, making known
And whole the blemished god.

In the Yukon

In Europe, you can't move without going down
    into history.
Here, all is a beginning. I saw a salmon jump,
Again and again, against the current,
The timbered hills a background, wooded green
Unpushed through; the salmon jumped, silver.
This was news, was commerce, at the end of the
    summer

The leap for dying. Moose came down to the
    water edge
To drink and the salmon turned silver arcs.
At night, the northern lights played, great over
    country
Without tapestry and coronations, kings crowned
With weights of gold. They were green,
Green hangings and great grandeur, over the north
Going to what no man can hold hard in mind,
The dredge of that gravity, being without
    experience.

In June and Gentle Oven

In June and gentle oven
Summer kingdoms simmer
As they come
And flower and leaf and love
Release
Their sweetest juice.

No wind at all
On the wide green world
Where fields go stroll-
Ing by
And in and out
An adder of a stream
Parts the daisies
On a small Ontario farm.

And where, in curve of meadow,
Lovers, touching, lie,
A church of grass stands up
And walls them, holy, in.

Fabulous the insects   ANNE
Stud the air   WILKINSON
Or walk on running water,
Klee-drawn saints
And bright as angels are.

Honeysuckle here
Is more than bees can bear
And time turns pale
And stops to catch its breath
And lovers slip their flesh

And light as pollen
Play on treble water
Till bodies reappear
And a shower of sun
To dry their languor.

Then two in one the lovers lie
And peel the skin of summer
With their teeth
And suck its marrow from a kiss
So charged with grace
The tongue, all knowing
Holds the sap of June
Aloof from seasons, flowing.

Leda in Stratford, Ont.

A silly country maiden went
A mile or so to Stratford, Ont.,
And here she found, as everywhere,
Things much too ordin'ry for her;
Yet from a Richard, Rex, or clown
She learned of Leda and the Swan,
And so admired their high-class union
That up and down the banks of Avon
She ogled those immaculate birds
That never turned to take her crumb

Or listen to her honeyed words
Of love, but simply swam.

ANNE
WILKINSON

A crow, observing her odd wish,
Laid the girl beneath a bush;
No sudden blow—the great wings beating—
More as a joke, a kind of larking.
And yet she doted on his action,
Tickled by such rare seduction,
Boasting to the birds, 'Black Swan,
Demon Lover urged me on.'
But no bird listened, for a caw,
Loud and rude, came from the crow.

The Red and the Green

Here, where summer slips
Its sovereigns through my fingers
I put on my body and go forth
To seek my blood.

I walk the hollow subway
Of the ear; its tunnel
Clean of blare
Echoes the lost red syllable.

Free from cramp and chap of winter
Skin is minstrel, sings
Tall tales and shady
Of the kings of Nemi Wood.

I walk an ancient path
Wearing my warmth and singing
The notes of a Druid song
In the ear of Jack-in-the-Green.

But the quest turns round, the goal,
My human red centre
Goes whey in the wind,
Mislaid in the curd and why of memory.

Confused, I gather rosemary ANNE
And stitch the leaves WILKINSON
To green hearts on my sleeve;
My new green arteries

Fly streamers from the maypole of my arms,
From head to toe
My blood sings green,
From every heart a green amnesia rings.

Lens

(I)

The poet's daily chore
Is my long duty;
To keep and cherish my good lens
For love and war
And wasps about the lilies
And mutiny within.

My woman's eye is weak
And veiled with milk;
My working eye is muscled
With a curious tension,
Stretched and open
As the eyes of children;
Trusting in its vision
Even should it see
The holy holy spirit gambol
Counterheadwise,
Lithe and warm as any animal.

My woman's iris circles
A blind pupil;
The poet's eye is crystal,
Polished to accept the negative,
The contradictions in a proof
And the accidental
Candour of the shadows;

127

The shutter, oiled and smooth   ANNE
Clicks on the grace of heroes   WILKINSON
Or on some bestial act
When lit with radiance
The afterwords the actors speak
Give depths to violence,

Or if the bull is great
And the matador
And the sword
Itself the metaphor.

(II)

In my dark room the years
Lie in solution,
Develop film by film.
Slow at first and dim
Their shadows bite
On the fine white pulp of paper.

An early snap of fire
Licking the arms of air
I hold against the light, compare
The details with a prehistoric view
Of land and sea
And cradles of mud that rocked
The wet and sloth of infancy.

A stripe of tiger, curled
And sleeping on the ribs of reason
Prints as clear
As Eve and Adam, pearled
With sweat, staring at an apple core;
And death, in black and white
Or politic in green and Easter film,

Lands on steely points, a dancer
Disciplined to the foolscap stage,
The property of poets
Who command his robes, expose
His moving likeness on the page.

ANNE
WILKINSON

Adam and God

On Monday man gave God
Dominion of the sky;
On Tuesday swore Him
President of waves;
On Wednesday crowned
Him Emperor
Of every creeping thing,
A monarch of the night
And King of day;
On Thursday
Man breathed into God
Man's anger, charged His gun
That God might fire from heaven;
On Friday
Bade Him eat the apple, fallen
From the Good and Evil
Tree in Eden;
On Saturday
Man grumbled, 'God
Is lonely, has no peer
To share His fate'
And cut the Devil
From a sleeping woman's rib;
On Sunday
God cried, 'Rest! Enough!'
And ran from man and hid.

Falconry

ANNE
WILKINSON

'*The* Boke of St Albans *had laid down precisely the
classes of people to whom any proper-minded mem-
ber of the* Falconidae *might belong . . . The list had
defined itself meticulously downward to the kestrel,
and he, as a crowning insult, was allowed to belong
to a mere knave—because he was useless to be
trained.*'—From T. H. WHITE'S *The Goshawk.*

(I)

Eagle for an Emperor
Peregrine is due an earl
Goshawk is the right of yeoman
Kestrel for a knave or no-man.

God's left hand must bear them all:
Eagle of the emperor,
Peregrine that's due an earl,
Yeoman's goshawk, and the knave's
Bating kestrel, no-man's slave.

Rather bating kestrel, I,
Than mind the fist beneath the glove.
I, a kestrel, God, the Knave—

And I will bate until I die,
And bite the leather of my jesses,
And starve before I eat His messes.
Can I do more? Sweet Knave, I'll try.

Yet that fist and glove are home,
For, banished, what could I bate from?

(II)

As falcon on a falconer's wrist,
So should I, on God's big fist;
Yet will I not or preen or sit
Or take His lure, the rabbit skull,

And dip my hawking beak in hell.   ANNE
WILKINSON
Rather would I bate :
Head-down hang and scream and squawk
And churn the air and rough my feathers,
For though the leash that holds my jesses
Ties me to the precincts of His glove,
I will not love.

If tidbits do not tame His falcon
God remembers Babylon
And proper ways to tease and starve
The lust upon His leather glove.
Regard me now; I quiet sit,
Brooding on the skulls I'll split.
Or watch my flight; its easy pause,
Angle of incidence inclined
Against the bitter wind
Before I dive, God's mercy in my claws.

Variations on a Theme

*'A man needs only to be turned around once with his
eyes shut to be lost in this world.'*—THOREAU

(1)

There is always a first flinging
Of the blood about in circles,
A falling down, a sickness ringing

In the ear, a swivelling eye
Uprooting tree whose tendrils flower
On sagging skin of sky.

Green blades cut, they spin so fast.
Round and round, a child on grass
Whose name in anagram is lost.

(II)

ANNE
WILKINSON

I turned round once; I shut my eyes;
I opened them on truth or lies.
And this is what I saw though
Cannot say : or false or true.

From arteries in graves, columns
Rose to soil the sky; and down
Their fluted sides the overflow
Slid to earth, unrolled and spread
On stalk and stone its plushy red.

Trees had shed their limbs, become
Mobile marble guards. Secret
Their manœuvres in this land;
And while they marched a mad dog's tooth,
Rabid violet, tore half my hand.

The wind blew from the south
Before I turned, but here a north
Wind blew, and I was lost. It blew
A milch cow dry, a new moon down;
Then higher roared until it blew
Seven fuses of the sun.

(III)

We shut our eyes and turned once round
And were up borne by our down fall.
Such life was in us on the ground
That while we moved, earth ceased to roll,
And oceans lagged, and all the flames
Except our fire, and we were lost
In province that no settler names.

132

(IV)

ANNE
WILKINSON

I shut my eyes and turned once round;
I opened them on alien air;
Sea had shrunk to farmer's pond
And sky was pink and distance near.
A forest and its nights were now
Woodpile for an old man's fire;
And where above me one black crow
Had cawed my spring, two dirty doves
Sang daintily. I stoned the birds
But no stone hit, for of white gloves
My hands were made; I stole a stick
To break the sky; it did not crack;
I could not curse—though I was lost,
Had trespassed on some stranger's dream
Where swan forswears his lust,
The gull his scream.

(V)

I shut my eyes and turned twice round;
Once for death, once for love.
I fell down twice upon the ground
But what I saw I cannot prove.

Death turned me first. When he had done
Black rings moved about the sun;
Love turned me next. I fell to rest
In quicksand, and was quickly lost.

Death turned me first, will twirl me last
And throw me down beneath the grass
And strip me of this stuff, this dress
I am, although its form be lost.

Invocation

Appear, O mother, was the perpetual cry
Of lost Aeneas, and you did take care of him;
Though Dido felt the iron of your whim.
Our shrouds are sea-rotten; and our keels
Are rust and weeds; broken is our limb;
Our winded oar is master of our wills.
You've let us go, and we are homeless men;
First pleasure our dreams, lady, and return
And let your worship kindling guide us in,
Renewed by your own apparition.
O love, teach us to love you, that we may
Through burning Carthage take our way.

Canticle of Darkness

(I)

Remind you, that there was darkness in my heart
And into the darkness in my heart
Sang light, and the singing light
Comprehended the darkness, but the darkness—
How could the darkness comprehend
The singing light ringing in my heart?
Which was not peace but storm, the gull
Flying, and the water pouring its wave
Into the wind's teeth, and the gull
Crying into the mouth of the harbour
Which was not peace but the sea's jaw

(II)

WILFRED
WATSON

Know you, that all knowing must sing again
In the love which sang, the first light commanded,
The waters divided, the earth parcelled out
For flowers, beasts and creeping things,
The air given for birds,
The sun made round and warm,
The moon mild as milk—but how can I begin?
For the singing light was wrath not peace—
O Venus, your love was the sea's jaw

(III)

Best you, might we not lie sleeping in the dark
Of darkness, in the nothing which is our womb?
Lie sleeping, and never cough at the air?
Lie sleeping soft, folded up quiet and warm?
And never suckle the teats of despair?
Does not the singing light, sing us into the storm,
Light us to the tomb? O Mary, the door
Of our home, O let the night cover
The light which is our doom

(IV)

Stand gentle in my words. It was
The Friday of roses. And there was a rose
Singing the red song of your blossom.
When I came to the rose, there was
Gethsemane. When I came to Gethsemane
There was the rose. Stand gentle in my words
It was the Friday of Golgotha, the place
Of skull. O cross of petals—
O crossed petals—
Stand gentle in my words. For I thought
It was the rose of crucifixion, till I knew
It was the rose of resurrection. Stand
Gentle in my words. Saying I saw

(v)

The things of the world drop their skins.
Saying I saw white wings swanning in
Endless flocks of white. Saying I saw
The earth like a white lamb walking
Beside the mother ewe. Saying I heard
The nations like a lost calf bawling
For the mud flanks of the cow. Stand
Gentle in my words. I saw the darkness
Tremble. I heard the darkness singing.

(vi)

Tell you, darkness was pierced by the rose
Which vanished in a sun. Tell you, it was
A sun of glory the singing rose was
Saying. From the rose to the woman.
From the woman to the man. From the man
To the sun. From the sun to the earth,
Beasts, and all creeping things. To the waters
Divided. To the light created. And the singing
Rose sang in the lap of Mary. Darkness
Sang to the light and the kiss of love was peace.

The White Bird

Because we were baffled
And somebody said,
What is that great white bird that flies overhead

We have shot the white bird
That flies overhead
And now we have done so, I'm glad it is dead.

Who shot the white bird
That flies overhead?
Why, no one at all, it was shot by the crowd.

Was no one arrested
That shot the bird dead?
Why no one, of course, for they thought it best
   dead.

And did you shoot the white bird
That flew overhead?
Did you drop your eyes and look on it dead?

I shot the white bird
That flew overhead.
And what was the use, now you've shot the bird
   dead?

There was no use at all
To shoot the bird dead.
Now get me a drink, for I shot the bird dead.

WILFRED
WATSON

Emily Carr

Like Jonah in the green belly of the whale
Overwhelmed by Leviathan's lights and liver
Imprisoned and appalled by the belly's wall
Yet inscribing and scoring the uprush
Sink vault and arch of that monstrous cathedral,
Its living bone and its green pulsing flesh—
Old woman, of your three days' anatomy
Leviathan sickened and spewed you forth
In a great vomit on coasts of eternity.
Then, as for John of Patmos, the river of life
Burned for you an emerald and jasper smoke
And down the valley you looked and saw
All wilderness become transparent vapour,
A ghostly underneath a fleshly stroke,
And every bush an apocalypse of leaf.

Le Jeu

Ne me dérangez pas je suis profondément occupé

Un enfant est en train de bâtir un village
C'est une ville, un comté
Et qui sait
                    Tantôt l'univers.

Il joue

Ces cubes de bois sont des maisons qu'il déplace
    et des châteaux
Cette planche fait signe d'un toit qui penche
    ça n'est pas mal à voir
Ce n'est pas peu de savoir où va tourner la route
    de cartes
Cela pourrait changer complètement
    le cours de la rivière
À cause du pont qui fait un si beau mirage
    dans l'eau du tapis
C'est facile d'avoir un grand arbre
Et de mettre au-dessous une montagne
    pour qu'il soit en-haut.

Joie de jouer! paradis des libertés!
Et surtout n'allez pas mettre un pied dans la
    chambre
On ne sait jamais ce qui peut être dans ce coin
Et si vous n'allez pas écraser la plus chère
    des fleurs invisibles

Voilà ma boîte à jouets
Pleine de mots pour faire de merveilleux
    enlacements

Les allier séparer marier,
Déroulements tantôt de danse
Et tout à l'heure le clair éclat du rire
Qu'on croyait perdu

Une tendre chiquenaude
Et l'étoile
Qui se balançait sans prendre garde
Au bout d'un fil trop ténu de lumière
Tombe dans l'eau et fait des ronds.

De l'amour de la tendresse qui donc oserait en
    douter
Mais pas deux sous de respect pour l'ordre établi
Et la politesse et cette chère discipline
Une légèreté et des manières à scandaliser les
    grandes personnes

Il vous arrange les mots comme si c'étaient de
    simples chansons
Et dans ses yeux on peut lire son espiègle plaisir
À voir que sous les mots il déplace toutes choses
Et qu'il en agit avec les montagnes
Comme s'il les possédait en propre.
Il met la chambre à l'envers et vraiment l'on ne
    s'y reconnaît plus
Comme si c'était un plaisir de berner les gens.

Et pourtant dans son œil gauche quand le droit rit
Une gravité de l'autre monde s'attache à la feuille
    d'un arbre
Comme si cela pouvait avoir une grande importance
Avait autant de poids dans sa balance
Que le guerre d'Éthiopie
Dans celle de l'Angleterre.

Nous ne sommes pas des comptables

Tout le monde peut voir une piastre de papier vert

Mais qui peut voir au travers
                    si ce n'est un enfant
Qui peut comme lui voir au travers en toute
    liberté
Sans que du tout la piastre l'empêche
                    ni ses limites
Ni sa valeur d'une seule piastre

Mais il voit par cette vitrine des milliers de jouets
    merveilleux
Et n'a pas envie de choisir parmi ces trésors
Ni désir ni nécessité
Lui
Mais ses yeux sont grands pour tout prendre.

SAINT-DENY
GARNEAU

Accompagnement

Je marche à côté d'une joie
D'une joie qui n'est pas à moi
D'une joie à moi que je ne puis pas prendre

Je marche à côté de moi en joie
J'entends mon pas en joie qui marche à côté de
    moi
Mais je ne puis changer de place sur le trottoir
Je ne puis pas mettre mes pieds dans ces pas-là
                    et dire voilà, c'est moi

Je me contente pour le moment de cette compagnie
Mais je machine en secret des échanges
Par toutes sortes d'opérations, des alchimies,
Par des transfusions de sang
Des déménagements d'atomes
                    par des jeux d'équilibre,

Afin qu'un jour, transposé,
Je sois porté par la danse de ces pas de joie,
Avec le bruit décroissant de mon pas à côté de
    moi

Avec la perte de mon pas perdu
                    s'étiolant à ma gauche
Sous les pieds d'un étranger
                    qui prend une rue transversale.

SAINT-DENYS
GARNEAU

Monde irrémédiable désert

Dans ma main
Le bout cassé de tous les chemins

Quand est-ce qu'on a laissé tomber les amarres
Comment est-ce qu'on a perdu tous les chemins

La distance infranchissable
Ponts rompus
Chemins perdus

Dans le bas du ciel, cent visages
Impossibles à voir
La lumière interrompue d'ici-là
Un grand couteau d'ombre
Passe au milieu de mes regards

De ce lieu délié
Quel appel de bras tendus
Se perd dans l'air infranchissable

La mémoire qu'on interroge
A de lourds rideaux aux fenêtres
Pourquoi lui demander rien ?
L'ombre des absents est sans voix
Et se confond maintenant avec les murs
De la chambre vide.

Où sont les ponts les chemins les portes
Les paroles ne passent pas
La voix ne porte pas

Vais-je m'élancer sur ce fil incertain
Sur un fil imaginaire tendu sur l'ombre

Trouver peut-être les visages tournés
Et me heurter d'un grand coup sourd
Contre l'absence

Les ponts rompus
Chemins coupés
Le commencement de toutes présences
Le premier pas de toute compagnie
Gît cassé dans sa main.

Un bon coup de guillotine
Pour accentuer les distances

Je place ma tête sur la cheminée
Et le reste vaque à ses affaires

Mes pieds s'en vont à leurs voyages
Mes mains à leurs pauvres ouvrages

Sur la console de la cheminée
Ma tête a l'air d'être en vacances

Un sourire est sur ma bouche
Tel que si je venais de naître
Mon regard passe, calme et léger
Ainsi qu'une âme délivrée

On dirait que j'ai perdu la mémoire
Et cela fait une douce tête de fou.

Poids et mesures

Il ne s'agit pas de tirer les choses par les cheveux
D'attacher par les cheveux une femme
    à la queue d'un cheval
D'empiler des morts à la queue-leu-leu
Au fil de l'épée, au fil du temps.

On peut s'amuser à faire des nœuds
    avec des lignes parallèles
C'est un divertissement un peu métaphysique

L'absurde n'étant pas réduit à loger au nez de
    Cyrano
Mais en regardant cela la tête à l'envers
On aperçoit des évocations d'autres mondes
On aperçoit des cassures dans notre monde
    qui font des trous

On peut être fâché de voir des trous dans notre
    monde
On peut être scandalisé par un bas percé un gilet
    un gant percé qui laisse voir un doigt
On peut exiger que tout soit rapiécé

Mais un trou dans notre monde c'est déjà quelque
    chose
Pourvu qu'on s'accroche dedans les pieds
    et qu'on y tombe
La tête et qu'on y tombe la tête la première
Cela permet de voguer et même de revenir
Cela peut libérer de mesurer le monde à pied,
    pied à pied.

From *La Mort grandissante*

(I)
Et jusqu'au sommeil perdu dont erre l'ombre
    autour de nous sans nous prendre
Estompe tout, ne laissant que ce point en moi
    lourd lourd lourd
Qui attend le réveil au matin pour se mettre
    tout à fait debout
Au milieu de moi détruit, désarçonné, désemparé,
    agonisant.

Ah ! ce n'est pas la peine qu'on en vive
Quand on en meurt si bien
Pas la peine de vivre
Et voir cela mourir, mourir
Le soleil et les étoiles

Ah ! ce n'est pas la peine de vivre
Et de survivre aux fleurs
Et de survivre au feu, des cendres
Mais il vaudrait si mieux qu'on meure
Avec la fleur dans le cœur
Avec cette éclatante
Fleur de feu dans le cœur.

C'est eux qui m'ont tué
Sont tombés sur mon dos avec leurs armes, m'ont
    tué
Sont tombés sur mon cœur avec leur haine, m'ont
    tué
Sont tombés sur mes nerfs leurs cris, m'ont tué

C'est eux en avalanche m'ont écrasé
Cassé en éclats comme du bois

Rompu mes nerfs comme un câble de fils de fer
Qui se rompt net et tous les fils en bouquet fou
Jaillissent et se recourbent, pointes à vif

Ont émietté ma défense comme une croûte sèche
Ont égrené mon cœur comme de la mie
Ont tout éparpillé cela dans la nuit

Ils ont tout piétiné sans en avoir l'air,
Sans le savoir, le vouloir, sans le pouvoir,
Sans y penser, sans y prendre garde
Par leur seul terrible mystère étranger
Parce qu'ils ne sont pas à moi venus m'embrasser

Ah ! dans quel désert faut-il qu'on s'en aille
Pour mourir de soi-même tranquillement.

Mais les vivants n'ont pas pitié des morts
Et que feraient les morts de la pitié des vivants
Maise le cœur des vivants est dur comme un bon
    arbre
  et ils s'en vont forts de leur vie
Pourtant le cœur des morts est déjà tout en sang
  et occupé d'angoisse depuis longtemps

Et tout en proie aux coups, trop accessible aux SAINT-DENYS
    coups GARNEAU
    à travers leur carcasse ouverte.
Mais les vivants passant n'ont pas pitié des morts
    qui restent avec leur cœur au vent sans abri.

—Nous avons mis à mort la pitié
Nous ne pouvons pas qu'elle soit
Nous sommes les orgueilleux
Nous nions les regards de pitié.

—Nous sommes les regards de pitié
Nous ne pouvons pas ne pas être sur terre
Les regards de pitié.

UN AUTRE ENCORE

ou

LE MOURANT QUI ME JOINT
ET M'ABREUVE DE CENDRE

Il y a certainement quelqu'un qui se meurt
J'avais décidé de ne pas y prendre garde
    et de laisser tomber le cadavre en chemin
Mais c'est l'avance maintenant qui manque
    et c'est moi
Le mourant qui s'ajuste à moi.

(II)

Nous avons attendu de la douleur
qu'elle modèle notre figure
    à la dureté magnifique de nos os
Au silence irréductible et certain de nos os
Ce dernier retranchement inexpugnable de notre
    être
qu'elle tende à nos os clairement la peau de nos
    figures
La chair lâche et troublée de nos figures
qui crèvent à tout moment et se décomposent
Cette peau qui flotte au vent de notre figure
    triste oripeau.

Faible oripeau à tous les vents qui nous trahit
Qu'elle l'assujettisse décidément
    à la forme certaine de nos os clairs.

Mais la douleur fut-elle devancée
Est-ce que la mort serait venue secrètement
    faire son nid dans nos os mêmes
Aurait pénétré, corrompu nos os mêmes
Aurait élu domicile dans la substance même de
    nos os
Parmi nos os
De sorte qu'arrivée là après toute la chair
    traversée
Après toutes les épaisseurs traversées
    qu'on lui avait jetées en pâture
Après toutes ces morsures dans notre chair molle
    et comme engourdie
La douleur ne trouve pas non plus
    de substance ferme à quoi s'attaquer
De substance ferme à quoi s'agripper
    d'une poigne ferme
Densité à percer d'un solide aiguillon
Un silence solide à chauffer à blanc
Une sensibilité essentielle et silencieuse
    à torturer sans la détruire

Mais elle ne rejoint encore qu'une surface qui
    s'effrite
Un édifice poreux qui se dissout
Un fantôme qui s'écroule et ne laisse plus que
    poussière.

Nous des ombres de cadavres elles des réalités
    de cadavres, des os de cadavres,
Et quelle pitié nous prend (et quelle admiration)
    ombres consciences de cadavres
Et terreur fraternelle nous prend
Devant cette réponse faite
Cette image offerte
Os de cadavres.

Quand on est réduit à ses os
Assis sur ses os
couché en ses os
avec la nuit devant soi.

SAINT-DENYS
GARNEAU

Nous allons détacher nos membres
    et les mettre en rang pour en faire un inventaire
Afin de voir ce qui manque
De trouver le joint qui ne va pas
Car il est impossible de recevoir assis
    tranquillement la mort grandissante.

Et cependant dressé en nous
Un homme qu'on ne peut pas abattre
Debout en nous et tournant le dos à la direction
    de nos regards
Debout en os et les yeux fixés sur le néant
Dans une effroyable confrontation obstinée et un
    défi.

.   .   .

GEORGE
WOODCOCK

b. 1912

Imagine the South

Imagine the South from which these migrants fled,
Dark-eyed, pursued by arrows, crowned with
    blood,
Imagine the stiff stone houses and the ships
Blessed with wine and salt, the quivering tips
Of spears and edges signalling in the sun
From swords unscabbarded and sunk in brine,
Imagine the cyclamen faces and yielding breasts
Hungered after in a dead desert of icy mists,
Imagine, for though oblivious, you too are cast
Exile upon a strange and angry coast.

147

Going into exile away from youth,
You too are losing a country in the South,
Losing, in the red daylight of a new shore
Where you are hemmed by solitude and fear,
The loving faces far over a sea of time,
The solid comfort and the humane dream
Of a peaceful sky, the consoling patronage
And the golden ladder to an easy age,
All these are lost, for you too have gone away
From your southern home upon a bitter journey.

GEORGE
WOODCOCK

There is no home for you marked on the compass.
I see no Penelope at the end of your Odysseys,
And all the magic islands will let you down.
Do not touch the peaches and do not drink the
   wine,
For the Dead Sea spell will follow all you do,
And do not talk of tomorrow, for to you
There will only be yesterday, only the fading land,
The boats on the shore and tamarisks in the sand
Where the beautiful faces wait, and the faithful
   friends.
They will people your mind. You will never touch
   their hands.

The Island

The oars fell from our hands. We climbed the dark
   Slopes of kelp to the stairway up the rock.
Scott went first, grasping the fraying rope.
   The rest of us followed, dragging the iron rack.

The crest was bare, but after scanty search
   In a bird's burrow we found the hunted man.
His flesh was naked and hard as barren earth
   His arms like scythes. His eyes spoke like a gun.

Before him we retired, unmanned by fear.

Unarmed, he seemed to move with harmful
   light.
Scott only stood, shaming us in the end.
   The fugitive surrendered without fight.

GEORGE
WOODCOCK

We laid him on the painful rack, stretched tight
   His limbs and bound his feet and wrists with
     wire.
Set leaden weights upon his sunken chest
   And tied his head down by the matted hair.

We turned the cranks and wrenched him hour
   by hour.
   In silence he endured. He would not speak
Of the hidden ore. At last his joints burst out
   And jetting from the ruptures fire broke.

Then lay before us on the rigid rack
   Straw limbs and a horse's polished skull.
Gulls mocked as walked away across the sea
   The man we hunted but could not keep or kill.

We threw the rack into the hungry surf
   And hacked the turf in anger with our swords.
Then, re-embarking on our fruitless voyage,
   We left the island to the mice and birds.

IRVING
LAYTON

b. 1912

The Birth of Tragedy

And me happiest when I compose poems.
     Love, power, the huzza of battle
     are something, are much;
yet a poem includes them like a pool
     water and reflection.

In me, nature's divided things—
    tree, mould on tree—
    have their fruition;
I am their core. Let them swap,
bandy, like a flame swerve
I am their mouth; as a mouth I serve.

IRVING
LAYTON

And I observe how the sensual moths
    big with odour and sunshine
    dart into the perilous shrubbery;
or drop their visiting shadows
    upon the garden I one year made
of flowering stone to be a footstool
    for the perfect gods :
    who, friends to the ascending orders,
sustain all passionate meditations
and call down pardons
for the insurgent blood.

A quiet madman, never far from tears,
    I lie like a slain thing
    under the green air the trees
inhabit, or rest upon a chair
    towards which the inflammable air
tumbles on many robins' wings;
    noting how seasonably
    leaf and blossom uncurl
and living things arrange their death,
while someone from afar off
blows birthday candles for the world.

Berry Picking

Silently my wife walks on the still wet furze
Now darkgreen the leaves are full of metaphors
Now lit up is each tiny lamp of blueberry.
The white nails of rain have dropped and the sun
    is free.

And whether she bends or straightens to each
   bush
To find the children's laughter among the leaves
Her quiet hands seem to make the quiet summer
   hush—
Berries or children, patient she is with these.

I only vex and perplex her; madness, rage
Are endearing perhaps put down upon the page;
Even silence daylong and sullen can then
Enamour as restraint or classic discipline.

So I envy the berries she puts in her mouth,
The red and succulent juice that stains her lips;
I shall never taste that good to her, nor will they
Displease her with a thousand barbarous jests.

How they lie easily for her hand to take,
Part of the unoffending world that is hers;
Here beyond complexity she stands and stares
And leans her marvellous head as if for answers.

No more the easy soul my childish craft deceives
Nor the simpler one for whom yes is always yes;
No, now her voice comes to me from a far way
   off
Though her lips are redder than the raspberries.

Cain

Taking the air rifle from my son's hand,
I measured back five paces, the Hebrew
In me, narcissist, father of children,
Laid to rest. From there I took aim and fired.
The silent ball hit the frog's back an inch
Below the head. He jumped at the surprise
Of it, suddenly tickled or startled
(He must have thought) and leaped from the wet
   sand

Into the surrounding brown water. But IRVING
The ball had done its mischief. His next spring   LAYTON
Was a miserable flop, the thrust all gone
Out of his legs. He tried—like Bruce—again,
Throwing out his sensitive pianist's
Hands as a dwarf might or a helpless child.
His splash disturbed the quiet pondwater
And one old frog behind his weedy moat
Blinking, looking self-complacently on.
The lin's surface at once became closing
Eyelids and bubbles like notes of music
Liquid, luminous, dropping from the page
White, white-bearded, a rapid crescendo
Of inaudible sounds and a crones' whispering
Backstage among the reeds and bulrushes
As for an expiring Lear or Oedipus.

But Death makes us all look ridiculous.
Consider this frog (dog, hog, what you will)
Sprawling, his absurd corpse rocked by the tides
That his last vain spring had set in movement.
Like a retired oldster, I couldn't help sneer,
Living off the last of his insurance:
Billows—now crumbling—the premiums paid.
Absurd, how absurd. I wanted to kill
At the mockery of it, kill and kill
Again—the self-infatuate frog, dog, hog,
Anything with the stir of life in it,
Seeing the dead leaper, Chaplin-footed,
Rocked and cradled in this afternoon
Of tranquil water, reeds, and blazing sun,
The hole in his back clearly visible
And the torn skin a blob of shadow
Moving when the quiet poolwater moved.
O Egypt, marbled Greece, resplendent Rome,
Did you also finally perish from a small bore
In your back you could not scratch? And would
Your mouths open ghostily, gasping out

Among the murky reeds, the hidden frogs,
We climb with crushed spines toward the
    heavens?

When the next morning I came the same way
The frog was on his back, one delicate
Hand on his belly, and his white shirt front
Spotless. He looked as if he might have been
A comic; tapdancer apologizing
For a fall, or an Emcee, his wide grin
Coaxing a laugh from us for an aside
Or perhaps a joke we didn't quite hear.

The Day Aviva Came to Paris

The day you came naked to Paris
The tourists returned home without their
    guidebooks,
The hunger in their cameras finally appeased.

Alone once more with their gargoyles, the
    Frenchmen
Marvelled at the imagination that had produced
    them
And once again invited terror into their apéritifs.
Death was no longer exiled to the cemeteries.

In their royal gardens where the fish die of old
    age,
They perused something else besides newspapers
—A volume perhaps by one of their famous
    writers.
They opened their hearts to let your tender smile
    defrost them;
Their livers filled with an unassuageable love of
    justice.
They became the atmosphere around them.

They learned to take money from Americans
And to think of themselves
As not excessively subtle or witty.
'Au diable with Voltaire,' they muttered,
'Who was a national calamity.
Au diable with la République.
(A race of incurable petits bourgeois, the French
Are happiest under a horse under a man)
Au diable with la Monarchie!
We saw no goddesses during either folly;
Our bald-headed savants never had told us
Such a blaze of pubic hair anywhere existed.'
And they ordered the grandson of Grandma Moses
To paint it large on the dome of le Sacré-Cœur.

My little one, as if under those painted skies
It was again 1848,
They leaped as one mad colossal Frenchman from
    their café Pernods
Shouting, 'Vive l'Australienne!
Vive Layton who brought her among us!
Let us erect monuments of black porphyry to
    them!
Let us bury them in the Panthéon!'

(Pas si vite, messieurs; we are still alive)

And when, an undraped Jewish Venus,
You pointed to a child, a whole slum starving in
    her eyes,
Within earshot of the Tuileries,
The French who are crazy or catholic enough
To place, facing each other, two tableaux
—One for the Men of the Convention, and one
    puffing the Orators of the Restoration—
At once made a circle wide as the sky around you
While the Mayor of the 5th Arrondissement
Addressed the milling millions of Frenchmen :

'See how shapely small her adorable ass is; IRVING
Of what an incredible pink rotundity each cheek.   LAYTON
À bas Merovingian and Valois!
À bas Charlemagne and Henri Quatre!
For all the adulations we have paid them
In our fabulous histoires
They cannot raise an erection between them. Ah,
For too long has the madness of love
Been explained to us by sensualists and curés.
À bas Stendhal! À bas Bossuet!

'Forever and forever, from this blazing hour
All Paris radiates from Aviva's nest of hair
—Delicate hatchery of profound delights—
From her ever-to-be-adored Arche de Triomphe!
All the languors of history
Take on meaning clear as a wineglass or the belch
    of an angel
Only if thought of as rushing
On the wings of a rhinoceros towards this
    absorbing event.
Voyeurs, voyez! The moisture of her delicate
    instep
Is a pool of love
Into which sheathed in candy paper
Anaesthetized politicians drop from the skies!'
(Word jugglery of course, my Sweet; but the
    French love it
—Mistake it in fact for poetry)

And the applaudissements and bravos
Bombinating along the Boulevard Saint-Germain
Made the poor docile Seine
Think our great Atlantic was upon it.
It overflowed with fright into the bookstalls
And sidewalk cafés.
Fifteen remaining Allemands with their cameras
Were flushed down the Rue Pigalle.

And when you were raised up
Into my hairy arms by the raving emotional
    crowds
Waving frenzied bottles of Beaujolais
And throwing the corks away ecstatically
(Not saving them !)
It was, my Love, my Darling,
As if someone had again ordered an advance
Upon the Bastille
Which we recalled joyously, face to face at last,
Had yielded after only a small token resistance.

A Tall Man Executes A Jig

(I)

So the man spread his blanket on the field
And watched the shafts of light between the tufts
And felt the sun push the grass towards him;
The noise he heard was that of whizzing flies,
The whistlings of some small imprudent birds,
And the ambiguous rumbles of cars
That made him look up at the sky, aware
Of the gnats that tilted against the wind
And in the sunlight turned to jigging motes.
Fruitflies he'd call them except there was no fruit
About, spoiling to hatch these glitterings,
These nervous dots for which the mind supplied
The closing sentences from Thucydides,
Or from Euclid having a savage nightmare.

(II)

Jig jig, jig jig. Like minuscule black links
Of a chain played with by some playful
Unapparent hand or the palpitant
Summer haze bored with the hour's stillness.
He felt the sting and tingle afterwards
Of those leaving their unorthodox unrest,

Leaving their undulant excitation
To drop upon his sleeveless arm. The grass,
Even the wildflowers became black hairs
And himself a maddened speck among them.
Still the assaults of the small flies made him
Glad at last, until he saw purest joy
In their frantic jiggings under a hair,
So changed from those in the unrestraining air.

(III)
He stood up and felt himself enormous.
Felt as might Donatello over stone,
Or Plato, or as a man who has held
A loved and lovely woman in his arms
And feels his forehead touch the emptied sky
Where all antinomies flood into light.
Yet jig jig jig, the haloing black jots
Meshed with the wheeling fire of the sun:
Motion without meaning, disquietude
Without sense or purpose, ephemerides
That mottled the resting summer air till
Gusts swept them from his sight like wisps of
    smoke.
Yet they returned, bringing a bee who, seeing
But a tall man, left him for a marigold.

(IV)
He doffed his aureole of gnats and moved
Out of the field as the sun sank down,
A dying god upon the blood-red hills.
Ambition, pride, the ecstasy of sex,
And all circumstances of delight and grief,
That blood upon the mountain's side, that flood
Washed into a clear incredible pool
Below the ruddied peaks that pierced the sun.
He stood still and waited. If ever
The hour of revelation was come

It was now, here on the transfigured steep.
The sky darkened. Some birds chirped. Nothing
    else.
He thought the dying god had gone to sleep:
An Indian fakir on his mat of nails.

(v)
And on the summit of the asphalt road
Which stretched towards the fiery town, the man
Saw one hill raised like a hairy arm, dark
With pines and cedars against the stricken sun
—The arm of Moses or of Joshua.
He dropped his head and let fall the halo
Of mountains, purpling and silent as time,
To see temptation coiled before his feet:
A violated grass snake that lugged
Its intestine like a small red valise.
A cold-eyed skinflint it now was, and not
The manifest of that joyful wisdom,
The mirth and arrogant green flame of life;
Or earth's vivid tongue that flicked in praise of
    earth.

(vi)
And the man wept because pity was useless,
'Your jig's up; the flies come like kites,' he said
And watched the grass snake crawl towards the
    hedge,
Convulsing and dragging into the dark
The satchel filled with curses for the earth,
For the odours of warm sedge, and the sun,
A blood-red organ in the dying sky.
Backwards it fell into a grassy ditch
Exposing its underside, white as milk,
And mocked by wisps of hay between its jaws;
And then it stiffened to its final length.
But though it opened its thin mouth to scream

A last silent scream that shook the black sky,
Adamant and fierce, the tall man did not curse.

IRVING
LAYTON

(VII)
Beside the rigid snake the man stretched out
In fellowship of death; he lay silent
And stiff in the heavy grass with eyes shut,
Inhaling the moist odours of the night
Through which his mind tunnelled with flicking
tongue
Backwards to caves, mounds, and sunken ledges
And desolate cliffs where come only kites,
And where of perished badgers and racoons
The claws alone remain, gripping the earth.
Meanwhile the green snake crept upon the sky,
Huge, his mailed coat glittering with stars that
made
The night bright, and blowing thin wreaths of
cloud
Athwart the moon; and as the weary man
Stood up, coiled above his head, transforming all.

b. 1913

Music on the Water

Saturday night she comes in her little boat
When the air is warm on the smoky river, afloat,
Making her presence felt in her flickering oars:
A journeying wound between the fragile shores.

Nights of splendour she's been to splendid men,
Swallowed them whole and spit them up again,
After which they've forgotten her perhaps—
As though she might have remembered them, poor
    chaps.

Now they're distributed about the town,
Two in a meeting, one in a dressing gown,
One in a hospital bed with stinking bones,
One in a radio drama, making groans.

One is a kind, white-eyebrowed public man,
Used to write poems and at times still can;
Fame is his breakfast food and evening prayer;
Saturday night he dozes in his chair.

Out on the skin of water she sings a song,
Sweet but a little bit flat and sometimes wrong;
Under the bridge it wobbles as she goes by
And wastes away in the willow trees and the sky.

The song she sings is a Pentecostal hymn
According to which Earth's glories are rather dim
Whereas the rewards of the just are very bright;
Low kind of song, but it serves her turn all right.

Noctambule

GEORGE
JOHNSTON

Mr Murple's got a dog that's long
And underslung and sort of pointed wrong;
When daylight fades and evening lights come out
He takes him round the neighbour lawns about
To ease himself and leak against the trees
The which he does in drops and by degrees
Leaving his hoarded fluid only where
Three-legged ceremonious hairy care
Has been before and made a solemn sign.
Mythology, inscrutable, canine,
Makes his noctambulation eloquent
And gives a power of meaning to his scent
That all who come and sniff and add thereto
And scratch the turf, may know they have to do
With Mr Murple's underslung long dog,
His mark, his manifesto and his log.

The Bulge

Nobody knows what's growing in Bridget,
    Nobody knows whose is, what's more :
Maybe a beauty queen, maybe a midget,
    Maybe a braided bloke to stand by the door.

Lovely full Bridget, her eyes are like figs,
    Her belly's an ocean, heaving with fish,
Her heart is a barnyard with chickens and pigs,
    Her outside's a banquet, her tongue is a dish.

Something enormous is bulging in Bridget—
    A milkman, a postman, a sugar-stick, a slop,
An old maid, a bad maid, a doughhead, a fidget.
    Multiple sweet Bridget, what will she drop ?

O Earth, Turn!

GEORGE
JOHNSTON

The little blessed Earth that turns
Does so on its own concerns
As though it weren't my home at all;
It turns me winter, summer, fall
Without a thought of me.

I love the slightly flattened sphere,
Its restless, wrinkled crust's my here,
Its slightly wobbling spin's my now
But not my why and not my how:
My why and how are me.

DOUGLAS
LE PAN

b. 1914

A Country Without a Mythology

No monuments or landmarks guide the stranger
Going among this savage people, masks
Taciturn or babbling out an alien jargon
And moody as barbaric skies are moody.

Berries must be his food. Hurriedly
He shakes the bushes, plucks pickerel from the
    river,
Forgetting every grace and ceremony,
Feeds like an Indian, and is on his way.

And yet, for all his haste, time is worth nothing.
The abbey clock, the dial in the garden,
Fade like saints' days and festivals.
Months, years, are here unbroken virgin forests.

There is no law—even no atmosphere
To smooth the anger of the flagrant sun.

November skies sting sting like icicles.   DOUGLAS
The land is open to all violent weathers.   LE PAN

Passion is not more quick. Lightnings in August
Stagger, rocks split, tongues in the forest hiss,
As fire drinks up the lovely sea-dream coolness.
This is the land the passionate man must travel.

Sometimes—perhaps at the tentative fall of
    twilight—
A belief will settle that waiting around the bend
Are sanctities of childhood, that melting birds
Will sing him into a limpid gracious Presence.

The hills will fall in folds, the wilderness
Will be a garment innocent and lustrous
To wear upon a birthday, under a light
That curls and smiles, a golden-haired Archangel.

And now the channel opens. But nothing alters.
Mile after mile of tangled struggling roots,
Wild-rice, stumps, weeds, that clutch at the canoe,
Wild birds hysterical in tangled trees.

And not a sign, no emblem in the sky
Or boughs to friend him as he goes; for who
Will stop where, clumsily constructed, daubed
With war-paint, teeters some lust-red manitou?

Coureurs de bois

Thinking of you, I think of the *coureurs de bois*,
Swarthy men grown almost to savage size
Who put their brown wrists through the arras of
    the woods
And were lost—sometimes for months. Word
    would come back:
One had been seen at Crève-cœur, deserted and
    starving,
One at Sault Sainte Marie shouldering the rapids.

Giant-like, their labours stalked in the streets of DOUGLAS
    Quebec LE PAN
Though they themselves had dwindled in
    distance : names only;
Rumours; quicksilvery spies into nature's secrets;
Rivers that seldom ran in the sun. Their resource
Would sparkle and then flow back under clouds
    of hemlock.

So you should have travelled with them. Or with
    La Salle.
He could feed his heart with the heart of a
    continent,
Insatiate, how noble a wounded animal,
Who sought for his wounds the balsam of
    adventure,
The sap from some deep, secret tree. But now
That the forests are cut down, the rivers charted,
Where can you turn, where can you travel ?
    Unless
Through the desperate wilderness behind your
    eyes,
So full of falls and glooms and desolations,
Disasters I have glimpsed but few would dream of,
You seek new Easts. The coats of difficult honour,
Bright with brocaded birds and curious flowers,
Stowed so long with vile packs of pemmican,
Futile, weighing you down on slippery portages,
Would flutter at last in the courts of a clement
    country,
Where the air is silken, the manners easy,
Under a guiltless and reconciling sun.

You hesitate. The trees are entangled with
    menace.
The voyage is perilous into the dark interior.

But then your hands go to the thwarts. You
   smile. And so
I watch you vanish in a wood of heroes,
Wild Hamlet with the features of Horatio.

DOUGLAS
LE PAN

An Incident

Arrange the scene with only a shade of difference
And he would be a boy in his own native
And fern-fronded providence,
With a map in his hand, searching for a portage
   overgrown
With brush. Slim he is as a moccasin-flower
With his throat open
To the winds, to the four winds, quivering,
Who alone by the worm-holed flower of the
   rose-pink house
Bears the weight of this many-ringed, foreign
   noon,
Shadowless, vast and pitiless.
Notched by the wedge of his frown, it takes no
   notice.
Light that, alive, would be pungent with resin,
Sapless, now weighs and ponders like limestone.

What is he waiting for
As he studies a map the colour of his youth?
Time stops and whirs in his ear like a humming-
   bird
As he gazes this way and that
For someone to relieve him
For someone to break through the thicket of his
   isolation.

In the silence
The grasshoppers crackle and crumble the
   summer

Between their thin wings
And their singing thighs.
And his head has begun to sing,
To sing with the heat.
Stampeding, his blood butts him like a bull-calf.
How should one so young have learned how to
    wait?
Ah! there is the relief.
A stray round has caught him at the nape of the
    neck
And splayed him flat on the earth,
His blood flung wide as a sunburst.

And the pink house, that eavesdropped
Through smoke-blackened holes to each
    palpitation,
Recovering its reserve,
Sucks in unblemished stillness;
While the wise light with petrified foliage
Having disposed of this awkward animal tremor
Again stands superb as a temple.

Nimbus

To dive for the nimbus on the sea-floor
    Or seek it in the sun
Calls for a plucky steeplejack
    Scaling sky's giddy ocean
Or dolphin-hearted journeyman
To swim from the foundered sunburst's roar
    With lost treasure on his back.

Ocean that slovens and sidles in vast
    Indifference, hides
In its sludge a wreath of drowning bells.
    Who in those tricky tides
Or up the slippery daybreak's sides
Can grapple the spices of morning fast
    That waste on the listless swells?

Smothered beneath a lowering ceiling
   All cock-crow crispness dies.
Bleary hordes are afraid to wake
   Into the mists that rise
From a palsied swamp where a marsh-bird cries.
Stranger, reconquer the source of feeling
   For an anxious people's sake.

Plunder the mind's aerial cages
   Or the heart's deep catacombs,
O daring's virtuoso, tossed
   Where the furious sunlight foams
Or through the instinct's twilit glooms,
Return with the sunburst's glistering pledges
   As a garland for the lost.

A bittern rustling in the reeds
   Is startled, and through the mist
Whirs screaming. Now, if now only, come
   With the nimbus in your fist.
Strike, strike the rust like a rhapsodist
And burnish gold each throat that pleads
   For dawn's encomium.

DOUGLAS
LE PAN

PATRICK
ANDERSON

b. 1915

From *Poem on Canada*

THE COMING OF THE WHITE MAN

Suppose it, for the last time, in that moment
when being undiscovered it lay quiet
and almost no other country, like the sea—
when resinous currents streaked its boughgreen
   waves and soundless arrows

were slipping like fish through fathoms of spruce
    and balsam :
the time of the tent, the shape of light in the
    water,
and the rustred encampment on the gravel shoal
with the glow of phosphorus from its deep
    drowned fire :
suppose it then, with its strange and primitive
    stillness
breathed awkwardly, with gills—not broken
by men brocaded with Renaissance lungs.
In that moment, the last in which it tested its
    silence
against the innumerable dialects of flowers
and birds, in pinprick crowds—
and deployed its multitudinous winds
gravely, amongst a few simple savages,
and slept the last immortal sleep of its childhood.

And then, when that moment hung like a cliff
and for miles and miles extended
westward its enormous capacity to be hurt
(for what is weaker than something that needs
only the casual eye to rupture its being
and luck to change it forever?) suppose,
suddenly, out of the haze,
come like a swimmer, the Renaissance man
aware of his Grecian whiteness—discovered!
At first his sea-head less important than gulls
then later nearer than ships
and standing out of the east, dripping with
    armour,
this conqueror with the marvelous corrupt face,
    drawing
soft Europe out of the water,
sanguine, scientific with flowers . . .
would not every movement of that first naked
    foot

utterly shatter
the white sand with the sound of a thunderbolt?

PATRICK
ANDERSON

That moment when l'uomo universale
crying with von Hutten 'It is a joy to be alive,'
captain and cousin of the Roman world,
coined in the delight of the Medici banks, lept
upon the white sand of the continent!
Yet shall we be in error if we say
that then—as though by arrow shot—he fell
down on his knees, God's cripple,
and the clean sands were
disordered by prayer and greed, as though by the
    wounded?
Planted a cross, claimed for a King, and stole
natives like curios, and hid his face
in the great purse of his soul?
For his America and Newfoundland
was not, after all, soft China like a girl's
expert monopoly in a lover's Trades,
but really the wrong country.
                              O here
in vast intervention island America
green as a tyro imposed her giant innocence
huge as the gardens of childhood. Was not
as easy Indies to his lover's hand
but always a trifle frigid like a gauche
but beautiful mirror, seeming shiningly empty
and keen, as a child does.
To which he comes, the prince adventurer,
competes his heart from that anarchic sea
where windy Luther and sleek Machiavelli
in a mess of sceptres a confusion of thrones
rise and are chaos to Christendom. Hacks
his private way, aches at his joint-stock frontier,
protests himself religious, prays for grace,
disrupts the forest in his monetary enterprise
and performs his prodigies

for the artists' banks, the commercial houses of
    Shakespeare.

And the moment not yet
fulfilment . . . nor northwest discovery
to those who see in plains the easier islands
only, and plot their rule and real estate
with gun, axe, bible, theodolite,
seignorial tenure. . . . Yet, historically,
one did what one could. The best was competition,
the winds particular, men against the sky,
the merchandise ordered. One was good at those
    things.
Sometimes one regretted the idyllic relations
and there were even those who talked for poetry
as Wolfe—before he died at Quebec.
'I had rather, etc. than take it,' he said
but, as the curfew tolled the knell of parting day,
he performed his historical function, and he was
    dead.

Others have also thought 'the Pen is mightier than
    the Sword'
or 'colonies are provincial,' but always there were
the things to be got; to be more particular
one thousand six hundred Beaver skins (for
    Europe's hats),
six thousand Lynx pelts, five hundred (superfine)
    Buffalo robes,
a quantity of castorum. And if one despaired
of the cutthroat pace, the raccoon and fox in the
    traps,
the pemmican on the trail, one could give the job
    up—
go native perhaps or become a Scottish laird.
And so a long paddle, a hard road
sweat blinding one.
                On the brave heart's investment
of energy sun's summer interest

pouring in palm, the finery of sex
and, cyclical, the slump of Fall—the leaves
devalued in their cashier's grilles—the boom
of early thaw. Spring and the luxury trades!
Powders and pollens brimming in the heat's
expanding market, August's mounting price
and far off thunder over crazy buying
of love, 'eternal moments,' gilt-edged stock
as fine and faithless as the goldenrod.
To own all this and then to own all Winter's
waspish gazette, from the first August rumours
to the inflation of maples, the scarlet spending, till
the empty safe, the shot of ice. And then
be tragic Hamlet, damned, Tory with death.
And so a hard and individual road
from the Portage de la Roche Capitaine to the
    Décharge of the Trou
with the water oftentimes awkward in channels
    and guts
of the pointed rocks, the oldest in the world:
a competition of hearts, a cruel journey:
the rapids of Matawoen a fierce lace
and Lake Nipissing a tough blue
and the beautiful hills cracking adventurous
    muscles.
And the Portage Pin de Musique and Mauvais de
    Musique,
many lost there, crushed by canoes,
and the Turtle, one thousand, five hundred and
    thirteen paces.
The far-flung heart in many awkward and
    beautiful
places and awkward beautiful waters before
they chose, at Grande Portage, from the
    pork-eaters
those who must go upon the western journey,
the winterers to the river of the rainy lake.

PATRICK
ANDERSON

And the North was. With winter the snow came.   PATRICK
Whole folios of it. Yet nothing written   ANDERSON
except one thing, a bleak expectancy—
the possible with its strenuous shade of whiteness,
where an intuition almost without equipment
could trek into the faint wind of the future,
getting its silence on the single track.
And the land was. And the Aurora came.
O then below the pale and famished lights
whose powder tremors and electric gales
hurled from the terrible fluted rays,
the wish hurt in the breast. For these
lights can illumine nothing but the spirit,
not lights but sketches of light,
naked, distant, uncertain,
to watch whose glacial radiance is an effort
never a peace, which to accept
is to be lone, lost in the spirit's hunger.
And the land was. And locked in all its lakes,
the land unseen. Although
by many needled tracks and snowy trails,
across tough ridges and down distances
of a green fatigue—in valleys of the yawn—
on plains spreading diffusion of desire—
discovered by a failure,
by the great captains of human weakness.

And the land was. And the people did not take it.
Wide was the land.
      And North.
        My Aunt bought lakes—
Aunt Hildegarde, living on Lincoln Terrace,
one of the genteel poor, unmarried,
playing at patience, stroked those cards
whose red is scarlet as the tongues of lovers
or as the autumn maples, with their dogs'
    tongues—
remembered the years in Ottawa, a Brockville
    childhood,

and sometimes opened the close cedar drawer   PATRICK
under the knickknacks between the aspidistras   ANDERSON
and showed me the deed. Crumpled it was and
    dusty—
deed to five thousand acres no one had ever seen
and three lakes, all unnamed.
               Aunt Hildegarde
had bought this stake in natural Canada
for a thousand dollars, timber and all.

I thought, as a child would, of her trees, her birds,
her streams, her little glaciers and her thaws
and of the beavers of Aunt Hildegarde.
When, as sometimes happened, she grew severe
I dreamt how seriously across her boundaries
a moose had stepped, and stood there gentle and
    grim.
In Spring she smiled as all her birds returned.
In Summer dozed, consulting butterflies—
an old lady, with a muskeg all her own.
When she sleeps, I thought, beside her medicine
    bottles,
It does not sleep. Maybe the Indians cross it
as shadows slur her features when she nods
by the parlour fire, reading the *Globe and Mail*.
When I grew older, I thought of those lakes as
    mirrors
in which Aunt Hildegarde had never seen
    herself—
brisk pits to show her soul and Canada's.
And, as a matter of fact, she often declared
she'd visit them one day. But she never did.
A cancer engrossed her, she grew thin and died.
Her lawyers, they say, had a hell of a time
trying to sell that marvellous empty
neck of the woods that no one had ever seen.

And the land was. And the people did not take it.

A Window on the North

Stirb und werde.—GOETHE

The whole landscape drifted away to the north,
To Moose Factory, hundreds of miles, to the pole
And beyond, to the Arctic ends of the earth,
Sullen, Siberian, grey, only the hills and
Humps of snow, and the frightening black
Of the evergreens before us.   The window
Was white with frost, inviting and beckoning the
Famishing cold into the room, into the very heart,
Into our true sadness, the gripping melancholy.

We drowsed with the languor of the battling
Heat from the ugly stove and the cramping
Weariness.   Three jays lay dead, their toes
Frozen to the icy juniper boughs, their blue
Plumage arranged artistically on the bush.
The uranium and gold capered like heroes
In a Chaplin film, and the Hollywood Indian
Rocked in the hush and dreamed of York boats
Down the Saskatchewan.

                    Die and become.
Die and become, Johnny Cree, the standing
    warrior.
Die and become in this vast waste of yours—
A blue-jay to come again in the sudden
Summer, now so lovely dead, a white fox
Out of the tundra, a mere thought over
The snow—warrior and wanderer once more
In the barrens of the world.

A geranium plant   R. A. D.
Stood on a shelf behind him.   Putney in extremis.   FORD
Suddenly it was all red with flower,
Glowing with magic, defiant to the great
White bear.   I thought of you in the sweet
South; and the wind at the window was only
A warm breeze to melt the icicles of sleep.

Back to Dublin

From Drogheda all along the coast, the Irish sea,
Followed by the ghost of the Marquis of I don't
Remember, but his car overwhelmed us with dust
Near Rush and his castle, a constant grey
Landmark all over Meath, appeared to say
Continually to us, second immigrants : what
Is the use of coming back to stare? While others,
     the poor
Relations, either jeered or seemed to think
We were there to gloat, had never heard
Of Joyce or Yeats, and glorified Thomas Moore,
Pointed out the shell marks in the Dublin streets,
And deferred the debate on the price of hogs
To show us where the Liffey meets with God.

No glory to come back, none to be there,
And none but the seer to tender why the
     pilgrimage
To the rain-washed isle; never got to the grave
Under Ben Bulben, nor Tara's Halls, nor Innisfree
In the heat of the year—but just to stand
Near the stained walls of the ancient town
And dream of sailing to Byzantium—
An old man and a damaged harp,
Weaving the sweetest pattern on the warp
Of a broken continent—that was the fee,
That was my ticket to come in.

Revenge of the Hunted

R. A. D.
FORD

The gun, the trap, the axe are borne
head high at dusk in triumph home—
the tramp of hunting boots,
the bloody mantle thrown
down, these challenge to the soul
the flagrant horn, and send
to the far bounds of the green
hills the trumpeting of death in shame.

There will be a beating out some day,
from bush to field to stone
farm; then, lugged in the mud,
spattered with wings torn and unclean
ugly parts of snake and lame
beasts, will with crude
arms barbarously destroy,
with fierce voices savagely proclaim:
Here lies the broken gun alone,
the green weeds sweeping it away,
and here the judgment of the wood.

GEORGE
WHALLEY
b. 1915

Affair of Honour

Eloquent between the formal hedges
The date of the year is grafted in the turf
With crossed swords
Calling back across three centuries
To this pastoral place above the sweet river
The carnal liturgy mortal in the dawn.

The principals, forthright in disaster and
Foreshortened to stone,
Gaze each other pale in the truculent light
Under the bright eyes of the hooded golden
    girlchild.
She at least is present,
Withdrawn a little to the company of stalking
    shadows,
Flattered to tears by the lion pride,
Enchanted by the dawning horror
Between the reticent formalities of the hedges.

For love's sake a virtuoso thrust
Asserts the crabbed and scrupulous logic of
    honour.
The casual enemy's plea is clenched on a gasp of
    silence
And gives no more evidence before the chief
    witness.
I see the agile figures
Sealed in the long stride of their companion
    shadows
Startled to stone;
And the drops of blood humbled by the girl's gaze
Blessing the grass.

Can seed and rain mingle aloud and flower
For pity at her frock's hem? or the eloquent
    blood
Spring into birdsong crying to plead
Stay of execution
In strictest confidence of the formal hedges?

The shadows are long, the dew astonishes the
    spiders,
The light shivers and falters, the thin pulse ebbs
    into silence;

GEORGE
WHALLEY

And she and the man,   GEORGE
WHALLEY
Braggart in their opening of the unstaunched vein,
Complacent as vultures, sardonic as astronauts,
Cut the date of the year for joy with crossed
   swords
In the dishonoured earth,
Laughing to think how it turns its face to the sky
   for good to celebrate
A brave encounter here on the grass where the
   blood dropped down
Between the formal hedges
Reticent these three centuries.

RINA
LASNIER

b. 1915

La Malemer

Je descendrai jusque sous la malemer où la nuit
jouxte la nuit — jusqu'au creuset où la mer forme
elle-même son malheur,

sous cette amnésique nuit de la malemer qui ne
se souvient plus de l'étreinte de la terre,

ni de celle de la lumière quand les eaux naissent
au chaos flexueux de l'air,

quand Dieu les couvrait du firmament de ses deux
mains avant la contradiction de Souffle sur les
eaux,

avant ce baiser sur la mer pour dessouder la mer
d'avec la mer — avant le frai poissonneux de la
Parole au ventre de l'eau la plus basse,

avant la division des eaux par la lame de la
lumière — avant l'antagonisme des eaux par
l'avarice de la lumière.

·   ·

Toute salive refoulée de silence — je regoûterai   RINA
aux eaux condamnées de ma naissance;   LASNIER

eau fautive de la naissance cernant l'innocence du
sang — et tu pends à la vie comme le fruit de
l'arbre contredit;

est-il nuit plus nouvelle que la naissance — est-il
jour plus ancien que l'âme?

maternité mystérieuse de la chair — asile ouvert
aux portes du premier cri, et la mort plus
maternelle encore!

        •   •   •

Face fiancée de la haute mer axée sur la spirale du
souffle — malemer séquestrée aux fosses marines
de la fécondité

haute mer! œil fardé du bleu des légendes — moire
des images et des étoiles éteintes;

eau joyeuse au trébuchet des ruisseaux —
danseuse au nonchaloir des fontaines;

chair plastique de ta danse — parole aventurière
de ta danse et phénix de ton esprit voyager par la
flamme verte de la danse;

amoureuse livrée au vertige des cataractes et tes
lentes noces au lit des fleuves — fidèle à la seule
alliance zodiacale comme à ta hauteur originelle;

eau circulaire et sans autre joug que le jeu de tes
voies rondes — c'est toi l'erre de nos fables et la
sécheresse de notre bouche;

à l'envers des nuages, nous avons vu tes
métamorphoses — et ton sommeil de cristal, ô
momie couchée sur les pôles; eau ascensionnelle

—j'ai entendu la rumeur de ton mensonge
redescendre dans l'oreille étroite de la conque;

tu joues aux osselets avec les coquillages — tes
mains jouent sur toutes les grèves du monde avec
le bois mort des cadavres;

sur toutes les tables de sable — tu prends l'aunage
de ta puissance et de ton déferlement;

tentative du guet des falaises — j'ai vu l'épaulée
féminine de tes marées pour effriter leur refus de
pierre;

fiancée fluente des vents durs et précaires —
comment te délieras-tu de la fatalité de ton
obéissance?

Purifiée par l'eau la plus lointaine — comment te
laveras-tu de la salure des morts?

Haute mer! je refuse ta rose d'argent dispersée sur
les sables — et ton essor dispersé en écume;

je ne serai plus la mouette de tes miroirs — ni
l'hippocampe droit de tes parnasses houleux;

haute mer! je salue la croix du sud renversée sur
ton sein — et je descends amèrement sous la
nuit océanique de la malemer!

Malemer, mer stable et fermée à la foudre comme
à l'aile — mer prégnante et aveugle à ce que tu
enfantes,

emporte-moi loin du courant de la mémoire — et
de la longue flottaison des souvenirs;

hale-moi dans ta nuit tactile — plus loin dans ton
opacité que la double cécité de l'œil et de l'oreille;

malemer, toi qui ne montes plus sur touffe fleurie
des prés — comme une pensée fatiguée des images,

toi qui ne laboures plus les grèves au cliquetis des cailloux — remuement de pensées au hasard des vocables,

toi que n'enchaîne plus la chaîne des marées — ni le bref honneur des révoltes verticales,

que je sois en toi ce nageur rituel et couché — comme un secret aux plis des étoffes sourdes;

sans foulée calculée — que je circule par tes chemins sans arrivages,

malemer — rature mon visage et noie cette larme où se refont des clartés,

que j'oublie en toi les frontières ambiguës de mon propre jour — et la lucide distance du soleil.

· · ·

NAISSANCE OBSCURE DU POÈME

Comme l'amante endormie dans l'ardente captivité — immobile dans la pourpre muette de l'amant,

fluente et nocturne à la base du désir — obscurcie de sommeil et travestie d'innocence,

ses cheveux ouverts à la confidence — telles les algues du songe dans la mer écoutante,

la femme omniprésente dans la fabulation de la chair — la femme fugitive dans la fabulation de la mort,

et l'amant pris au sillage étroit du souffle — loin de l'usage viril des astres courant sur des ruines de feu,

elle dort près de l'arbre polypier des mots

médusés — par l'étreinte de l'homme à la cassure
du dieu en lui,

par cette lame dure et droite de la conscience —
voici l'homme dédoublé de douleur,

voici la seule intimité de la blessure — l'impasse
blonde de la chair sans parité;

voici l'évocatrice de ta nuit fondamentale,
malemer — la nuit vivante et soustraite aux
essaims des signes,

malemer, mer réciproque à ton équivoque
profondeur — mer inchangée entre les herbes
amères de tes pâques closes,

toute l'argile des mots est vénitienne et mariée au
limon vert — tout poème est obscur au limon de
la mémoire;

malemer, lent conseil d'ombre — efface les images,
ô grande nuit iconoclaste !

.   .   .

Malemer, aveugle-née du mal de la lumière —
comment sais-tu ta nuit sinon par l'œil circulaire
et sans repos de paupière?

pierrerie myriadaire de l'œil jamais clos —
malemer, tu es une tapisserie de regards te
crucifiant sur ton mal;

comment saurais-tu ta lumière noire et sans
intimité — sinon par le poème hermétique de tes
tribus poissonneuses?

ô rime puérile des étages du son — voici
l'assonance sinueuse et la parité vivante,

voici l'opacité ocellée par l'œil et l'écaille —
voici la nuit veillée par l'insomnie et l'étincelle;

RINA
LASNIER

entre les deux mers, voici le vivier sans servitude
— et le sillage effilé du poème phosphorescent

mime fantomatique du poème inactuel — encore
à distance de rose ou de reine,

toute la race du sang devenue plancton de mots —
et la plus haute mémoire devenue cécité vague;

pierre à musique de la face des morts — frayère
frémissante du songe et de la souvenance;

malemer, quel schisme du silence a creusé ta babel
d'eau — négation à quels éloges prophétiques?

assises du silence sur le basalte et le granit — et
sur les sinaïs noirs de tes montagnes sans
révélation,

le vent n'a point de sifflement dans ton herbage
— la pluie est sur toi suaire de silence,

veille la parole séquestrée dans l'éclair — faussaire
de tes silences catégoriques,

tu l'entendras draguer tes étoiles gisantes, tes
soleils tout démaillés — la haute mer lui portera
ferveur,

pleureuse de la peine anonyme — la nuit lui est
remise à large brassée amère,

chanteuse encore mal assurée — et c'est toi socle
et cothurne inspiré,

fermentation de la parole en bulles vives — roses
hauturières et blanches pour une reine aveugle.

·   ·   ·

Qui donc avant nous a fait vœu au large de la nuit
— sans route ni courant vers le bruissement de
l'aube?

qui donc a fait vœu d'enfance et d'images — par
la mer portante?

vœu de risque et de plénitude — par la mer
submergeante?

par l'échelle liquide, croisement d'ailes et de
monstres — manifestation de l'étoile par
l'araignée d'eau et l'astérie,

lassitude des naissances de haute mer — par le sel
des sargasses atlantiques,

surfaces mensongères des métropoles étoilées —
feux froids de leurs reflets nocturnes,

d'avoir touché terre, la mer a touché le mensonge
— la foudre la nettoie des images riveraines,

tendue dans l'orage par ses nerfs végétaux — la
mer se lave avec ses mains brisées,

par le miel viril de ses varechs — elle se guérit des
odeurs terriennes,

ni rives ni miroirs — mais le seul faîtage marin des
bras levés;

que la mer haute aille à la mer basse — qu'elles
brûlent ensemble dans les aromates
incorruptibles!

ni le vent ni le soleil ne sécheront la mer, marée
sur marée — ni le gibier des songes, banc sur banc,

ni la mer ne sortira du sel et du foudroiement —
ni le poème de la chair et de la fulguration du
verbe;

bois ta défaite avec le sable échoué — refuse le   RINA
calfat des mots pour tes coques crevées;   LASNIER

cécité sacrée d'une charge de lumière — ouvre tes
yeux sur les cavernes de ta nuit,

ni le soleil ni le vent n'ordonnent la terre — mais
la rosée née de la parfaite précarité,

ni la lumière ni l'opacité n'ordonnent la mer —
mais la perle née de l'antagonisme des eaux,

maria, nom pluriel des eaux — usage dense du
sein et nativité du feu.

ANNE
HÉBERT

b. 1916

La Chambre fermée

Qui donc m'a conduite ici?
Il y a certainement quelqu'un
Qui a soufflé sur mes pas.
Quand est-ce que cela s'est fait?
Avec la complicité de quel ami tranquille?
Le consentement profond de quelle nuit longue?

Qui donc a dessiné la chambre?
Dans quel instant calme
A-t-on imaginé le plafond bas
La petite table verte et le couteau minuscule
Le lit de bois noir
Et toute la rose du feu
En ses jupes pourpres gonflées
Autour de son cœur possédé et gardé
Sous les flammes oranges et bleues?

Qui donc a pris la juste mesure
De la croix tremblante de mes bras étendus?
Les quatre points cardinaux
Originent au bout de mes doigts
Pourvu que je tourne sur moi-même
Quatre fois
Tant que durera le souvenir
Du jour et de la nuit.

ANNE
HÉBERT

Mon cœur sur la table posé,
Qui donc a mis le couvert avec soin,
Affilé le petit couteau
Sans aucun tourment
Ni précipitation?

Ma chair s'étonne et s'épuise
Sans cet hôte coutumier
Entre ses côtes déraciné.
La couleur claire du sang
Scelle la voûte creuse
Et mes mains croisées
Sur cet espace dévasté
Se glacent et s'enchantent de vide.

Ô doux corps qui dort
Le lit de bois noir te contient
Et t'enferme strictement pourvu que tu ne bouges.
Surtout n'ouvre pas les yeux !
Songe un peu
Si tu allais voir
La table servie et le couvert qui brille !

Laisse, laisse le feu teindre
La chambre de reflets
Et mûrir et ton cœur et ta chair;
Tristes époux tranchés et perdus.

Le Tombeau des rois

ANNE
HÉBERT

J'ai mon cœur au poing
Comme un faucon aveugle.

Le taciturne oiseau pris à mes doigts
Lampe gonflée de vin et de sang,
Je descends
Vers les tombeaux des rois
Étonnée
À peine née.

Quel fil d'Ariane me mène
Au long des dédales sourds?
L'écho des pas s'y mange à mesure.

(En quel songe
Cette enfant fut-elle liée par la cheville
Pareille à une esclave fascinée?)

L'auteur du songe
Presse le fil,
Et viennent les pas nus
Un à un.
Comme les premières gouttes de pluie
Au fond du puits.

Déjà l'odeur bouge en des orages gonflés
Suinte sous le pas des portes
Aux chambres secrètes et rondes,
Là où sont dressés les lits clos.

L'immobile désir des gisants me tire.
Je regarde avec étonnement
À même les noirs ossements
Luire les pierres bleues incrustées.

Quelques tragédies patiemment travaillées,
Sur la poitrine des rois, couchées,
En guise de bijoux
Me sont offertes
Sans larmes ni regrets.

Sur une seule ligne rangés :
La fumée d'encens, le gâteau de riz séché
Et ma chair qui tremble :
Offrande rituelle et soumise.

Le masque d'or sur ma face absente
Des fleurs violettes en guise de prunelles,
L'ombre de l'amour me maquille à petits traits
    précis;
Et cet oiseau que j'ai respire
Et se plaint étrangement.

Un frisson long
Semblable au vent qui prend, d'arbre en arbre,
Agite sept grands pharaons d'ébène
En leurs étuis solennels et parés.

Ce n'est que la profondeur de la mort qui persiste,
Simulant le dernier tourment
Cherchant son apaisement
Et son éternité
En un cliquetis léger de bracelets
Cercles vains jeux d'ailleurs
Autour de la chair sacrifiée.

Avides de la source fraternelle du mal en moi
Ils me couchent et me boivent;
Sept fois, je connais l'étau des os
Et la main sèche qui cherche le cœur pour le
    rompre.

Livide et repue de songe horrible
Les membres dénoués
Et les morts hors de moi, assassinés,
Quel reflet d'aube s'égare ici ?
D'où vient donc que cet oiseau frémit
Et tourne vers le matin
Ses prunelles crevées ?

Vie de château

ANNE
HÉBERT

C'est un château d'ancêtres
Sans table ni feu
Ni poussière ni tapis.

L'enchantement pervers de ces lieux
Est tout dans ses miroirs polis.

La seule occupation possible ici
Consiste à se mirer jour et nuit.

Jette ton image aux fontaines dures
Ta plus dure image sans ombre ni couleur.

Vois, ces glaces sont profondes
Comme des armoires
Toujours quelque mort y habite sous le tain
Et couvre aussitôt ton reflet
Se colle à toi comme une algue

S'ajuste à toi, mince et nu,
Et simule l'amour en un lent frisson amer.

La Fille maigre

Je suis une fille maigre
Et j'ai de beaux os.

J'ai pour eux des soins attentifs
Et d'étranges pitiés.

Je les polis sans cesse
Comme de vieux métaux.

Les bijoux et les fleurs
Sont hors de saison.

Un jour je saisirai mon amant
Pour m'en faire un reliquaire d'argent.

Je me pendrai
À la place de son cœur absent.

Espace comblé,
Quel est soudain en toi cet hôte sans fièvre?

Tu marches
Tu remues;
Chacun de tes gestes
Pare d'effroi la mort enclose.

Je reçois ton tremblement
Comme un don.

Et parfois
En ta poitrine, fixée,
J'entr'ouvre
Mes prunelles liquides

Et bougent
Comme une eau verte
Des songes bizarres et enfantins.

Mystère de la parole

Dans un pays tranquille nous avons reçu la
passion du monde, épée nue sur nos deux mains
posée

Notre cœur ignorait le jour lorsque le feu nous fut
ainsi remis, et sa lumière creusa l'ombre de nos
traits

C'était avant tout faiblesse, la charité était seule
devançant la crainte et la pudeur

Elle inventait l'univers dans la justice première et
nous avions part à cette vocation dans l'extrême
vitalité de notre amour

La vie et la mort en nous reçurent droit d'asile, se

regardèrent avec des yeux aveugles, se touchèrent ANNE
avec des mains précises HÉBERT

Des flèches d'odeur nous atteignirent, nous liant à
la terre comme des blessures en des noces
excessives

O saisons, rivière, aulnes et fougères, feuilles,
fleurs, bois mouillé, herbes bleues, tout notre avoir
saigne son parfum, bête odorante à notre flanc

Les couleurs et les sons nous visitèrent en masse
et par petits groupes foudroyants, tandis que le
songe doublait notre enchantement comme l'orage
cerne le bleu de l'œil innocent

La joie se mit à crier, jeune accouchée à l'odeur
sauvagine sous les joncs. Le printemps délivré fut
si beau qu'il nous prit le cœur avec une seule
main

Les trois coups de la création du monde sonnèrent
à nos oreilles, rendus pareils aux battements de
notre sang

En un seul éblouissement l'instant fut. Son éclair
nous passa sur la face et nous reçumes mission du
feu et de la brûlure

Silence, ni ne bouge, ni ne dit, la parole se fonde,
soulève notre cœur, saisit le monde en un seul
geste d'orage, nous colle à son aurore comme
l'écorce à son fruit

Toute la terre vivace, la forêt à notre droite, la
ville profonde à notre gauche, en plein centre du
verbe, nous avançons à la pointe du monde

Fronts bouclés où croupit le silence en toisons
musquées, toutes grimaces, vieilles têtes, joues

d'enfants, amours, rides, joies, deuils, créatures, ANNE
créatures, langues de feu au solstice de la terre HÉBERT

O mes frères les plus noirs, toutes fêtes gravées en
secret; poitrines humaines, calebasses musiciennes
où s'exaspèrent des voix captives

Que celui qui a reçu fonction de la parole vous
prenne en charge comme un cœur ténébreux de
surcroît, et n'ait de cesse que soient justifiés les
vivants et les morts en un seul chant parmi l'aube
et les herbes

Ève

Reine et maîtresse certaine crucifiée aux portes de
la ville la plus lointaine

Effraie rousse aux ailes clouées, toute jointure
disjointe, toute envergure fixée

Chair acide des pommes vertes, beau verger
juteux, te voici dévastée claquant dans le vent
comme un drapeau crevé

Fin nex de rapace, bec de corne, nous nous en
ferons des amulettes aux jours de peste

Contre la mort, contre la rage, nous te porterons
scapulaires de plumes et d'os broyés

Femme couché, grande fourmilière sous le mélèze,
terre antique criblée d'amants

Nous t'invoquons, ventre premier, fin visage
d'aube passant entre les côtes de l'homme la dure
barrière du jour

Vois tes fils et tes époux pourrissent pêle-mêle
entre tes cuisses, sous une seule malédiction

Mère du Christ souviens-toi des filles dernières-
nées, de celles qui sont sans nom ni histoire, tout

de suite fracassées entre deux très grandes pierres

Source des larmes et du cri, de quelles parures
vives nous léguas-tu la charge et l'honneur.
L'angoisse et l'amour, le deuil et la joie se
célèbrent à fêtes égales en pleine face gravées,
comme des paysages profonds

Mère aveugle, explique-nous la naissance et la
mort et tout le voyage hardi entre deux barbares
ténèbres, pôles du monde, axes du jour

Dis-nous le maléfice et l'envoûtement de l'arbre,
raconte-nous le jardin, Dieu clair et nu et le péché
farouchement désiré comme l'ombre en plein midi

Dis-nous l'amour sans défaut et le premier homme
défait entre tes bras

Souviens-toi du cœur initial sous le sacre du matin,
et renouvelle notre visage comme un destin pacifié

La guerre déploie ses chemins d'épouvante,
l'horreur et la mort se tiennent la main, liés par
des secrets identiques, les quatre éléments bardés
d'orage se lèvent pareils à des dieux sauvages
offensés

La douceur sous le fer est brûlée jusqu'à l'os, son
cri transperce l'innocent et le coupable sur une
seule lame embrochés

Vois-nous, reconnais-nous, fixe sur nous ton
regard sans prunelle, considère l'aventure de nos
mains filant le mystère à la veillée comme une
laine rude

L'enfant à notre sein roucoule, l'homme sent le
pain brûlé, et le milieu du jour se referme sur nous
comme une eau sans couture

Ève, Ève, nous t'appelons du fond de cette paix   ANNE
soudaine comme si nous nous tenions sans peine   HÉBERT
sur l'appui de notre cœur justifié

Que ta mémoire se brise au soleil, et, au risque de
réveiller le crime endormi, retrouve l'ombre de la
grâce sur ta face comme un rayon noir.

ELDON
GRIER

b. 1917

'More than most people'

More than most people,

the artist

is afraid of the gold gone from his eye
and the plum coloured tendrils grown
where once a god had sat transfixed.

He may feel something great and close to nothing,

a rare expanse of innocence.

To be lost is perhaps to stumble
                    on the Garden.
It has always been there
even before that first dramatic reporting.

How revealing it would be to find

carved into the trees

the signs and hearts of those who have known
its incomparable spell.

'Sensible is the label'

ELDON
GRIER

Sensible is the label which most suits us—

especially the men

who lay great stock in honesty and good sense.

It never amounts to a passion
but you can see it on them,
　　　　　a fine grey pencilling.

As a poet I need to experience ecstasy.

(English poetry never went crazy, a Frenchman
　　said. It was not a compliment.)

Our poets must give themselves to a kind
of unsensible madness;
they must hear music not meaning as they write.

Words must be clear bells,
or sound gravely along like horns.
They should detonate, explode like lightning
　　　　　　　under the sea,
be silver wire, silk thread suspended,

sardonyx,

layers of white alternated with sard.

There are words that are the incomparable beasts
　　　　　of our imagination.

Sound them.
Revel in the extravagance.

I wish to make literature, you say.

Oh, if only we could.

'I am almost asleep'

ELDON
GRIER

I am almost asleep
with your poems on my chest,

Apollinaire

I am almost asleep,
but I feel a transfusion of fine little letters
dripping slantwise into my side.

On the Subject of Waves . . .

Mountain teeth, tips of anemious rippled stone,
a glacier of white cloud settled into the tilting
    passages :

Are you there, Li?

Are you there in the mists, Li Po?

If I ring your two-change name against the
    massive greys will you answer?
On this day and in this location can you see
    how it is with us humans?

There are greens about me here, and the pressure
    of the soft gloom,
animals in the rising fields.
            Men I shall never see
stand in the doorways of their huts like true
    sentinels of life.
There are chimneys behind me rolling up the first
    balls of pale smoke.
A high plateau above, ceaselessly swept with
    tears of anemia,
before me, and always in my mind is the shape
    of peninsulas
as insistent as a black mirror.

The empty truck, traumatically still;   ELDON
A score of men loosely grouped beneath a tree.   GRIER
           The stillness is the echo of an explosion!

I find the burlap square in the centre of the road
and I know that beneath it there is a dead child.

Is this what you meant by 'waves,' Li Po?

P. K.
PAGE

b. 1917

Element

Feeling my face has the terrible shine of fish
caught and swung on a line under the sun
I am frightened held in the light that people make
and sink in darkness freed and whole again
as fish returned by dream into the stream.

Oh, running water is not rough : ruffled to eye,
to flesh it's flat and smooth; to fish
silken as children's hands in milk.

I am not wishful in this dream of immersion.
Mouth becomes full with darkness
and the shine, mottled and pastel, sounds its
     own note, not
the fake high treble thrown on resounding faces.

There are flowers—and this is pretty for the
     summer—
light on the bed of darkness; there are stones
that glisten and grow slime;
winters that question nothing, are a new
night for the passing movement of fine fins;

and quietly, by the reeds or the water fronds
something can cry without discovery.

Ah, in daylight the shine is single
as dime flipped or gull on fire or fish
silently hurt—its mouth alive with metal.

Images of Angels

Imagine them as they were first conceived:
part musical instrument and part daisy
in a white manshape.
Imagine a crowd on the Elysian grass
playing ring-around-a-rosy,
mute except for their singing,
their gold smiles
gold sickle moons in the white sky of their faces.
Sex, neither male nor female,
name and race, in each case, simply angel.

Who, because they are white and gold, has made
    them holy
but never to be loved or petted, never to be
    friended?

Not children, who imagine them more simply,
see them more coloured and a deal more cosy,
yet somehow mixed with the father, fearful and
    fully
realized when vanishing bed
floats in the darkness,
when the shifting point of focus, that drifting
    star,
has settled in the head.

More easily, perhaps, the little notary
who, given one as a pet, could not
walk the sun-dazzled street
with so lamb-white a companion.

For him its loom-large skeleton—
one less articulated than his own—
would dog his days with doom
until, behind the lethal lock
used for his legal documents
he guiltily shut it up.
His terror then that it escape
and smiling call for him at work.
Less dreadful for his public shame,
worse for his private guilt
if, in that metal vault
it should die mute
and in the hour that he picked it up
he found it limp and boneless as a flower.

Perhaps, more certainly perhaps, the financier.
What business man would buy as he buys stock
as many could cluster on a pin?
Angels are dropping, angels going up.
He could not mouth such phrases and chagrin
would sugar round his lips as he said 'angel.'
For though he mocks their mention he cannot
tie their tinsel image to a tree
without the momentary lowering of his lids
for fear that they exist in worlds which he,
uneasy, reconstructs from childhood's memory.

The anthropologist with his tidy science,
had he stumbled upon one unawares,
found as he finds an arrowhead, an angel,
a—what of a thing—
primitive as a daisy
might with his ice cold eye have assessed it coolly.
But how, despite his detailed observations,
could he face his learned society and explain?
'Gentlemen it is thought that they are born
with harps and haloes

as the unicorn with its horn.
Study discloses them white and gold as daisies.'

P. K.
PAGE

Perhaps only a dog could accept them wholly,
be happy to follow at their heels
and bark and romp with them in the green fields.

Or, take the nudes of Lawrence and impose
asexuality upon them; those
could meet with ease these gilded albinos.

Or a child, not knowing they were angels could
wander along an avenue hand in hand
with his new milk-white playmates,
take a step
and all the telephone wires would become taut
as the high strings of a harp
and space be merely the spaces between strings
and the world mute, except for a thin singing,
as if a sphere—big enough to be in it
and yet small
so that a glance through the lashes
would show it whole—
were fashioned very finely out of wire
and turning in a wind.

But say the angelic word
and *this* innocent
with his almost unicorn
would let it go
for even a child would know
that angels should be flying in the sky,
and, feeling implicated in a lie,
his flesh would grow
cold
and snow
would cover the warm and sunny avenue.

Puppets

P. K.
PAGE

See them joined by strings to history :
their strange progenitors all born full-grown;
ancestors buried with the ancient Greeks—
slim terra-cotta dolls with articulate limbs
lying like corpses.
                    Puppets in Rome
subject to Papal laws, discreet in tights.
And see the types perpetuate themselves
freed from the picket prejudice of race.
The seaside Punch with his inherited nose
carried from Pulcinella round the globe
ends up in Bexhill, enters English eyes.

While here in a Sunday drawing room beside
the bland Pacific and its rain come two
emerging full-grown from their dark cocoons—
two whose blasé antecedents once
performed for Pepys' mistress, or, in silk,
were bawdy for bored Royalty at court;
escaped and raided country fairs and spread
the world with areas of Lilliput.
Now—brought forth after toast and tea, these two
reduce the room to their immediate size
and own it like inhabitants with their
indelible characters deep in their rags as dye.

Before our eyes the twelve inch clown grows large
and dances on his rubber feet and kicks
pneumatic legs, thumbs his enormous nose;
lies down for push-ups, and, exhibitionist,
suddenly turns and waves.
More clown than clowns, he is all laughter,
is buoyed by it and brilliant in its light.
Unlike his living prototype has no
dichotomy to split him : this is all.

He calls your laughter out without reserves;
is only and always feet and a vulgar streak
and his music—brass.

The negro does a tap dance and his toes
click on the parquet.
Music moves in him and explodes in his toes
and somehow he is two-fold, though he grins
his hands are stripped of humour,
they are long
and lonely attached to him.
He is himself and his own symbol,
sings
terribly without a voice, is so
gentle it seems that his six delicate strings
are ropes upon him;
but still he grins, he grins.

Oh, coming isolated from their plays but not
isolated from their history,
shaped and moulded by heredity—
negro and clown—oh, these
small violent people shake the quiet room
and bring all history tumbling about
a giant audience that almost weeps.

Man with One Small Hand

One hand is smaller than the other. It
must always be loved a little like a child;
requires attention constantly, implies
it needs his frequent glance to nurture it.

He holds it sometimes with the larger one
as adults lead a child across a street.
Finding it his and suddenly alien
rallies his interest and his sympathy.

Sometimes you come upon him unawares
just quietly staring at it where it lies
as mute and somehow perfect as a flower.

But no. It is not perfect. He admits
it has its faults : it is not strong or quick.
At night it vanishes to reappear
in dreams full-size, lost or surrealist.

Yet has its place like memory or a dog—
is never completely out of mind—a rod
to measure all uncertainties against.

Perhaps he loves it too much, sets too much stock
simply in its existence. Ah, but look !
It has its magic. See how it will fit
so sweetly, sweetly in the infant's glove.

Arras

Consider a new habit—classical,
and trees espaliered on the wall like candelabra.
How still upon that lawn our sandalled feet.

But a peacock rattling its rattan tail and screaming
has found a point of entry. Through whose eye
did it insinuate in furled disguise
to shake its jewels and silk upon that grass ?

The peaches hang like lanterns. No one joins
those figures on the arras.
                    Who am I
or who am I become that walking here
I am observer, other, Gemini,
starred for a green garden of cinema ?

I ask, what did they deal me in this pack ?
The cards, all suits, are royal when I look.
My fingers slipping on a monarch's face
twitch and go slack.

I want a hand to clutch, a heart to crack.   P. K.
PAGE

No one is moving now, the stillness is
infinite. If I should make a break. . . .
take to my springy heels . . . ? But nothing moves.
The spinning world is stuck upon its poles,
the stillness points a bone at me. I fear
the future on this arras.
                    I confess :
It was my eye.
Voluptuous it came.
Its head the ferrule and its lovely tail
folded so sweetly; it was strangely slim
to fit the retina. And then it shook
and was a peacock—living patina,
eye-bright—maculate!
Does no one care?

I thought their hands might hold me if I spoke.
I dreamed the bite of fingers in my flesh,
their poke smashed by an image, but they stand
as if within a treacle, motionless,
folding slow eyes on nothing. While they stare
another line has trolled the encircling air,
another bird assumes its furled disguise.

MIRIAM
WADDINGTON

b. 1917

Catalpa Tree

Catalpa, in you a song, a cache
A secret story hidden,
A cat, an alp to climb, an ahhh—
Winedrinker's joy and almost the apache
Of violent lunges, whisperings backstage.

And still the greenery, the lacings of the leaves MIRIAM
WADDINGTON
With quiet, wind outside
And inside cool, cool as caves
Or water, cool as waves
And welcome as water is
On salted skin and ankle.

Here is everness,
And gliding of the light
Into some brilliant world where it enjoys
Its own infinity, here I taste the grass
And touch the springy blossoms dry as silk,
Think such was I and such my child may be
If grace grows leaves and listening multiplies
And trees yield up their wordless therapy.

My Lessons in the Jail

Walk into the prison, that domed citadel,
That yellow skull of stone and sutured steel,
Walk under their mottoes, show your pass,
Salute their Christ to whom you cannot kneel.

In the white-tiled room arrange the interview
With the man who took his daughter, and learn
That every man is usual but none are equal
In the dark rivers that in them burn.

And take this man's longest, bleakest year,
Between done act and again-done act, and take
His misery and need, stand against his tears
And transform them to such a truth as slakes

The very core of thirst, and be you sure
The thirst is his and not your own deep need
To spurt fine fountains; accept, accept
His halting words—since you must learn to read

Between the lines his suffering and doubt.
Be faithful to your pity, be careworn,

Though all this buffet you, and beat, and cruelly

MIRIAM
Test you—you chose this crown of thorns. WADDINGT

Wear it with grace and when you rise to go
Thank him, and don't let yourself forget
How hard it is to thank, and to beholden be
One to another, and spin your role out yet

For moments in the hallway, compose your face
To false good humour, conceal your sex :
Smile at the brute who runs the place
And memorize the banner, *Christus Rex*.

The Season's Lovers

In the daisied lap of summer
The lovers lay, they dozed
And lay in sun unending,
They lay in light, they slept
And only stirred
Each one to find the other's lips.
At times they sighed
Or spoke a word
That wavered on uneven breath,
He had no name and she forgot
The ransomed kingdom of her death.

When at last the sun went down
And chilly evening stained the fields,
The lovers rose and rubbed their eyes :
They saw the pale wash of grass
Heighten to metallic green
And spindly tongues of granite mauve
Lick up the milk of afternoon,
They gathered all the scattered light
Of daisies to one place of white,
And ghostly poets lent their speech
To the stillness of the air,
The lovers listened, each to each.

Into the solid wall of night
The lovers looked, their clearer sight
Went through that dark intensity
To the other side of light.
The lovers stood, it seemed to them
They hung upon the world's rim—
He clung to self, and she to him;
He rocked her with his body's hymn
And murmured to her shuddering cry,
You are all states, all princes I,
And sang against her trembling limbs,
Nothing else is, he sang, *but I.*

They lifted the transparent lid
From world false and world true
And in the space of both they flew.
He found a name, she lost her death,
And summer lulled them in its lap
With a leafy lullaby.
There they sleep unending sleep,
The lovers lie
He with a name, she free of death,
In a country hard to find
Unless you read love's double mind
Or invent its polar map.

MIRIAM
WADDINGTON

MARGARET
AVISON

b. 1918

Intra-Political

AN EXERCISE IN POLITICAL ASTRONOMY

Who are we here?
boxed, bottled, barrelled
in rows?

Comestibles with the trick   MARGARET
of turning grocer, shoplifter   AVISON
or warehouse trucker, or sometimes,
in faery-false springtime
the lion-hearted four-foot haggler
with a hot dime?

Games are too earnest.
These packaged us-es
are to the gamboling of real nourishment
as mudcake to transmuted sun.
Truth is, men chew and churn (in rows
or squares, or one by one
like a domino on a walled tennis-court)
galactic courses:
chlorophyll, mutton, mineral salts
pinpoint multiple sunrise, and
cram us with incendiary force;
or we ingesting cede
the solar plexus its serenes of sky,
till every sunborn creature
may lume deepforest pools, and floodlight
his architects; find, too,
lenses for micro-astronomical
amaze (he—transport!—
SNEEZES).

Who plunges away
from the inexorable of
weaving orbits, like a colt
hurtled from his gentle pasturing
by a through freight?
(Space with its purple eye
marks his fixed field
and not his helter-skelter heels.)
Fixity of our sun-selves in our courses—
that willed harmonics—is
nothing we know to date,

nothing we know
who do know fearful things.

MARGARET
AVISON

Look at that platinum moon,
the sky still muslin pale inspiring
doom-sweet violation.
But ask the lone balloonist.
Zones of ultramarine
clutch at his jugular,
and when he engineers his venture,
a Vandal, loving, he lays waste;
the fields and folds Horace could celebrate
strip back to rainsoak
and Rome still baldly suns in its
imperial distances.
(Nothing inert may, in stone, space, exist—except
as our clocking selves insert it.
We move too far from ways of weightlessness.)
Space is a hazard.

Yet this pre-creation density
presses : our darkness dreams of
this heavy mass, this moil, this self-
consuming endless squirm and squander, this
chaos, singling off
in a new Genesis.
(Would it perhaps set swinging
the little horn-gates to new life's
illumined labyrinths if, released
from stifling,
creatures like us were planet-bathed
in new-born Light?)
(Glee dogs our glumness so.)

Dreams, even doubted, drive us.
Our games and grocery-store designs
are nursery-earnest,
evidence.

209

Strait thinking set us down in rows
and rigged the till.
But being bought and eaten
is, experienced, enough
to change this circular exchange.
And cringeing from such courses
compounds confusion :
a new numerical excess
of us-es.

MARGARET
AVISON

We set up shop after,
poach as we might, nothing else much remained
but tufts of fur and insect skeletons?
And energy hasn't minded
phoenixing for us in our nonce?

But even our own energy
will out. String beans
and coronal pyres of sleep
keg up. These city shelves,
this play emporium,
wobble on nitroglycerine.

If, with dainty stepping, we unbox ourselves
while still Explosion slumbers,
putting aside mudcakes,
the buying, selling, trucking, packaging
of mudcakes,
sun-stormed, daring to gambol,
might there not be an immense answering
of human skies?
a new expectant largeness?
Form has its flow,
a Heraclitus-river with no riverbank
we can play poise on now.

(George Herbert—and he makes it plain—
Guest at this same transfiguring board
        Did sit and eat.)

Voluptuaries and Others

MARGARET
AVISON

That Eureka of Archimedes out of his bath
Is the kind of story that kills what it conveys;
Yet the banality is right for that story, since it is
    not a communicable one
But just a particular instance of
The kind of lighting up of the terrain
That leaves aside the whole terrain, really,
But signalizes, and compels, an advance in it.
Such an advance through a be-it-what-it-may but
    take-it-not-quite-as-given locale :
Probably that is the core of being alive.
The speculation is not a concession
To limited imaginations. Neither is it
A constrained voiding of the quality of
    immanent death.
Such near values cannot be measured in values
Just because the measuring
Consists in that other kind of lighting up
That shows the terrain comprehended, as also its
    containing space,
And wipes out adjectives, and all shadows
        (or, perhaps, all but shadows).

The Russians made a movie of a dog's head
Kept alive by blood controlled by physics,
    chemistry, equipment, and
Russian women scientists in cotton gowns with
    writing tablets.
The heart lay on a slab midway in the apparatus
And went phluff, phluff.
Like the first kind of illumination, that successful
    experiment
Can not be assessed either as conquest or as defeat.
But it is living, creating the chasm of creation,
Contriving to cast only man to brood in it, further.

History makes the spontaneous jubilation at such
    moments less and less likely though,
And that story about Archimedes does get into
    public school textbooks.

MARGARET
AVISON

In a Season of Unemployment

These green painted park benches are
all new. The Park Commissioner had them
planted.
Sparrows go on
having dust baths at the edge of
the park maple's shadow, just where
the bench is cemented down, planted
and then cemented.

    Not a breath moves
    this newspaper.
    I'd rather read it by the Lapland sun at
        midnight. Here we're
    bricked in early by a
    stifling dark.

On that bench a man in a
pencil-striped white shirt
keeps his head up and steady.

    The newspaper-astronaut says
    'I feel excellent under the condition of
        weightlessness.'
And from his bench a
scatter of black bands in the hollow-air
ray out—too quick for the eye—
and cease.

    'Ground observers watching him on a TV
        circuit said

At the time of this report he
was smiling,' Moscow ra-
dio reported.
I glance across at him, and mark that
he is feeling
excellent too, I guess, and
weightless and
'smiling.'

MARGARET
AVISON

A Story

Where *were* you then?
      At the beach.
With your crowd again.
Trailing around, open
to whatever's going. Which one's
calling for you tonight?
      Nobody.
I'm sorry I talk so. Young
is young. I ought to remember
and let you go and be glad.
      No. It's all right.
      I'd just sooner stay home.
You're not sick? did you
get too much sun? a crowd,
I never have liked it, safety in numbers
indeed!
      —He was alone.
Who was alone?
      The one
      out on the water, telling
      something. He sat in the boat that
      they shoved out for him, and told
      us things. We all just stood there
      about an hour. Nobody
      shoving. I couldn't see

very clearly, but I listened
the same as the rest.
What was it about?
About a giant, sort of.
No. No baby-book giant.
But about a man. I think—
You *are* all right?
Of course.
Then tell me
so I can follow. You all
standing there, getting up
out of the beach-towels and gathering
out of the cars, and the ones
half-dressed, not even caring—
Yes. Because the ones
who started to crowd around were
so still. You couldn't
help wondering. And it spread.
And then when I would have felt out of it
he got the boat, and I could
see the white, a little, and
hear him, word by word.
What did he tell the lot of you
to make you stand? Politics?
Preaching? You can't believe everything
they tell you, remember—
No. More, well, a
fable. Honestly, I—
I won't keep interrupting.
I'd really like you to tell.
Tell me. I won't say anything.
It is a story. But
only one man comes.
Tall, sunburnt, coming
not hurried, but as though
there was so much power in reserve
that walking all day and night

would be lovelier than sleeping if
sleeping meant missing it, easy
and alive, and out there.

Where was it?
On a kind of clamshell back.
I mean country, like round about here,
but his tallness, as he walked there
made green and rock-gray and brown
his floorway. And sky a brightness.

What was he doing? Just walking?
No. Now it sounds strange
but it wasn't, to hear.
He was casting seed,
only everywhere.
On the roadway, out
on the baldest stone,
on the tussocky waste
and in pockets of loam.

Seed? A farmer?
A gardener rather
but there was nothing
like garden, mother.
Only the queer
dark way he went
and the star-shine of
the seed he spent.

(Seed you could see that way—)
In showers. His fingers
shed, like the gold
of blowing autumnal
woods in the wild.
He carried no wallet
or pouch or sack,
but clouds of birds followed
to buffet and peck
on the road. And the rock
sprouted new blades

and thistle and stalk   MARGARET
matted in, and the birds   AVISON
ran threading the tall grasses
lush and fine
in the pockets of deep earth—
You mean, in time
he left, and you saw
this happen?
          The hollow
          air scalded with sun.
          The first blades went sallow
          and dried, and the one
          who had walked, had only
          the choked-weed patches
          and a few thin files
          of windily, sunnily
          searching thirsty ones
          for his garden
          in all that place.
          But they flowered, and shed
          their strange heart's force
          in that wondering wilderness—
Where is he now?
          The gardener?
No. The storyteller
out on the water?
          He is alone.

          Perhaps a few
          who beached the boat and
          stayed, would know.

The Word

'*Forsaking all*'—You mean
head over heels, for good,
for ever, call of the depths
of the All—the heart of one

216

who creates all, at every
moment, newly—for
you do so—and
to me, far fallen in the
ashheaps of my
false-making, burnt-out self and in the
hosed-down rubble of what my furors
gutted, or sooted all
around me—you implore
me to so fall
in Love, and fall anew in
ever-new depths of skywashed Love till every
capillary of your universe
throbs with your rivering fire?

'*Forsaking all*'—Your voice
never falters, and yet,
unsealing day out of a
darkness none ever knew
in full but you,
you spoke that word, closing on it forever:
'Why hast Thou forsaken . . .?'

This measure of your being all-out, and
meaning it, made you
put it all on the line
we, humanly, wanted to draw—at
having you teacher only, or
popular spokesman only, or
doctor or simply a source of sanity
for us, distracted, or only
the one who could wholeheartedly
rejoice with us, and know
our tears, our flickering time, and
stand with us.

But to make it head over heels
yielding, all the way,
you had to die for us.

The line we drew, you crossed,
at the faintest stirring of what
you know is love, is One
whose name has been, and is
and will be, the
I AM.

For Dr and Mrs Dresser

Your doctor, Lord,
from West Irian,
brought pictures of a leaf that served as plate,
and grubs, fat, silkily hirsute, that men
need there for nourishment.
Whoever speak your word
along that coast must share
that feast of fatness first
for love of you and them
who offer from your provenance their best.
The gorge that finds your natural good
in food that squirms is
given aptitude, surely, by grace. . . .

As that doctor, Lord,
learned to subsist, in order
to love first-hand, for you, and tell
how God, to His plain table
invites them too, and will
dwell among them who offer Him their all,
You, once for all,
offered and dwelt—you, fairest beyond call
              of mortal imagining :
here, taking on yourself not only
our spoiled flesh, but the lonely
rot of the rebel, of the solitary,
of all not-God on earth, for all

who claim, in all your range of time. And still MARGARET
without one queasy tremor, you could wholly   AVISON
swallow our death, take on our
lumpish wingless being, darkened out
to cold and night—except for
the timeless love
even for us, my Lord.
And having suffered us to glut
the pure well-spring, and having
plumbed even hell, for us, you could
come back, in flesh, living, and
open out the shaft and sweep
of clarity and scope,
flooding us with your risen radiance,
can bid us, now, in turn, o gentle Saviour :
'take, eat—
live.'

LOUIS
DUDEK

b. 1918

García Lorca

It was as if the devil of evil had got
the God of all that is good by the throat
and shot
the garden with his breath,
Adam the boy and Eve his girl,
scorched like a but through space.

The end of a world.

And yet, just as the fascists, firing, were only
an ignorant audience, breaking
to bits his stage.

219

that was such a friendly comedy
of loving creatures, of flowers and happy people,

LOUIS
DUDEK

and the poet
with notes in his fingers
was something on a stem,

a fire
in cups of flowers,

so, of us, many wise as candle wicks
in our halos while round us the insect wheels
in violence, kill what we can
alone, with subtle and selfish claws;
set up ourselves a single majority,
usurp the soul with a dollar,
the dictator for the ruling class of greeds;
and intent on the growth of percentage
and drawing a little blood from friends,
prepare the squeaking gallows
where soon, like innocent lilies, our children
will weep, bewildered and wondering why.

Each man's struggle against the pack
is the futile and dispersed class war. Could we but
concentrate violence, press out this pus
in one shock ! But we make
a nest for germs, saving our inch of skin,
a home for killers paid by generous bankers,
ready to belt on their holsters and say, 'I am the
    law.'

So it grows to insanity, the furious stars
in our ears ringing, the poet's roses
ripped and scattered apart, as Federico
García Lorca was shot that morning,
an agile songster dropped in the damp grass.

What if from bloody Granada
the black bullets sped

like lights from a mirror, knocking
at doors and at window ledges
with knuckles bleeding and red?

LOUIS
DUDEK

The news is a prophecy
no one heard :
a child had been taken from bed
and broken in our hands.

From *Provincetown*

FISHING VILLAGE

And then the old inhabitants, so kind,
or bigoted, after their kind,
stick-to-itive as grass,
        the Acadians, Portuguese, English
who built the white town
now placarded with whimsical art-work (not art),
the gentry, wrinkled with work
                on the white whittling foam,
and their descendants
        the ladies of the land :
the bent little old one, who made a meticulous
    point
            of not overcharging
(the Fathers at least would have been cheered,
but not by the gin bottles
        lying on the bank,
nor the beauties walking the streets . . .)
So the shaping spirit of work
        can make a town;
but we have made all of our world
        with our own machines,
and now the unnatural man

must come to the plain old town, to see how it
    was,
quiet and quaint old streets
        and honest people,
from whom he can learn less than nothing—
        not even the good manners
to bathe himself and leave the ocean clean.

NEWS

He fell from the roof
        of the dock-shed onto the wharf
hitting it with his knees—
           one of the boys
        diving all day into the deep water
and climbing on odd corners, to do it,
        I saw him
lying on the fish-cart,
his legs tied up in a towel,
and his arms terribly shaking, the eyes closed,
           it comes like that
some little accident to prove
the genial power over us
        that death preserves :
the mourning sister so beautiful,
the silent bathers,
and the pale lips of the boy.
The ocean cannot come near to it, in
    magnificence,
           nor can we degrade it
               by using it for our pleasure.

THE OCEAN

But when the water roars around us
and the sky bellows,
the sea-birds mewing

        falling upon the minnows,
the seagulls resting against the wind
        and the small scallops, the crabs, the
           crustaceans
heaving and falling, torn upon the tide
        rolling in,
that gives them its shape, of a tiara,
        or a chandelier of jelly,
           a groping claw—
I think of man,
        prone under striped umbrellas
        and oily with lotions,
who has outdone the speed of the mackerel
        and the sea robin,
has filed the tooth of the tiger
and made a fibre of sharkskin : the winner,
        the wordy vanquisher
of the streaming kingdoms,
of the armoured, the swift, and sharp-clawed—
        man in a bathing suit,
        looking out over the ocean.

AVANT GARDE

We can't give them up, though,
        the middle classes
           of this America.
In Provincetown, home of the Fathers,
        coming to meet the old
        out on a sand bar
in the steps of the Pilgrims
        to the first sweet water,
        on the barbs of whalers;
knobby in knickers, they talk to each other,
        looking at relics :
        'What does it prove?'
        'That it's shock-proof and water-proof'
        (a watch in a window);

but somewhere the area   LOUIS
      of difference widens   DUDEK
      (the old and the new)
         enough for an ocean,
and children go dizzy
seeing their fathers
      astride on a yew tree—
      ridiculous posture!
They, like the fishermen,
spit with the wind now,
and what all the artists
know, they won't stoop to tell you.

Look, how the birds
are diving against each other!
Almost, the curved wave catches them.
That's how we are, in the void,
      between the now and hereafter!

'Good morning, Mr. Greenpepper.'

The Marine Aquarium

FROM *Atlantis*

I have been in a marine aquarium and I have seen
    LOLIGO VULGARIS
     TRACHINUS ARANEUS
    SCORPAENA SCROFA
    SCYLLARIDES
    ANEMONIA SULCATA
    ASTEROIDES CALYCULARIS
    MAJA SQUINADO
    MUSTELLUS LAEVIS
    THALASSOCHELIS CARETTA
    TRIGLA CORAX
    TRYGON VIOLACEA
    HYPPOCAMPUS BREVIROSTRIS
    SPIROGRAPHIS SPALANZANII

ACTINIA CARI   LOUIS
MURAENA HELENA   DUDEK
SYNGNATUS ACUS
RETEPORA MEDITERRANEA
PELAGIA NOCTILUCA
PARAMURICEA CHAMALEON

Of a very graceful undulant movement
        of a pale white colour
                with translucent fins

Fish that lie buried in the sand, on the sea bottom,
        with only their eyes peering out

Or long and thin as a pencil
        flexible in movement

Or absurd, barnacled, monstrous bulldogs of the
    deep,
            and sea-spiders of gigantic size.

Red flowers of the sea
            (or orange coloured)
            like carnations, like broken pieces of
    pomegranate

(I too was once a fish

I rubbed myself on the sea bottom, leaping
    gracefully
            A large fish, about two feet long)

There was one like a great sturgeon
            constantly moving and twisting its
    muscular body

And a fish with tentacles under the fins
            on which it walks on the sea floor !
It has a blue fin, that opens when it swims

And speckled fish, too, with the eyes of snakes
            at the bottom of the sea, their heads gently
    bobbing

And an octopus   LOUIS
with saucer-like suckers, a paunchy body,   DUDEK
            huge eyes on great mounds,
blowing out of intestinal tubes,
            coiling the tips of his tentacles like a
    seashell.

He looked intelligent
Maybe he is intelligent, I thought, like a poet
            or a philosopher
who understands, but cannot act to circumvent
    clever men.

The octopus opened his magnificent umbrella,
pushed the belly forward, and bumped into a
    sleeping fellow
Then he went behind a pilaster
            because I had been watching him too long.

A magnificent creature.

And I saw beautiful tiny sea-horses
            with a fin on the back
                vibrating like a little wheel

And a ghostly shrimp six inches long
            light pink and white
and graceful as a star, or the new moon

And a whorl of delicate white toothpicks
And brown stems, with white strings like Chinese
    bean-sprouts, long and graceful.

And I saw a wonderful turtle.

But I have seen fish, turtle, octopus, with dead eyes
            looking out at the world.
What is life doing? Waiting for something to
    come?

Are we all stepping-stones to something still
  unknown?
Is man, when he is glad, when he is in love or
  enthralled
At last getting a glimpse of it?
Are the birds? Are the swift fish?

LOUIS
DUDEK

(Or perhaps they know they are captive. Who can
  tell,
even a fish may know when it is not at home.)

Then I saw a thin, thin thing
undistinguishable from a twig (just a few inches
  long)
but on close inspection very beautiful.

Since he has disguised himself to look so
  unremarkable,
        for whom does he keep that secret form?

There was a light green jelly
        PHYSOPHORA HYDROSTATICA

And a kind of huge one-foot-long paramecium
        PYROSOMA GIGANTEUM

And a thread-like plant with fragile white hair
(They say the chromosomes are such a thing of
  diminutive size,
        the whole life contained in their genes!)

And a coral that was a true artistic design
        made by a growing plant—
            a Persian decorative motif.

And many other intelligent plants, animals,
  and fish.

ALFRED
PURDY
b. 1918

Evergreen Cemetery

I guess it is ever green. . . .
What's sure if green isn't?
Me standing here in death's
ceded town
          in full summer
the dead down there unfreezing comfortably
the cold miserable rain untouching them—
outnumbering all to hell the last newcomers:
1 human, 2 chipmunks, some squirrels. . . .
Child me (subtract 30 years)
yelling down the rotting mausoleum vent;
          'Hoo, hoo—wake up!'
The dead inside silent
          silent now.

So—So the swaggerers flaunt
over graves an appropriate green panache—
so the braggarts delve into dumb roots—
so the lovers join an unemotional passion
as earth shapes and reshapes itself
          again and again—

But the dead are wholehearted about being dead,
no half measures, no shilly-shallying:
they're committed, dedicated
          to purposelessness. . . .
And I get a grim glee from all the high sounding
old aspirations and clichés ending in damp ground,
glee close to grief maybe, a hangman's gladness—
if that's being human it's best done with—

But it's too complicated to sum up
in telling phrase or easy pessimism,

syllogism or dénouement—
I've seen this same graveyard sunlight
at a beach mottled on a girl's flesh,
and groped for it under a blanket—
I've seen these trees spilling down mountains
that I trudged up sweating,
and loved for their banners' brightness. . . .

Well
      I've no business in this damned place,
not yet anyway with the taverns open,
tho my mother has :
inept christian that she was
bumbling among the granite colossi
searching for her redeemer—
  But I remember her savage grey face
before she died in a drugged fever,
and nurse telling me she'd stuffed her false teeth
up her rectum (in a pleased shocked voice) :
          that sharpened elemental
          grinning face
          with empty jaws which
          almost as I watched bit
                    hard on death. . . .
Which reminds me I'd better hurry and get out
of here before the gates close.

ALFRED
PURDY

Wilderness Gothic

Across Roblin Lake, two shores away,
they are sheathing the church spire
with new metal. Someone hangs in the sky
over there from a piece of rope,
hammering and fitting God's belly scratcher,
working his way up along the spire
until there's nothing to nail on—
Perhaps the workman's faith reaches beyond :

touches intangibles, wrestles with Jacob,
replacing rotten timber with pine thews,
pounds hard in the great cave of the sky,
contends heroically with difficult problems
of gravity, sky navigation and mythopoeia,
his volunteer time and labour donated to God,
minus sick benefits of course on a non-union job—

ALFRED
PURDY

Fields around are yellowing into harvest,
nestling and fingerling are sky and water borne,
death is yodeling quiet in green woodlots,
and bodies of three young birds have disappeared
in the sub-surface of the new county highway—

That picture is incomplete, part left out
that might alter the whole Dürer landscape:
gothic ancestors peer from medieval sky,
dour faces trapped in photograph albums escaping
to clop down iron roads with matched greys:
work-sodden wives groping inside their flesh
for what keeps moving and changing and flashing
beyond and past the long frozen Victorian day.
A sign of fire and brimstone? A two-headed calf
born in the barn last night? A sharp female agony?
A drooling idiot kept in the parsonage attic?
An age and a faith moving into transition,
the dinner cold and new-baked bread a failure,
deep woods shiver and water drops hang pendant,
double-yolked eggs and the house creaks a little—
Something is about to happen. Leaves are still.
Two shores away, a man hammering in the sky.
Perhaps he will fall.

Dead Seal

He looks like a fat little old man
an 'Old Bill'   sort of face
both wise and senile   at the same time

with an anxious to please expression ALFRED
PURDY
    in fact a clown
which is belied on account of the dark slow worm
of blood crawling down his forehead
that precludes laughter
or being anything   but a dead animal
tho perhaps part of a fur coat

Often I want to pet something
that looks like this
(and been warned the Eskimo dogs are dangerous)
which appeals to me on common ground i.e.
they unsure of what being an animal consists of
I equally unsure of what a human being is
    supposed to be
(despite the legal and moral injunctions that say
        'Thou Shalt Not'
nobody says or is likely to say with real conviction
        'Thou Shalt—go ahead and Shalt'
        or 'shall' as the case may be)
On the other hand it would be ridiculous
to pat the head of a dead seal
touch the wet blood that streams back from the
    boat
a feather of smoky brown in the water widening
into a crude trailing isosceles triangle
with mathematically impossible fish
re-tracing the seal's ghost past not
knowing they're involved in anything
And here he is now
        casually taking a nap
with flippers like futile baby hands
and clown look   of just pretending
    I shan't wake him
for it would be disgusting to touch the blood
and it's unnecessary to prove anything
even to myself
        Then change my mind

'I (damn well) Shalt'
—reach out as if the head were electric
with a death-taboo invisibly attached
dark and dank-cold with the hair on it
sticky where the bullet touched
                less gently
smooth elsewhere like an intimate part
                of the human body
that must be touched with delight in living
not curiosity and defiance of breaking rules
—But I am no hunter
        of any kind
go back to the tent
            to sit for a few minutes
inside the white canvas blindfold and wonder
what got into me?

What Do the Birds Think?

Are they exiles here from the rest of the world?
Déjà vu past egg and atom
from the yellow Sahara-ocean
or farmlands in Ontario
a witness   hanging   daubed
in the rural blue
while a plowman half a mile down
in the dark field with a snoring tractor
moves in circular sleep?
Or exiles from the apple country
where Macs and Spies plop soft
on wet ground in slow autumn days
with the rotten tangy odour
of cider rising on moonswept nights?
Have they lists and a summary
of things elsewhere and
remember the crimson racket
encountering tropic strangers

or nests of an old absence
lined with a downy part of themselves
far south?
And being south do they think sometimes
of the rain and mists of Baffin
and long migrations wingtip to wingtip
a mile high
and mate to mate in the lift and tremble
of windy muscles pushing them
pushing them where?
And do they ever
an arrow leader pointing the way
touch wearily down on ships passing?
—'Rest here a while and go on!'
(Forgotten in the hurry
of their streaming generations
another captain
called Noah
& Bjarni Herjolfsson
in horned helmet
and the sweeps' silver lifting
to a luring Hyperborean ocean
or whaling ships' myopic stumbling
from dull wave to dull wave and the
paint of the bright-over-the-horizon-gazing
woman flaked with salt)
How are we kept here
by what bonds
are we always exiles
a chirping roar in the silence
of foxes and watery romp of walrus
in the long sea lands
or perched on rubbery muskeg
like blue teacups
or lost brown mittens
by what agency of restlessness
in the driftwood heart?

ALFRED
PURDY

Until on a day the eggs hatch   ALFRED
and the young are trained to endurance   PURDY
ice rattles the shroud of summer
the flight plans sent
the log book sand is scribbled on
'Goodbye—we are going—Hurry'
and mounting a shaft of sunlight or
the mizzen mast of the sky
they climb and go
And that is the way it is?
Except perhaps I wonder
do they ever
remember down there in the southland
Cumberland Sound
and the white places
of Baffin
that I will remember soon?

The Winemaker's Beat-étude

I am picking wild grapes last year
in a field
            dragging down great lianas of vine
tearing at 20 feet of heavy infinite purple
having a veritable tug-o-war with Bacchus
who grins at me delightedly in the high branches
of one of those stepchild apple trees
unloved by anything but tent caterpillars
and ghosts of old settlers
become such strangers here—
I am thinking what the grapes are thinking
become part of their purple mentality
that is
      I am satisfied with the sun and
eventual fermenting bubble-talk together
then transformed and glinting with coloured
   lights in a
      GREAT JEROBOAM

that booms inside from the land beyond the world   ALFRED
PURDY
in fact
I am satisfied with my own shortcomings letting
myself happen
              then I'm surrounded by cows
black and white ones with tails—
At first I'm uncertain how to advise them
in mild protest or frank manly invective
then realize that the cows are right
it's ME that's the trespasser—
              Of course they are curious
perhaps wish to see me perform
              I moo off key
              I bark like a man
              laugh like a dog
              I talk like
              God hoping
they'll go away so Bacchus and I can get on with
    it—
Then I get logical thinking if there was ever a
feminine principle cows are it and why not but
what would so many females want?
I address them like Brigham Young hastily
              'No, that's out! I won't do it!
              Absolutely not!'
Contentment steals back among all this femininity
thinking cows are together so much they must be
    nearly
all lesbians fondling each other's dugs by
    moonlight why
Sappho's own star-reaching soul shines inward and
    outward
from the soft Aegean islands in these eyes and
I am dissolved like a salt lick instantly oh
              Sodium chloride!
              Prophylactic acid!
              Gamma particles (in suspension)!
              After-shave lotion!

235

Rubbing alcohol !
suddenly
I become the whole damn feminine principle so
happily noticing little tendrils of affection steal
out from each to each unshy honest encompassing
golden calves in Israel and slum babies in Canada
 and
a millionaire's brat left squawling on the toilet
 seat in
Rockefeller Center
   O my sisters
   I give purple milk !

PETER
MILLER

b. 1920

The Prevention of Stacy Miller

For a minute, daughter, for an afternoon
you existed. And with you capered a host
of merry phantoms, with picayune
troubles among the leaves, engrossed

in innocency; orient, airy,
things to be cared for. You had a brother,
his name was Ian. Ordinary
pleasures surrounded you : a mother

who loved you as she loved me not,
even in the myth (though there she tried
to be patient, to be kind); a forget-me-not
of a father (that was I, squint-eyed,

stiff-jointed from standing your sentry
against harm). Your window framed
woods, your woods, and the entry
to them was through trilliums. Tamed

at last for the slender family
was the tiger Life, lying with its paws
crossed on the hearth, like our pedigree
poodle. . . .
             But all, figures of gauze. . . .

PETER
MILLER

Stacy, you danced on the distant side
of a curtain of dream. Your little person
was immaterial : an infanticide
your mother, having of you and her son

brief conception; husband-killer
too, and uprooter of fair trees.
But, prevented sprite, O Stacy Miller,
you swing forever on your high trapeze.

The Capture of Edwin Alonzo Boyd

15TH MARCH, 1952

The hunt was up, the hunt was up
    for Edwin Alonzo Boyd,
the leader of ten robberies,
    of whom all the jails were void.

For Edwin Boyd the master-crook
    the hue and cry was on;
for Edwin Boyd who lately had
    slid down the walls of the Don.

They tracked him through an advertisement
    in the Toronto Daily Star;
for it was his wife who advertised
    for the sale of her used car,

and a detective and a lady cop
    went up to answer the ad.
From that day on, Mrs Doreen Boyd
    wore policemen's eyes for a plaid.

They saw her and Edwin's brother Norm
    take a house on Heath Avenue
and register as missionaries,
    quiet citizens, true-blue.

PETER
MILLER

Those missionaries by the name of Hall
    expected a brother soon,
and he was to come and share with them
    their cosy silk cocoon.

The brother came on a Friday night,
    and his surname was not Hall,
but his name was Boyd, and he packed a gun
    readied for a free-for-all.

When they saw him go in, the cops radioed
    to their Chief, 'The Big Boy's here!',
and the squad cars moved in silently,
    and grim was the atmosphere.

The neighbourhood bristled with sixty police
    when by midnight the trap was laid,
and all night long they were all around
    but never a sound they made.

At 6 a.m. the trap was sprung,
    and Sergeant Adolphus Payne
with Kenneth Craven (no craven, he!)
    slipped into the Boyds' domain.

They picked the lock and climbed the stairs,
    each with their gun in hand,
and tiptoed into every room
    just as they both had planned.

They found the Boyds asleep in bed
    in a state of full surprise,
for Ed sat up, tired and tame,
    rubbing his sleepy eyes,

and asked as though in a dream, 'What's up?'
   'Look, Boyd', said the sergeant, 'It's Payne.'
He shone a flashlight on Ed's face,
   saying again, 'It's Payne!'

While Ed Boyd clambered out of bed
   in long wool underwear,
his wife, in a yellow Chinese gown,
   could only sit and stare.

There was $25,000 in cash
   in a briefcase by the bed,
and a loaded pistol was in it too,
   but Ed reached for his pants instead.

And as Edwin Boyd, who was damned annoyed,
   put his city clothes back on,
a committee waited down the stairs
   to welcome him back to the Don.

The Mayor and the Chief and the sixty police
   were fidgeting round about,
and no-one could tell whether Boyd or the Mayor
   was the keener photographer's tout.

Said Boyd to the Mayor, 'I never thought
   we would meet over something like this.'
And the Mayor grinned at the newsmen
   and almost blew them a kiss.

Then as a photographer moved close
   Ed Boyd asked 'Shall I smile?'
'In your case, better not!' said the Mayor
   with photogenic bile.

'You can be thankful you're alive', added he,
   'and not torn apart by a mob.'
'Why, yes', said Boyd with a gracious bow,
   'you fellows did a fine job!'

Sémaphore

(I)

Les signes vont au silence
Les signes vont au sable du songe et s'y perdent
Les signes s'insinuent au ciel renversé de la pupille
Les signes crépitent, radiations d'une essence
  délétère,
chimie de formes cinétiques, filigranes d'aurores
  boréales.
Et tout se tisse de souvenirs feuillus, de gestes palmés
éventant l'aire des lisses liesses.
Les signes sont racines, tiges éployées, frondaisons de
signaux dans le vent qui feuillette son grimoire.
C'est l'hiver et le pays revêt sa robe sans couture
  dans
un grand envol de feuilles et de plumes, dans un
  geste
de sorcier saluant les derniers spasmes de la flamme.
Sous la voussure du ciel
S'allume une bourrasque de sel
Signe d'un silence qui sourd du songe et de l'ennui
Le silence darde sa lance au cœur du paysage
  soudain
cinglé de souffles véhéments et la tempête monte
  comme une
écume de légende pour ternir les bagues de la nuit.
L'homme dans le mitan de son âge ne sait plus
de quelle rive lui vient la vie.

(II)

Signes, silence, fumées
Songe désert, page blanche
Sphère soudain pleine d'une solitude grumeleuse
comme on voit aux boules de verre où
    tourbillonnent
des astérisques d'ivoire
Moment d'extrême nudité sous le halo des
    réverbères
seuls signes au loin d'une humaine sollicitude
Les hurlements ne sont que les voix de chiens
    crevés
depuis longtemps quand au claquement d'une
    rafale
se lève la meute des longues années perdues au
    jour le jour
des gestes éperdus
Toute mouvance se givre et la durée, la durée se
    fige
au lac de mémoire.

(III)

Signes au silence
Silence dispersé au long des litanies neigeuses
Semaille de froidure au long des routes venteuses
où l'homme perd la trace de lui-même, ô dérision
    des pas
pris aux pièges des tourbillons
car la mémoire même du feu vacille et l'avenir
est constellé d'éphémères
Le voir et le boire sont désirs d'eunuque
au sein d'un présent cerclé d'épouvante
Verticale, la vie se néantise.

(IV)

La neige violente la face tendue vers la dernière
   feuille
qui tient tête à l'automne
vers la tendresse des soirs violacés
vers l'encens sylvestre qui coule tout au long des
étés résineux
Vers la petite joie pointue du dernier cri d'oiseau
Cri gelé, jet glacé, prisme d'une chanson spoliée
Le bruit clouté du vent fait éclater la rêverie
Signaux, songes évanouis
Le froid creuse de lentes galeries dans le minable
homme des neiges
Le voici tout poreux
grotte sonore hérissée de stalactites.

(V)

Signaux venus d'une vive mer qu'êtes-vous
   devenus ?
Tout le pays a le vague à l'âme
Fausse vierge, vestale sacrilège
la tempête déchire ses vêtements de lavandière
aux pointes des Rocheuses
Tempête, folle tempête va te jeter dans la mer
où la vague profère ses incantations démentes
L'homme dans sa conque neigeuse l'entend bruire
Elle lui conte des contes venus d'une enfance
   alifère
si bien qu'il ne sait plus si la mer bat de l'aile
ou si la mémoire enfin fait craquer la porte du gel.

(VI)

Signe souverain
L'horloge marque l'heure nacrée au solstice
   d'hiver

Et ce n'est rien de voir se dérouler les volutes
car le temps se fige
La méditation désoperculée du sage se vide
comme un gâteau de cire
Dans son alvéole de froid l'homme songe au miel
    de l'été
Le visage tendu comme un drap sous la piqûre
des abeilles de neige
sous l'essaimage des images
Le sommeil est une pâte dont il ferait son pain
Empalé sur le glaçon d'une attente austère
il n'ose bouger
Cloisonné
une feuille de glace le sépare de la mort
feuille translucide, vitrail où se dessinent déjà
les pâles arabesques d'une absence
Signes néfastes
premières leurs d'outre-songe.

(VII)
Et pourtant nous avions fait cargaison de vives
amitiés de silex. Qu'est-il donc advenu des étincelles
—pierres froides, silex désertés du feu, armes à
blessures—Rien n'est si tranchant qu'une haine
bien aiguisée, sinon les cristaux du silence. En
toute autre saison l'amour survit comme le sisal ou
l'avocatier sous les grandes vitres blanches et
bleues des regards voilés. Mais rien ne croît sous
l'arcade du froid, sous la paume d'un hiver qui
gèle toute ardeur au lit même des rivières.

(VIII)   GILLES
HÉNAULT

Signe d'abandon

L'hiver distribue l'usufruit de son fief à tout vent
Rien n'échoit en partage aux âmes roturières
sauf l'essaim des paillettes évanescentes
Pour qui voit voltiger la théophanie des cristaux
s'anime la rosace des merveilles
Les signes les plus fastes sont arcanes pour les
    regards éteints
Mais l'âme sans dol frappe toutes choses à son
    effigie
Ah la soudaine flambée du rire au versant de
    l'accueil !
En la courbure de l'espace la lumière éploie sa
    chrysalide
Son aile encore moite couvre l'arbre du matin
D'Ouest en Est court un vent de lessive
une senteur de linge frais
un crissement de drapeau gelé à la hampe du
    vertige
Le paysage est vernissé de verglas
couvert d'idéogrammes et nul n'y peut vivre
sinon dans le cercle de clarté d'un regard d'amante.

(IX)

Signes mués en sigles
Quel paléographe saura lire la toundra dénudée ?
Grand alphabet de glace parcouru par des loups
qui tentent d'en formuler le sens en longs
    hurlements lunaires
Faim froid paroles venteuses plus légères que balle
    de mil
toute la douceur de vivre est passée au crible des
    forêts
C'est alors que se love l'amour aux paumes des
    maisons luisantes

Un couple à la barre du jour se penche sur un
    avenir de jardins
dont la dernière brindille était garante.

(x)

Signe d'errante mort
Le temps fait table rase
Hier est porte close
Le vent redit toujours la même phrase cendreuse
les mêmes paroles charbonneuses
Alphabet de tisons morts
de joies éteintes comme lucioles noyées au plus
    noir de l'été
Les glaçons percent doucement le cœur
le sang charrie des alluvions vers l'amère morte
    saison
Il neige de mesquines petites aiguilles sur un
    paysage
tout faufilé de fil de fer
L'espace a la dimension du froid.

(xi)

Nuage neige nuit
le mot naître gèle dans la bouche
l'homme gît l'âme à vif sous l'opacité des jours
Mais une dalle se lève au fleuve du devenir
une dalle d'aube se lève pour la résurrection des
    sèves
pour la métamorphose des rêves en signes
    dénombrables.
L'inondation délie la langue.

(xii)

Signes et sortilèges
Entre la lampe et le lit la femme agite des
    oriflammes

GILLES
HÉNAULT

Et c'est un bercement de hanches qui annonce la
   marée
aux charnelles anses
La femme de proue dénoue les amarres de l'amour
et lance un vol de mouettes à la rencontre du mâle
Signes de la main
survol plané de paroles empennées qui vont droit
   au cœur
Débâcles d'énigmes
Sous l'éclair du désir s'abolit la distance, la
   chaleur
pénètre aux chambres neigeuses, le flot du fleuve
   clame
soudain la plus haute chanson de délivrance, un
   courant porte
sur son échine la passion des vagues et c'est
   l'heure
de la grande insurrection des sèves.
Glaces, miroirs tout se brise et se brouille
Le fleuve harnaché se cabre sous la bride du
   barrage
et comme une armée rompant ses lances au soleil
la saison luit sous le signe du Bélier.

GILLES
HÉNAULT

·   ·   ·

Coup de grisou des frondaisons
Qu'adviendra-t-il de nous sous la mitraille du
   pollen?

Bestiaire

Un seul cri,

grogner, chuinter, miauler, bêler, aboyer, hennir,
glapir, siffler, rugir,

un seul cri

246

suffit à l'animal, un seul cri viscéral, une seule expression de tout son être, un seul cri qu'il module selon les méandres de son instinct, les frissons de son poil, l'intensité de sa rage, les fêlures de ses images biologiques, le tremblement de sa peur,

un seul cri

et son peuple dresse l'oreille, les ailes s'affolent, les échines se cabrent, les galops battent le tambour des plaines, les courses font flèche de tout bois, les paniques moutonnent vers les précipices,

un seul cri

et c'est l'appel au combat des mâles agglomérés par l'aimant du rut, c'est l'orientation vers les sources qui luisent déjà aux naseaux des chefs de files, c'est l'acheminement millénaire vers le cimetière où l'éléphant lance le barrissement final. Mais nous sommes aphones.

Il faudrait trouver le cri qui rallie toutes les angoisses, qui exprime toutes les joies, qui fasse enfi communiquer l'homme avec l'homme par les entrailles de ses plus secrètes convoitises.
La parole articulée sèche à mesure qu'elle étend ses rameaux.

Trop d'arabesque nous trompent sur le sens caché des mots, trop de fleurs de rhétorique tressent des couronnes artificielles aux plus dévêtus sentiments.
Il me faut la parole nue

Il me faut des mots comme des balles et des cris purs qui transpercent. La poésie cherche à bercer l'âme, alors qu'elle devrait pétrir les choses, faire entendre au-dessus des cacophonies religieuses, philosophiques, morales et politique le cri nu de

l'homme qui affirme son existence singulière et GILLES
grégaire.   HÉNAULT

Ah que choient enfin les fruits pourris du
désespoir; que se blessent aux plus dures épines
les enchantements factices; que s'affolent les
idées fixes aux lointains sidéraux de nos crânes;
que s'apprivoisent les cataclysmes; que la joie
nous éclabousse de son sang, même s'il faut qu'elle
en meure.

On n'a pas fini d'inventorier le monde, et je me
fous du vent de l'esprit quand soufflent sur ma
face les vraies tourmentes minérales qui font
crisser entre mes dents les Sahara et les Gobi,
quand je reçois l'énorme soufflet d'algues et de sel
des tempêtes marines, ô larmes noyées dans les
ressacs à l'abordage des navires de haut bord.
Toute la mer se mutine et fait claquer le drapeau
gelé des glaces polaires. Les mouvements de l'âme
sont des mouvements de lames. Et si je sens
soudain l'étendue m'envahir, mes veines se
confondre aux fleuves du monde, c'est que mon
corps est marée, c'est que je baigne dans la lymphe
universelle, c'est que les fibres de mon être sont
immergées dans l'écoulement du temps physique
et que je suis poreux.

Je veux lever toutes les défenses, brûler tous les
interdits, dévêtir tous ceux qui se parent
d'ornements de mages et qui vaticinent depuis des
siècles sous prétexte qu'ils ont un plumage
multicolore.

Je veux rogner tous les dieux, demi-dieux et
quarts-de-dieux jusqu'à ce qu'il n'en reste plus
qu'un petit tas de scories.

Je veux que ma colère se transforme en pierres
sous mes paumes.

Notre Jeunesse

GILLES
HÉNAULT

Nous avons quitté ces climats
où la terre s'étend nue
sous un ciel qui ne sourit pas
où l'homme est un inconnu

pour l'homme, où le monde
est irréel et grimaçant
où la sonde plonge
au mirage d'un impossible océan.

En ce temps-là, tous les paysages
n'étaient que le ciel mouvant de nos fièvres
et nous cherchions en vain des visages
pour notre soif de regards et des lèvres . . .

Les mains fraternelles
n'étaient que branches brisées . . .

Dans ce pays, dépaysés,
pleins de désirs paralysés,
nous avons tant cherché à vous briser
miroirs affolants de nos amours déguisées.

Nous étions sourds au monde et insonores,
Vieilles guitares désaccordées,
Nous disions la vie finie, le ciel incolore
et le bonheur, pur coup de dé.

Avons-nous assez joué les Crusoé
les nègres blancs, les insulaires
qui n'avaient jamais navigué
sauf pour la chasse à la Chimère !

Notre sécheresse nous rendait les yeux vitreux.
Notre petit monde intérieur
devenait sec et sonnait creux
notre petit monde intérieur

dont nous étions les demi-dieux
n'était que vieille calebasse

de faux complexes, de vieux
mythes et préjugés tenaces.

GILLES
HÉNAULT

Il fallait voir à marée basse
comme nous étions rongés d'amertume
dans le marais salant de nos larmes !

Nous pensions être pour toujours encalminés
dans quelque mer ses Sargasses,
Port d'attache des illuminés
du bal rimbaldien.

Les hiers nous servaient d'amarres,
et casqués de souvenirs, scaphandriers,
bêtement nous replongions aux mares
de nos angoisse où croissaient les polypiers
de nos philosophies barbares.

Le monde sous-marin
Le monde transhumain
Les désirs fous, les idées fixes, les oiseaux rares

nous faisaient une âme de panoplie
fixée aux parois du cœur.
Rien n'existe, disions-nous, sinon les folies
qui mènent leur ronde au petit monde intérieur.

From *Le Voyage d'Arlequin*

(VIII)

Mes mains sont si pleines de roses
Que j'improvise le bonheur.
Plénitude des portes closes
Et des bras tombants de douceur.

La fenêtre, à pas lents, s'avance
Dans le ciel. Tout comme un bateau
Nouvel et incertain qu'on lance.
Enfermez-moi dans le château !

L'hiver viendra laver la terre.
Et, sur les meubles du printemps,
On posera, la main légère,
Des pots de fleurs dans tous les champs.

(IX)

L'aurore était pâle et ravie.
Or, le matin a dévêtu
La nuit. Que maintenant la vie
Marche nue au soleil pointu !

La campagne passe joyeuse
Avec ses larmes dans les yeux.
Un peu comme un pas de danseuse,
Le regard monte dans les cieux.

Les bras lentement qui se tendent
Dénouant l'amour d'autrefois
Sont des voyageurs qui attendent
Les doigts dans le cœur, tant de fois !

251

(x)

Combien d'étincelles sont mortes
Dans cette large mer du soir ?
Les livres s'avancent, m'apportent
Le chant inconnu d'un pas noir.

Leur fantôme s'en vient qui danse,
Visage couvert de la main.
J'ai peur de l'étrange cadence
Qui pourrait bien mourir demain.

Couleur d'un parfum débonnaire,
La lune a démasqué la mer
Et de son œil cherche la terre.
Ce pied dans le ciel est amer.

Le Chasseur

Ce grand-père, un joyeux sportif,
Un gars qui adorait la chasse.
Il prenait un fusil (pas fou
Le vieux) et il partait. Eh hop !
Le fusil, lui aussi, partait.

Il a tué un orignal,
Un chevreuil et douze bouvreuils,
Une gazelle, la plus belle,
Quatre lapins sur son lopin,
Trois canards et plusieurs coin-coin

Je me suis tué au travail,
Disait-il. Aujourd'hui, repos.
Et pour tuer le temps, je tue.

Or, un soir, en rentrant chez lui,
Il tua grand-mère, sa femme,
Sans y penser, distraitement.
L'habitude, vous comprenez ?
Hé ! hé ! il fut pendu quand même
C'est bien fait. Ça lui apprendra.

Les Parents exemplaires

ÉLOI DE
GRANDMONT

Il y a des parents qui punissent les enfants.
D'autres qui les grondent, les
Gourmandent, les
Réprimandent, les
Morigènent, les
Révoltent, les
Domptent, les
Matent, les
Soumettent
Et leur tirent les oreilles.

D'autres qui les raisonnent, les
Taquinent, les
Asticotent, les
Empoisonnent, les
Emprisonnent, les

Enquiquinent, les
Séquestrent, les
Maltraitent, les
Maudissent et les
Déshéritent.

Il y a aussi des parents qui les corrigent,
Des parents qui les pincent, les
Frappent, les
Giflent, les
Fessent, les
Torturent, les
Martyrisent, les
Assassinent, les
Déposent à l'assistance publique et vont
Ensuite dormir pour en faire d'autres.

Par ailleurs, il y a ceux qui les privent
De désert, les
Empêchent de dormir, leur

Défendent de sortir, leur
Coupent l'argent de poche et leur
Coupent le sifflet.

Enfin, il y a ceux qui leur donnent de
Grands coups de pieds au derrière et la
Bénédiction paternelle au Jour de l'An.

ÉLOI DE
GRANDMONT

RAYMOND
SOUSTER

b. 1921

May 15th

May 15th :
        the birds begin to nudge me
awake before the dawn. When I look out finally
into the morning, the Manitoba maples
have at last put out
their first clusters of leaves,
shape of a clenched fist. A squirrel
climbs warily up to the white-faced oval
of the bird-bath and takes
a long cool drink, the same
as the birds. The cats are a different matter.
In no time at all they've sensed
the possibilities — one of them is always lurking
not too far off, hoping for a kill . . .

Kill or be killed,
that's the law of nature, and the law
of the lawless of this world, with their
        inter-continental
missiles, their bombers, their bombs, all trigger-
        ready to prove it :
            but it's not *my* law, even though

the only ones listening to the poets these days
are the poets themselves, inbred generation
of lost souls, with their 'little' magazines,
their private presses, their government grants,
to get away from a country they secretly hate,
don't know how to come to terms with :

RAYMOND
SOUSTER

and they've taken poetry
into the universities, buried it
under text-books, mythologies,
so what comes out is as dead as the walls
they hide behind, as brittle as the chairs
their fat asses vegetate on, as pointless
as the anthologies they edit, one eye
on the Foundations. . . .
            (But why the hell talk
about poetry on such a day?)
                  Over in Geneva
the statesmen of the power cults are assembling
behind round and square tables to decide
the fate of the world — state regimentation
or capitalistic automation — which will be decided
more by the fitness of livers
after a month of vodka and Canadian Club
than by any honesty, humanity. . . .
            (But why the hell talk
about Geneva and the statesmen of death
on such a day?)
      Here in Toronto
the long-hanging green flags of the willows
almost arouse the muck and filth of the Don,
and for a moment bring life back
into this cancerous stream : the sky above Queen
    Street is so maiden blue one can almost forget
the bug-crawling food in these windows, the spit
    on the sidewalks
and the worn lungs coughing it up : while at noon
a naked woman clad only

in three yards of ticker-tape stands up

RAYMOND
SOUSTER

in the Stock Exchange and cries out :
how much am I offered? (She is sold
for ten thousand shares of a penny mining stock
and trading resumes as usual.)
                    I myself
take the road along the Humber Valley, where
    workmen
struggle with huge concrete blocks, changing now
the course of this river (pus carrier,
garbage dump of excrement), where still a few
    birds
keep to the trees, where there's no stench of
    gasoline,
where ducks can waddle up on the shale
without being fired at, where sky is still visible,
    sun warm,
with no buildings cornering the spring air,
    distilling it
with furnace ash, street dust, exhaust fumes.
                    I look down
into the depths of a green-slimed, rock-clustered
    pool,
where nothing moves to the eye but small bubbles
    rising rising
to the surface, now here, now there . . .
                    in these times
keep your mind calm as this pool, go out into life
letting it burst around you, let it blossom
through your heart like this spring that today
promises never to end :
                    and be earth's forerunner.

MAY 1959

256

Ladybug

RAYMOND
SOUSTER

Pull me down, ladybug,
pull me down among your jungles
your rivers :
    let me be the one
closest to the sun and the rain;
never let me go, ladybug,
even if you have to strap me
to a toadstool,
    even if you have
    to make love to me, ladybug,
your husband watching you
not a weed's width away.

The Six-Quart Basket

The six-quart basket
one side gone
half the handle torn off

sits in the centre of the lawn
and slowly fills up
with the white fruits of the snow.

Ties

New ties, fifteen each, ten
For a dollar (he said),
Holding them up in bunches of I suppose
Five each for us to see : and they did look new,
Like good ties, cheap at double the price.
But we didn't buy any; I because I had only
A dime left for a beer, the others—well,
They'd been stung too many times before,
   bargains

Not bargains, something like that. It's the same
As marriage or joining the army
They might have said, joking, but not really
     joking
As much as telling a fact, the essential fact
Of their lives: nothing wonderful, nothing in
     their favour
Liable ever to happen; life like these ties
Passed round in front of us, difficult to judge,
     uncertain, open
To the greatest suspicion, a jungle of dark-twisting
     lies.

RAYMOND
SOUSTER

Choosing Coffins

The funeral gent led us
to the room where the coffins were displayed
like a furniture store, price-tags in evidence
among the fancy-coloured linings
                    and at once my father
spotted a polished beauty, which he stroked
down its smooth mahogany length like you would
     a cat,
explaining that he'd had this same wood
in a canoe forty years ago
                    (the canoe had cost
eighty dollars, this casket was twenty-four
     hundred
'complete with burial')
                    we moved around the room
to look at the others, but I knew my father
couldn't wait to circle back to that casket,
to fondle the close-rubbed grain, push back time
to his young manhood, Rouge River, Humber
     nights
those sweaty black-fly northern portages. . . .

258

Minotaur Poem II

My father was always out in the garage
building a shining wing, a wing
that curved and flew along the edge of blue air
in that streamed and sunlit room
that smelled of oil and engines
and crankcase grease, and especially
the lemon smell of polish and cedar.
Outside there were sharp rocks, and trees,
cold air where birds fell like rocks
and screams, hawks, kites, and cranes.
The air was filled with a buzzing and flying
and the invisible hum of a bee's wings was honey
in my father's framed and engined mind.
Last Saturday we saw him at the horizon
screaming like a hawk as he fell into the sun.

Four Songs from
the Book of Samuel

(I)

THE WITCH OF ENDOR

every path a green lady
but I abandon green hair
for the wretch of winter
I handle a cold stone
take up the cold stones of her breast
my hands move in her icy hair

I walk over the stony harp
she plays in her cage of ribs

she casts down her spears
she waters my heart with ice

ELI
MANDEL

in the cave of her eyes
I see the coiling bed
she beckons me to with a hand of boughs
she is the black tree of winter

(II)

a cave of eyes : here is the bed
here the springs where the youth fed
here the lilt of the king
the huddled clothes like a sleeping girl
the crows clawing their songs on the wall
the boneless millions slain in the dream
the young slayer on his springing horse

this is the nation's hope : here is the bed
here the murdering dreamer lay in his dream

(III)

the intellect does not age, the body dies
daily the mind declares its lies
about the soul, about the self
about the body and its ageless cries

now mind grows freer as the body dies
daily the body ages in its lies
about the mind, about the self
about the mind's clear sense of paradise

(IV)

I forgive the adulterer, I forgive the song
I forgive the straw man in my bed
I forgive the old man his lies about the bed
I forgive my armies for their arms

I forgive the generals for their boots ELI
and the mayors for their homes MANDEL
and the councillors
      my mother
for her prophecies, my father
for his mistaken comfort in failure
my teachers for their religion
I forgive the girl's face in the flower
the instrumental poet hung on his strings
the colonies for the times they did not eat
I forgive the food of the armies
and the carpets under the general's feet
I forgive the poet for lying about god
I forgive god for tomorrow
I forgive the arisen prophet
the man who is a weapon
the weapon
death
the song
the singer dying in his song
even myself

Song

When the echo of the last footstep dies
and on the empty street you turn empty eyes
   what do you think that you will see?
     A hangman and a hanging tree.

    When there are no more voices
    and yet you hear voices singing
      in the hot street,
what do you think will be their song?
Glory to the hangman who is never wrong.

When on the hot sands of your burning mind
   the iron footsteps clang no more

261

and blind eyes no longer see
    and hot voices end,
what do you think will be your plea?
    Hanging isn't good enough for me.

ELI
MANDEL

MILTON
ACORN

b. 1923

I ve Tasted My Blood

If this brain's over-tempered
consider that the fire was want
and the hammers were fists.
I've tasted my blood too much
to love what I was born to.

But my mother's look
was a field of brown oats, soft-bearded;
her voice rain and air rich with lilacs:
and I loved her too much to like
how she dragged her days like a sled over gravel.

Playmates? I remember where their skulls roll!
One died hungry, gnawing grey porch-planks;
one fell, and landed so hard he splashed;
and many and many
come up atom by atom
in the worm-casts of Europe.

My deep prayer a curse.
My deep prayer the promise that this won't be.
My deep prayer my cunning,
my love, my anger,
and often even my forgiveness
that this won't be and be.
I've tasted my blood too much
to abide what I was born to.

The Fights

MILTON
ACORN

What an elusive target
the brain is ! Set up
like a coconut on a flexible stem
it has 101 evasions.
A twisted nod slues a punch
a thin gillette's width
past a brain, or
a rude brush-cut to the chin
tucks one brain safe under another.
Two of these targets are
set up to be knocked down
for 25 dollars or a million.

In that TV picture in the parlour
the men, who linked move to move
in a chancy dance,
are abstractions only.
Come to ringside, with two
experts in there ! See
each step or blow pivoted,
balanced and sudden as gunfire.
See muscles wriggle, shine
in sweat like windshield rain.

In stinking dancehalls, in
the forums of small towns,
punches are cheaper but
still pieces of death.
For the brain's the target
with its hungers
and code of honour. See
in those stinking little towns,
with long counts, swindling judges,
how fury ends with the last gong.
No matter who's the cheated one
they hug like a girl and man.

It's craft and
the body rhythmic and terrible,
the game of struggle.
We need something of its nature
but not this;
for the brain's the target
and round by round it's whittled
till nothing's left of a man
but a jerky bum, humming
with a gentleness less than human.

MILTON
ACORN

PIERRE
TROTTIER

b. 1925

Femme aux couleurs de mon pays

Femme aux couleurs de mon pays
Voici qu'un peuple entier me porte
Sur les épaules de ses vagues
Et me remplit le cœur à déferler
D'amour d'un océan à l'autre

Ne vas pas replier sur toi-même les ailes
De ce château que tu habites que tu laisses
Envahir par la brousse et les ronces rebelles
Rebelles trop à mes caresses jardinières

Ne me refuse pas d'entendre ce poème
Que fait le vent d'automne aux flancs de tes
     montagnes
En vers émerveillants de couleurs et de chutes
De feuilles que j'emprunte aux vignes de tes murs
De feuilles dont tes pas redoutent la douceur

Reconnais-les de ton château de mon pays
Et ne crains point d'y perdre tes propres couleurs

N'impose plus à mes forêts
La pénible morsure d'une patience
Aux dents de jour aux dents de nuit qui rongent
Les arbrisseaux des heures virginales
Pour les abattre une à une aux rives du temps

PIERRE
TROTTIER

Les Malédictions

SERMON SUR LE MONT-ROYAL

Au nom du ciel et de la terre et des étoiles ainsi
   soit-il

Malheur à nous
Si nous voyons nos villes endormies
Toujours rouler du côté de la nuit
Toujours ouvrir de grandes mains de rêve
Pour effeuiller entre les doigts de leurs clochers
Quelques étoiles-marguerites

Malheur à nous
Si nous voyons nos temples devenir musées
Où nos curés surveillent des collections d'âmes

Malheur à nous
Si nous ne savons pas quoi dire aux pauvres
À tous ceux qui demandent l'heure aux autres
Lorsque nos montres marquent l'heure
D'un empire qui n'est pas le nôtre

Malheur à nous
Si notre amour n'a pas encor forcé les portes
D'une Cité que nous n'avons bâtie qu'en rêve

Malheur à nous
Si nous fuyons l'épreuve de la connaissance
Et le péché qui donne une présence au monde

Malheur à nous
Si nous guettons aux fenêtres d'avril
Une saison qu'ici les regrets seuls connaissent

Malheur à nous
Si notre haine ne fait pas d'hivers si froids
Que le printemps ne les dissipe en vaine pluie

PIERRE
TROTTIER

Malheur à nous
Si nos saisons dérivent sans peser sur la terre
Et si nos nuits d'amour l'amour lui-même les
    oublie

Nous qui n'avons que par la grâce de nos pas
Le sol que nous foulons en ce monde loué
Nous nous multiplions pour mieux porter nos
    morts
Pour mieux mourir encore que tous nos ancêtres
Mais sans qu'à force de mourir une lumière
Une raison de vivre éclaire nos tombeaux

Au nom du ciel et de la terre et des étoiles ainsi
    soit-il

Le Soldat inconnu

J'ai cru qu'il suffirait sur la place publique
D'étendre les deux bras comme aiguilles d'horloge
Pour dire aux gens l'heure que je vivais
Mais tout le monde avait sa montre à soi

J'ai cru qu'il suffirait de joindre les deux mains
Au dessus de ma tête pour me faire
Un arc de triomphe mais personne
N'est venu allumer la flamme sur la tombe
Du soldat inconnu que toujours je demeure

J'ai cru qu'il suffirait d'un bon lit chaud
Pour attirer toutes les femmes dans mes bras
Et pour me réveiller en berçant des enfants
Hélas mes nuits jamais ne durèrent assez
Pour empêcher les femmes de s'enfuir
Et les enfants de naître loin de moi

J'ai cru qu'il suffirait d'une table accueillante PIERRE
Pour que mon pain réjouisse un grand nombre TROTTIER
   d'amis
Mais on me l'a volé pour le manger ailleurs
Et je suis resté seul avec des miettes pour les rats

Ô mon heure mon arc de triomphe
Mes amours et mon pain solitaires
N'y a-t-il que ma mort qui vous reste fidèle

De tout ce que je suis de ma mort même
Ne restera-t-il rien qui puisse faire l'envie
Du soldat inconnu dont tout le monde
Dont tout le monde au moins sait qu'il est mort

Le Temps corrigé

Or je suis revenu sur mes pas
Je suis revenu jusqu'à ma naissance
Et j'ai refoulé jusqu'à la leur
Ma famille et tous mes ancêtres

J'ai chanté une messe à l'envers
Pour que le sang goûte le vin
Pour que la chair goûte le pain
Pour revenir au nom du Père
Et ne plus dire ainsi-soit-il

J'ai tout rendu ce que j'avais
Ma foi au roi des cieux ma langue au roi de France

J'ai rendu Rome à ses collines
J'ai dispersé les douze Apôtres
J'ai renvoyé chez eux les bergers et les Mages
J'ai démoli Babel étage par étage
Et j'ai rendu la pierre à la montagne
J'ai ramené sa colombe à Noé
Et j'ai bu toute l'eau du déluge
J'ai replacé dans l'arbre le fruit défendu

PIERRE
TROTTIER

Et remis à Satan le péché de science
J'ai fait rentrer en moi la première Ève
Et j'ai rendu le sexe à l'unité

Alors il ne me resta plus
Pour souffler la lumière
Qu'à rendre le premier soupir
Et tout rentra dans les ténèbres

FRANCIS
SPARSHOTT
b. 1926

Entanglement

My thought is caught in the eyes of love
Like mist caught in a tree's branches;
A ragged sky whistles above
Where wind tugs and rain drenches.
No one I care for calls for me.
Heavy-winged, the little dove
Sighs for an olive-naked sea.
My thought is caught in the eyes of love.

The Lord speaks in the burning bush,
The whale spouts in the freezing sea,
Wires whine in winter wind;
I cannot speak, I cannot see.
In a thicket of thorn the tangled ram
Watches the blade and never flinches.
My thought is caught in the eyes of love
Like mist caught in a tree's branches.

Crowds collect at Bloor and Yonge,
Waiting, crossing when they can;
Love lives in a furnished room
With an empty grate and an ottoman.
Lobsters creep in the hollow rocks.

Tramps lie awake on park benches.   FRANCIS
My thought is caught in the eyes of love   SPARSHOTT
Like mist caught in a tree's branches.
I cannot speak, I cannot move,
I am caught in the eyes of love.

Improperia

Hung between thief and thief
Swung between wind and wind
Slung between rock and sky
        Jesus my own one
        Jesus my dear son
        Hear your mother's cry

By pains of bearing
By joys of suckling
By cares of rearing
        Jesus my dear one
        Jesus my darling son
        Hear your mother's cry

By the trial of my waiting
By the wrench of our loving
By the shame of your spurning
        Jesus my darling one
        Jesus my own son
        Hear your mother's cry

Come on, now, Jesus, remember your Dad:
Let's show them all:
Screw world and sky into one crumpled ball
And come down off that cross like a good lad.
        Jesus my own one,
        Jesus my dear son,
        Hear a mother's prayer.

I hear, I hear, what though I hear,
Since my corpse jerked to the corporal's spear
I am harrowed and harrow, I am in hell and here.

The cross is old, the nails are new.
I cannot come to you.

While man turns vermin : streams choked,
    fruitful land
Bulldozed and bungalowed, all beasts killed but
    his kind,
His bombs and smokes clogging the common
    wind :
            The cross is old, the nails are new,
            I cannot come to you.

While I am racked between Geneva and Rome
And cannibal sects lie in my hated name;
While my come kingdom waits till kingdom
    come :
            The cross is old, the nails are new,
            I cannot come to you.

Caught between thieves, wind-spun, speared
    between earth and sky
By hunger and envy, greed and grief, weakness
    and cruelty,
Behold your son : your God : good creature, pity
    me.
            The nails are new. The cross is old.
            I cannot come though I be called.

Paysage choisi

AFTER PAUL VERLAINE

Her soul is a select district
Where they give the most charming dances.
They do not enjoy them, exactly, but do their best
To keep up appearances,

Speaking in carefully modulated voices
Of the latest engagements and life's little chances;

Or, weary of walled prosperity,
Dream of dim landscapes where a sick moon
  glances
On birds and fountains singing in their sleep,
And halls of black marble where nothing is ever
  done.
One is not encouraged to raise children, or
  whistle, or make a noise :
The district is so select, one must keep up the
  tone.

FRANCIS
SPARSHOTT

JAMES
REANEY

b. 1926

The Katzenjammer Kids

With porcupine locks
And faces which, when
More closely examined,
Are composed of measle-pink specks,
These two dwarf imps,
The Katzenjammer Kids,
Flitter through their Desert Island world.
Sometimes they get so out of hand
That a blue Captain
With stiff whiskers of black wicker
And an orange Inspector
With a black telescope
Pursue them to spank them
All through that land
Where cannibals cut out of brown paper
In cardboard jungles feast and caper,
Where the sea's sharp waves continually
Waver against the shore faithfully
And the yellow sun above is thin and flat

With a collar of black spikes and spines JAMES
To tell the innocent childish heart that REANEY
It shines
And warms (see where she stands and stammers)
The dear fat mother of the Katzenjammers.
Oh, for years and years she has stood
At the window and kept fairly good
Guard over the fat pies that she bakes
For her two children, those dancing heartaches.
Oh, the blue skies of that funny-paper weather!
The distant birds like two eyebrows close
    together!
And the rustling paper roar
Of the waves
Against the paper sands of the paper shore!

From *A Suit of Nettles*

BRANWELL'S SESTINA

My love I give to you a threefold thing,
A jewsharp serenade, a song I've made
And a sparkling pretty rose diamond ring.
To haste your love to me by fate delayed.
Zing zing zing zing, azeezing, azeezing,
Azuggazing, azeezug-zug-azing.

Six reasons are there for my loving you:
Your eyes, voice, beak, legs, mind and feathers
    white;
Feathers like snow, like cloud, like milk, like salt,
White white against the green grass in the spring.
Oh white angel in bethlehems of grime
Teach my slow wits to understand your worth.

With only reckless hope, not the true worth
That should raise up a suitor wooing you,
I try to know that stainless mind, so white

That crystal shafts and lily mines of salt   JAMES
Seem when compared coal black : and in love's   REANEY
   spring
I beg forgiveness for my own mind's grime.

Your paddling legs do even cleanse that grime;
When I scan all your parts and all your worth,
Sometimes they seem the prettiest part of you,
Those orange sticks beneath your body white,
Those sturdy swimming oars that somersault
Above your body at the pond in spring.

When your swift beak dives down for frog
   offspring,
Oh resting in his bathos hut of muddy grime
How sweet to be a frog that's nothing worth
Lifted to the sublime up up by you
By your fox orange beak and neck so white,
Your beak so bright it hurts the eye like salt.

Venison needs a humble pinch of salt;
You need the sounds that from your beak do
   spring,
Bragful when your feet feel spring's first
   thaw-grime,
Stout and most vigorous and strong when worth
We argue among us; rasping when you
See robbers in the yard with moonlight white.

But most I love—that's neither orange nor
   white—
Your circular blue eyes intense as salt :
They shot and caught my blizzardheart for spring,
First sky they cracked into my egg of grime,
First rain they let from out your storms of worth.
For these six things then I praise and love you
And now I beg you, my dread goddess white,
To slake my dry salt lips with mercy's spring
And touch my cold grime with your golden
   worth.

Le Tombeau de Pierre Falcon

JAMES
REANEY

Pierre Falcon,
You say here along with this unsingable music
That on June nineteenth these Burnt Wood people
Ah yes, the Métis were dark, so called Bois-Brûlés,
Arrived near this settlement of Lord Selkirk's
Fort Douglas
You say in this second verse that your Burnt
    Woods
Took three foreigners prisoner at Frog Plain.
These foreigners were Scotchmen from the
    Orkneys
Who had come, as you put it, to rob your—Pierre
    Falcon's—
Country.

Well we were just about to unhorse
When we heard two of us give, give voice.
Two of our men cried, 'Hey ! Look back, look
    back !
      The Anglo-Sack
      Coming for to attack.'

Right away smartly we veered about
Galloping at them with a shout !
You know we did trap all, all those Grenadiers !
      They could not move
      Those horseless cavaliers.

Now we like honourable men did act,
Sent an ambassador—yes, in fact !
'Monsieur Governor ! Would you like to stay ?
      A moment spare—
      There's something we'd like to say.'

Governor, Governor, full of ire.
'Soldiers !' he cries, 'Fire ! Fire !'
So they fire the first and their muskets roar !

They almost kill
Our ambassador!

JAMES
REANEY

Governor thought himself a king.
He wished an iron rod to swing.
Like a lofty lord he tries to act.
    Bad luck, old chap!
    A bit too hard you whacked!

When we went galloping, galloping by
Governor thought that he would try
For to chase and frighten us Bois-Brûlés.
    Catastrophe!
    Dead on the ground he lay.

Dead on the ground lots of grenadiers too.
Plenty of grenadiers, a whole slew.
We've almost stamped out his whole army
    Of so many
    Five or four left there be.

You should have seen those Englishmen—
Bois-Brûlés chasing them, chasing them.
From bluff to bluff they stumbled that day
    While the Bois-Brûlés
    Shouted 'Hurray!'

To the Avon River
Above Stratford, Canada

What did the Indians call you?
For you do not flow
With English accents.
I hardly know
What I should call you
    Because before
I drank coffee or tea
    I drank you
    With my cupped hands

And you did not taste English to me

JAMES
REANEY

And you did not taste English to me
    And you do not sound
    Like Avon
    Or swans & bards
But rather like the sad wild fowl
    In prints drawn
    By Audubon
And like dear bad poets
    Who wrote
    Early in Canada
And never were of note.
You are the first river
    I crossed
And like the first whirlwind
    The first rainbow
    First snow, first
    Falling star I saw,
You, for other rivers are my law.
    These other rivers :
    The Red & the Thames
    Are never so sweet
To skate upon, swim in
    Or for baptism of sin.
    Silver and light
The sentence of your voice,
    With a soprano
Continuous cry you shall
    Always flow
    Through my heart.
The rain and the snow of my mind
Shall supply the spring of that river
    Forever.
Though not your name
Your coat of arms I know
    And motto :
A shield of reeds and cresses
    Sedges, crayfishes
The hermaphroditic leech

Minnows, muskrats and farmers' geese
And printed above this shield
One of my earliest wishes
'To flow like you.'

JAMES
REANEY

PHYLLIS
GOTLIEB
b. 1926

This One's On Me

1. The lives and times of Oedipus and Elektra
   began with bloodgrim lust and dark carnality
   but I was born next to the Neilson's factory
   where every piece is different, and that's how I
       got
   my individuality.

2. I lived on Gladstone Avenue,
   2 locations on Kingston Rd
   2 crescents, Tennis and Chaplin
   Xanadu, Timbuktu,
   Samarkand & Ampersand
   and many another exotic locality.

3. My grandparents came from the ghettos
   of Russia and Poland with no mementos
   one grandfather was a furrier, one a tailor,
   grey men in dark rooms tick tack to
   gether dry snuffy seams of fur and fibre
   my father managed a theatre

4. which one day (childhood reminiscence
       indicated) passing
   on a Sunday ride, we found
   the burglar alarm was ring
   alingaling
   out jumped my father and ran for the front
       door

Uncle Louie ran for the back
siren scream down the cartrack Danforth
and churchbells ding dong ding
(ting a ling)
and brakescreech whooee
six fat squadcars filled with the finest
of the force of our fair city
brass button boot refulgent
and in their plainclothes too
greysuit felthat and flat black footed
and arrested Uncle Louie

Oh what a brannigan
what a brouhaha
while Mother and Aunt Gittel and me
sat in the car and shivered
delicious
ly

because a mouse bit through a wire.

5. For some the dance of the sugar-plum fairies
   means that.
   but the Gryphons and Gorgons of my dreams
   dance in the salon of Miss Peregrine Peers
   stony eyed, stone footed on Church Street
   up grey stairs
   where two doors down at Dr Weams I
   gnawed his smoky fingers and followed
   the convolutions of his twisted septum
   as he stretched and knotted little twines of
      silver
   on the rack of my oral cavity
   and all the while Miss Peregrine Peers
   tum tiddy tum tiddy TUM TUM TUM
   O Peregrine O Miss Peers
   I find you no longer in life's directories

may you rest in peace
and I do mean

6. Where, oh where are the lovely ladies who
      taught me
   to break the
   Hearts And trample the *Flowers* of the muses?
                              Mrs Reeves
   gracile, a willow on a Chinese plate, who
   winced with an indrawn gasp when I struck a
      wrong
   note, or blew my nose in her handkerchief
   absentmindedly?
   Miss Marll, under whose tutelage icecubes
   popped from the pores of my arm
   pits and slid down to drop from my
   ELBOWS HELD HIGH FINGERS CURVED ON THE
      KEYS
   may you rot in hell
   subtly, Miss Marll.

7. O child of the thirties
   of stonewarm porches and spiraea snowfalls
   in print cotton dress with matching panties
      hanging well down
   (the faded snapshot says)
   hand on the fender of the Baby Austin
   (feel the heat and glare)
   gaptooth grin to be converted by braces
   myopic eyes fit for glasses
   and tin ears waiting to be bent
   by the patient inexorable piano teacher
   the postered car advertises in innocence:
   LADIES OF LEISURE
   See it at the Eastwood Theatre, friends,
   next time 1930 rolls around.

DAVID
KNIGHT

b. 1926

'When the Students Resisted, a Minor Clash Ensued'

Students, like students, form and fly.
Cops are like cops. Tear-gas and I
Met twenty years ago; today
We circulate along the way
Without acknowledging ourselves.
The students' books are on the shelves.
The owners, like a single beast,
Rustle their feet, and are policed.
Typewriters, windows, hopes and heads
Are broken. Some are in their beds.
The rest have nothing left to do
But laugh, and can't quite do it. Who
Am I, to bring my children here
And ask for mail, beside this fear?
For this is fear, this silent rage
That turns them to another age
Than undergraduate. Myself?
One of the books upon the shelf,
One of the reasons uniforms
March in tight shuffle and small swarms
And do a kind of baby drill :
Police who do not shoot to kill,
Police who hit and run awry
And panic in the sun — and I,
Who have as yet taught none of these,
Am still one reason why they seize
Anger and fear, and outrage, and,
So orderly, get out of hand.
I and the tear-gas do not meet.
I am a tourist on their street,
I and my children. Still, they guess

There must be one thing I profess   DAVID
As a professor : truth — so I   KNIGHT
Am smiled upon and let go by,
A petty talisman, to find
A smell of tear-gas in the mind
And ghost of it upon the street
(For students ran here in the heat,
Heart-sick, half-scared, one-quarter-glad,
Pursued by what the helmets had :
The right, in law, to go too far).
I close the windows of the car.
Is there a truth for me to name,
Since truth is a professor's game ?
Should I back up, and just get out,
And show I have, besides my doubt,
Courage to stand, and stare, and see ?
The undergraduates, not me,
Are here at bay with liberty.
Respect, and prudence, and the rules
For loving such a crop of fools
Mean that I turn the car again
And leave the students to be men.

The Chief of the West, Darkling

A high-speed metal snake switches its tail
Down all the angles of the road; multiple-fanged,
Multiple-eyed at night, it sweeps, thrown, bowled,
(Greased curving lightning) down the road,
    suddenly,
In a bending carnival invisible tunnel of air,
Sucked headlong forwards by vacuum, travelling,
    oh travelling,
Swift segmented serpent : don't touch ! don't pass !
    Glass-clear
Water-bright staccato blue-sapphire interrupted
    light
Flicks jewelled air, a hysterical star, travelling,

Oh travelling, traceless: don't pass! Fast, fast, the DAVID
   snake   KNIGHT
Streaking from unremembered curved basking ease
Somewhere, some garden somewhere, doesn't
   matter where . . .
To be protected, go fast, flicker the blue light, run
The rolled footless tormented unhunted swift
Unable-ever-to-rest tenanted trainlike convoy
Of limousines on a road at night, with a manned
   brain:
Has it a hole? a house? Hide, root fangs; hide.
   And hide
The tick-tock, tell-tale trick-time God-I'm-afraid
   blue
(Cops!) overspeed metronome miraculous blue
   (look!) light
Chipping the mechanical night (long snake-rear
   tire-sung
Horn-voiced bright whine: I'm scared, I'm tired):
   anything to say,
Bright black snake, road-driven? 'Don't pass?
   don't touch? *Noli me tangere?*'
Not you, not here, not in the night, not in the
   wild-eyed, car-stared
Road-swung (nobody pass!) clear God's-night:
   convoy, convoy,
Convoy: rib guards rib guards head guards tail
   belly-plates
Flicker-tongue fang eyes cop-light! stored stomach
   brain
Soul?
     And may God remember the rivers of Eden's
Slow silver meandering snake-tracks out — and
   then this:
So smooth-fast bead-strung-sliding. The road's
   home!
Only the road's home: home free! Run, slip, slide,
   scurry,

Twist winding, hurry! carrier of the blue light   DAVID
Hyphening night-time, road-time, danger-time.   KNIGHT
    And the stopped towns
Stop, look, light, listen, measure, and know. So.
    Go, cars,
Illusion of a trafficked black unimaginable damned
    quick beast
Driven, propelled, sucked vacuum-seeking and
    stopless,
Fleeing from a garden no part of your generation
(Time or begetting) was ever part of : go on.
Nothing stops you, nor can you stop. All the full
Mouthfuls of dark air are your own shed dry skins.
You are broken : in the perfect image the snake
    is hooped,
Motionless, and in pursuit, and with its enemy
    known, forever.

Ibadan, Nigeria
10 Jan. 1965

In Memoriam S. L. Akintola
January 15, 1966

Who shot the snake? beat it to death on the road?
Ran over it (or whatever happened)? because the
    snake's
        Dead, in a wild cock-crow.
Who killed the snake? People in their worst
    clothes
Dance, sing, wave ripped-down palm-leaves, and
    threaten
        Others, and the cocks crow.
Have they looked at a dead snake lately? all that
    tense grey
Striving against softness? that taut knot suddenly
    dropped?
        They are like cocks crowing
Dunghill-high, scruffy feather-proud scurriers.
The snake's dead, all his scale-proud chill patterned
    malice

Broken for the flies and vultures. Shout with the
    roosters.
Dance and wave yellowed palm-fronds : the snake
    won't bite.
        Clash palms, shriek cock-crow . . .
The venom of the snake bites asphalt through
    smashed skin.
And the scraggly roosters square to their own
    battles
        In rank envious cock-crow
As the always part-dead palm-tops batter in wind
And the crowing humans caper palm-forested.
        Before the cock crows
Three times, you will deny anything, any
    knowledge.
The snake killed, glistened, tyrannized, struck, and
    died,
        In a wild cock-crow,
In the morning, and this day belongs to the dignity
Of the reptile, for the roads are free of him. He is
    dead.

The Palms

This is what is was like? God on a donkey,
In a white robe, with choirs of pastel people
Modulating hosannas in clean clothes,
With a brocade of palms, a frieze of palms
Waving stately hello, a carpet-pattern
Of palms in reverence on a spotless road :
The decorous discipline of the parade? No?
I have seen it.
        The palms were every different colour,
And half of them weren't palms at all : pawpaw,
Flame-tree, anything with a leaf and a long stick,
The palm-leaves tattered, discoloured, bruised,
    broken, grabbed

To be whips, cudgels, fly-swatters, noisemakers.   DAVID
Decorum? they dance, their feet stamp, they shout   KNIGHT
    drums.
The eye-whites burn: 'Hosanna!' Voices break
    loose.
Branches lash: banners of insult, fronds like
    placards,
Bodies for road-blocks.
      Deep in the foundered traffic
In the sleeve of mob, one man comes face-to-face
With a smooth-barked shattered piece of young
    tree-trunk,
And that's a palm: three leaves on a gaunt stem
Stick out of it: 'Hosanna!' And he can't cry.
And the arms spread into gripping hands, and the
    torso
Hunches, and the balls of the feet spring fidgety
Far apart, and the three leaves quiver in jerks,
Hefted one-handed. And the praise-cry roars,
    challenging.
God on a donkey? No, he wasn't here,
Nor did they cry for him. They cried for politics,
Vengeance, and triumph, and a righteous cleansing
    army.
'Minding true things by what their mockeries be?'

But the other was this way too . . .

PHYLLIS
  WEBB

b. 1927

Propositions

I could divide a leaf
and give you half.

Or I could search for two leaves
sending you one.

Or I could walk to the river
and look across

and seeing you there,
or not there,

absence or presence,
would spring the balance to my day.

Or I could directly find you and take your hand
so that one hand would be given

and one kept, like a split leaf
or like two leaves separate.

These would be signs and offerings :
the just passion, just encountering.

Or we perhaps could speed four eyes,
the chariot horses of our dreams and visions,

in them direction and decision find.
The split leaf floating on the river,

the hand sketching in the air
a half-moon, its hidden wholeness there.

'The Time of Man'

Extrapolations from an article by
DR LOREN EISELEY

'The little toe is attractive

    to the student of rudimentary
and vanishing organs,'

and whooping cranes claxon

    to the spellbound preservers
of what would naturally vanish.

When the adored ones

    pass through the door ('the future
of no invention can be guaranteed')

who does not follow them,

half in love with his tears,
tickled by the lower brain,
    'the fossil remnant',
        claws

    scratching at the large
        symbolic order,
animal sad, watching the members
        fade :

    clitoral love, the royal we
        stumbling :

'The perfectly adjusted perish with their
    environment'

        —then take me with you
            crying
                take me with you—

The brain when it began to grow

    was 'shielded by a shell of bone
as thick as a warrior's helmet'.

Poetics Against the Angel of Death

I am sorry to speak of death again
(some say I'll have a long life)
but last night Wordsworth's 'Prelude'
suddenly made sense—I mean the measure,
the elevated tone, the attitude
of private Man speaking to public men.
Last night I thought I would not wake again
but now with this June morning I run ragged to
    elude
The Great Iambic Pentameter
who is the Hound of Heaven in our stress
because I want to die
writing Haiku
or, better,
long lines, clean and syllabic as knotted bamboo.
    Yes!

Rien à manger
la main de l'oiseau de satin
porte sa récolte aux limites du rivage
sa récolte et son nid
dans l'espace le plus libre qui soit

envolée innocente
d'une main porte-bonheur
à travers la grande mer de l'air

je vois d'ici
le feu dans la chair du fruit

feu bleu comme des flèches suspendues
aux crochets des îles de vapeur
feu comme du pain dans la bouche
de ceux qui ont le pouvoir de se nourrir
à même les champs du ciel

    moi
    je reste
    à l'intérieur de ma porte de verre
    seul
    avec les quelques bouchées de nacre chaude
    laissées au hasard
    sur la grève mouvante

le jeu du plus humble de ces vieux
c'est moi qui l'ai joué
en silence
je suis revenu à mon pieu coutumier
pour dormir alentour
de mon tapis battu

    Fidèle
    on m'appelle Fidèle
    parce que j'ai le teint vert dit-on
    d'une petite bête dressée
    dans sa serre de plomb

Géographie du labeur quotidien

JEAN-PAUL
FILION

à chaque jour
mes bras largement appuyés sur une île

une île-ville immense
avec son bleu son blanc son noir
ses rivières en colliers
et tous ses lamentables îlots

à chaque jour
mon visage parallèle aux chemins de terre et de
    fer
aux ponts comme des bandages
sur l'eau glauque de mes heures affreusement
    tendues

à chaque jour
le cri de l'aube à tous les détenus de la raison
    commune
il faut plonger
plonger passer son corps
de la falaise à l'eau brune de poussière
son corps enlisé embastillé emmuselé
submergé par la force du Pain Tout-Puissant
et meurtri par la force de sa propre impuissance

ici le corps sert le pain
comme un sacristain le Monseigneur

le pain
ce pauvre petit dieu orgueilleux
couronné d'amertume
enfariné de douleur
et gagné par simple amour des siens

le cri de l'aube
il faut plonger
il faut suer
il faut pétrir
pétrir l'argile d'un monde qui n'est pas au monde
pétrir le ciel
pétrir l'enfer

à chaque jour JEAN-PAUL
ma tête lourdement renversée sur une île FILION
  stérile
j'ai voulu reculer la mer
en dressant les ports de la survivance
les quais comme des dents d'engrenage
les bateaux comme des maillons d'espérance

au premier voyage sur le bel océan du repos
mes doigts suivront minutieusement
chacune des veines de la grève
mes doigts comme des bâillons
sur les bruits sourds de la mort délaissée

Feu contre fer

comme dans un courant d'air
j'avançai mon corps jusque dans les caveaux de
  la ville
mon corps et mes désirs promenés
dans la nuit
comme un troupeau sans abri

les femmes ne m'ont montré que le fer de leur
  chair
et la roche de leurs faux yeux
m'ayant frappé au visage
à la tempe je sentis battre le feu
le feu de la guerre
et du sang et de la rage

autour de moi les hommes
comme de vieux enfants suppliants
avaient soif de bière
de rêve amer
et de froide lumière

GILLES
VIGNEAULT

b. 1928

Mon pays

Mon pays ce n'est pas un pays c'est l'hiver
Mon jardin ce n'est pas un jardin
          c'est la plaine
Mon chemin ce n'est pas un chemin
          c'est la neige
Mon pays ce n'est pas un pays c'est l'hiver

Dans la blanche cérémonie
Où la neige au vent se marie
Dans ce pays de poudrerie
Mon père a fait bâtir maison
Et je m'en vais être fidèle
À sa manière à son modèle
La chambre d'amis sera telle
Qu'on viendra des autres saisons
Pour se bâtir à côté d'elle

Mon pays ce n'est pas un pays c'est l'hiver
Mon refrain ce n'est pas un refrain
          c'est rafale
Ma maison ce n'est pas ma maison
          c'est froidure
Mon pays ce n'est pas un pays c'est l'hiver

De mon grand pays solitaire
Je crie avant que de me taire
À tous les hommes de la terre
Ma maison c'est votre maison
Entre mes quatre murs de glace
Je mets mon temps et mon espace
A préparer le feu la place
Pour les humains de l'horizon
Et les humains sont de ma race

Mon pays ce n'est pas un pays c'est l'hiver

GILLES
VIGNEAUL

Mon jardin ce n'est pas un jardin
                    c'est la plaine
Mon chemin ce n'est pas un chemin
                    c'est la neige
Mon pays ce n'est pas un pays c'est l'hiver.

Mon pays ce n'est pas un pays c'est l'envers
D'un pays qui n'était ni pays ni patrie
Ma chanson ce n'est pas ma chanson
                    c'est ma vie
C'est pour toi que je veux posséder
                    mes hivers . . .

Chanson

J'ai fait mon ciel d'un nuage
Et ma forêt d'un roseau.
J'ai fait mon plus long voyage
Sur une herbe d'un ruisseau.

D'un peu de ciment : la ville.
D'une flaque d'eau : la mer.
D'un caillou, j'ai fait mon île;
D'un glaçon, j'ai fait l'hiver.

Et chacun de vos silences
Est un adieu sans retour,
Un moment d'indifférence
Toute une peine d'amour.

C'est ainsi que lorsque j'ose
Offrir à votre beauté
Une rose, en cette rose
Sont tous les jardins d'été.

Quelqu'un était ici

GILLES
VIGNEAULT

Quelqu'un était ici.
Quelqu'un s'en est allé
Pour chercher un pays
Dont nul n'avait parlé.

En buvant de la bière,
Il s'en est souvenu,
Puis il a disparu
Par le chemin de pierre.

S'il passe à votre porte
Dites-lui que naguère
J'ai perdu de la sorte

Une île et deux rivières
A poursuivre ces terres
Que l'horizon transporte.

PAUL-MARIE
LAPOINTE

b. 1929

Arbres

j'écris arbre
arbre d'orbe en cône et de sève en lumière
racines de la pluie et du beau temps   terre
    animée

pins blancs   pins argentés   pins rouges et gris
pins durs à bois lourd   pins à feuilles tordues
potirons et baliveaux
pins résineux   chétifs et des rochers   pins du lord
    pins aux tendres pores   pins roulés dans leur
    neige   traversent les années   mâts fiers voiles
    tendues   sans remords et sans larmes

équipages armés
pins des calmes armoires et des maisons pauvres
bois de table et de lit
bois d'avirons de dormants et de poutres   portant
le pain des hommes dans tes paumes carrées
cèdres de l'est   thuyas et balais   cèdres blancs
bras polis   cyprès jaunes   aiguilles
couturières
emportées   genévriers cèdres rouges   cèdres
bardeaux parfumeurs   coffres des fiançailles
lambris des chaleurs
genévrier qui tient le plomb des alphabets

épinettes grises   noires   blanches   épinettes de
savane
clouées

épinette breuvage d'été   piano   droit   tambour
fougueux

sapins blancs   sapins rouges   concolores et
gracieux
sapins grandissimes   sapins de Babel coiffeurs
des saisons   pilotis des villes fantasques
locomotives gercées   toit des mines
sapin   bougie des enfances

conifères d'abondance espèces hérissées crêtes
vertes des matinaux   scaphandriers du vent
conifères dons quichottes sans monture sinon
la montagne   clairons droits foudroyant le
ciel
conifères   flammes pétrifiées   vertes brûlantes
gelées de feu   conifères
arêtes de poissons verticaux dévorés par l'oiseau

j'écris arbre
arbre pour l'arbre

bouleau   merisier jaune et ondé   bouleau
      flexible
      acajou sucré   bouleau   merisier odorant
      rouge   bouleau rameau de couleuvre
         feuille-
      engrenage vidé   bouleau cambrioleur à
         feuilles
      de peuplier   passe les bras dans les cages du
      temps   captant l'oiseau captant le vent

bouleau à l'écorce fendant l'eau des fleuves
bouleau fontinal   fontaine d'hiver   jet figé
      bouleau des parquets   cheminée du soir
      galbe des tours et des bals
albatros dormeur

aubier entre chien et loup
aubier de l'aube aux fanaux

j'écris arbre
arbre pour le thorax et ses feuilles
arbre pour la fougère d'un soldat mort   sa
         mémoire
      de calcaire et l'oiseau qui s'en échappe avec
      un cri

arbre
peuplier   faux-tremble   trembleur à grands crocs
      peuplier-loup   griffon troubleur   arracheur
      immobile de mousse et de terre   peuplier
         feuilles
      étroites   peuplier au front bas   peuplier
      ligne droite cheval séché œillères rances
peuplier baumier   embaumeur des larmes
         peuplier
      aux lances-bourgeons   peuplier fruit de
         coton
      ouates désintéressés   langues de chattes
         pattes
      d'oiselle rachitique   peuplier allumettes

PAUL-MARIE
LAPOINTE

coupe-vent des forêts   garde-corps et
    tonnelier
    charbon blanc des hivers

arbre

arbre pour l'arbre et le Huron
arbre pour le chasseur et la hache
arbre pour la sirène et le blé   le cargo le cheval

noyers circassiens masseurs d'azur   noyers à noix
    longues   noyers gris   noyers tendres
      noyers
    noyade heureuse   minéraux éclairés par le
    centre   fabricants de boules   noyers goélette
    aérée   noyers eaux-fortes

saule écorce amère   saule aux rameaux grêles
    cassants
    comme paroles en l'air graine-coq à aigrette et
    paon fugace   saules noirs   saules à feuilles de
    pêcher   saules à feuilles mortelles   saules
      blancs
    fragiles et pleureurs   pendeloques des morts

caryer ovale noir amer   caryer écailleux   caryer à
    noix piquées au vif   caryer des pourseaux
      noix
    douces   caryer sportif cible élastique

charme bois dur   bois de fer   narcisse plongeur
    humide   égoïste à la plainte suffoquée

aunes   vernes   aunes à bourrelets   rameaux
poilus
    tortues décapitées   raies échouées   aune
      fragile
    aux clous   aune émailleur ébéniste   aune à
    feuilles minces   aune verrerie profonde
      aune
    crispé   lisse   antennes arrachées à l'insecte

arbre

l'arbre est clou et croix
croix de rail et de papier
croix de construction   d'épée   de fusil
croix de bombardier   téléphone   haut-fourneau
    sémaphore
croix d'aluminium et de néon
croix de gratte-ciel et de chien   de torture et de
    faim

chênes musclés   chiens gendarmes chevaux
chênes
    aux gros fruits   photographes et tournesols
    têtes franciscaines chênes-fruits blancs ou
    bicolores   selon le délire ou rien
blanc frisé ou bleu   chêne prin à la coque polic
    chinquapin mosaïque

chêne boréal   tronc labours d'automne   chêne
    écarlate   chêne-baiser   chêne des marais
        fusant
    au sud
constructeur   transport de soif   bloc habitable
    tan des cuirs et des plages

hêtres brous ouverts   faines épousailles à plumes
châtaignier   marronnier fruiteur aux envols de
    drapés à stries
hêtres filtreurs de vinaigre   fûts à liqueur

j'écris arbre
arbre   bois de loutre et d'ourson
bois de femme et de renard

cerisiers noirs   cerisiers d'octobre à l'année
        longue
    cerisiers merisiers petits   cerisiers à grappes et
    sauvages   cerisiers à confiture   cerisiers
        bouche
    capiteuse et fruits bruns   mamelons des
        amantes

chicots   gymnoclades   fèviers   palettes au
      pinceau
      picoreur

vinaigrier beau feuillage   vinaigrier   sumac du
      sable et de la pierre

aune à trois feuilles   frère du houblon

orme   acier timide   bois lumineux   orme
      utilitaire
      orme aux feuilles d'œuf   scies grugeuses de
      vent   orme fauve   orme roux   orme liège
      arme indécise   arme de cidre et de faiblesse

rosacées
hanches et mousse

cerisiers   pruniers   aubépines
sorbiers
pommetiers nains et sauvages   grisailleurs à
      crachats
      fleuris   fillettes à la misère amoureuse

décorateur   magnolias   tulipier   sassafras
      roi-mage
      caravanier d'aromates   encensoir
      savonnier

hamamélis coupant le sang des blessures

sorbier des oiseaux   cormier   mascous amers et
      polaires tirant l'amant vers le baiser

pommier croqueur

j'écris arbre   animaux tendres   sauvages
      domestiques

frênes gras   frênes à feuilles de sureau
tilleul tisane de minuit

érables à épis   parachuteurs d'ailes et samares
érable barré   bois d'orignal   nourriture d'été

PAUL-MARIE
LAPOINTE

fidèle au gibier traqué dans les murs et la
    fougère
érable à feu   érable argenté   veines bleues dans le
    front des filles
érables à feuilles de frêne   aunes-buis qui poussent
    comme rire et naissent à la course
érable à sucre   érable source

sureau bleu   alouette   sifflet dans les doigts

arbres

les arbres sont couronnés d'enfants
tiennent chauds leurs nids
sont chargés de farine

dans leur ombre la faim sommeille
et le sourire multiplie ses feuilles

ROLAND
GIGUERE

b. 1929

Vivre mieux

La lumière avait su me prendre
en plein délire
les yeux droits dans les miroirs
les mains au cœur du torrent

je détournai de moi
les palmes noires que l'on m'offrait
je quittai pour toujours
les routes jalonnées de feux morts
pour d'autres routes plus larges
où mon sang confondait le ciel
comme une flèche confond sa cible

je commençai à vivre mieux.

Mémoire d'ombre

ROLAND
GIGUERE

Ombre et mémoire illusoire
l'amer des jours sans feu
en pays déserté
en forêt muette
en présence inoubliable d'aigles repus

ombre et mémoire des demeures
hautes en plaisir
capitales en amour
aux portes mêmes de la douleur

ombre et mémoire d'avant l'ombre
quand l'aube se multipliait avec nous
sur la pente d'un avenir transparent
quand la tour la carène l'émeraude et la mouette
étaient de verre

ombre et mémoire du désir
d'une voix sans mots au cœur de la furie
de l'écho des mers dans les palais
du sang précieux des pierres
libre de toute alliance
d'or rose
et libre

ombre et mémoire idéale
pour les rêves d'Aline nue
au lit de cristal

ombre et mémoire d'ailleurs
au lieu-dit l'Étang-Noir
où naguère ton visage embrasait
les chemins de sombres fougères

ombre et mémoire polaire
en ces jours de givre sur nos lèvres
pour sceller un silence parfait
sans secret
sans regret.

La Vie dévisagée

ROLAND
GIGUERE

(I)

Le matin se lève
les yeux cernés d'une nuit blanche
petit matin sans aube matin décapité
et figé dans l'orbite ce paysage de bitume
coup de grisou dans la cervelle grisée

l'homme s'engouffre dans son obscur tunnel
quotidiennement il s'enfourne
se remet à vaciller de paupière en paupière
à louvoyer d'une heure à l'autre jusqu'à la lune
louvoie louvoie sans rien voir que la tombée du
    soir
aux mains de la vorace nuit

(II)

Traces de boue traces atroces traces de loups
ceux qui ne savent pas jouer ruinent tout

les grands défigurés s'avancent
dans un infernal et habituel nuage de cendre
tristes habitués des ténèbres
habitants des noirs cratères
où le feu n'a plus rien de sa magie
feu sans joie sans flamme et sans dieux

longs visages de pierre ponce
mains d'ardoise friable
visages de pierre tombale où vous rompez le pain
visages sans tain
ne reflètent plus rien

(III)

On s'enferme dans les silos
mêlés aux derniers épis de blé
on engrange la révolte de l'amour

pendant que d'autres tricotent des mailles de
    chaînes
pendant que d'autres préparent des mois de haine

de temps en temps un couteau dans l'aine
de temps en temps dis-moi que tu m'aimes

(IV)

Il nous faut sans cesse tenir l'équilibre
entre l'horizon disparu et l'horizon imaginé
avec la crainte de perdre pied à la terre
de n'avoir plus le pied marin
de ne pouvoir plus marcher sur les fils de fer
de ne savoir plus marcher sur les mains

malheureux fils d'équilibristes
nés en plein ciel
au temps mémorable de l'absence des filets

(v)

Le vertige nous prend par la taille et nous renverse
nous tournons autour des tiges
pendant que nos mains tissent les minces fils de
    l'espoir
qui nous retiendront à la vie

lianes lianes d'espoir lianes
léger fil d'Ariane

(VI)

Il faudra dérouler les rails de la patience
prendre le jour par la main et lui montrer le
    chemin
qui mène aux hommes chancelants sur les bords
    de la nuit

le souffle trop longtemps contenu nous défigure

la vie face aux murs prend figure de défaite
s'il n'y a dans quelque fissure l'apparence d'un
    espoir
l'espoir de l'amour l'espoir de la liberté
l'espoir qu'un jour nous vivrons tous pour aimer.

ROLAND
GIGUÈRE

Roses et ronces

À DENISE

Rosace rosace les roses
roule mon cœur au flanc de la falaise
la plus dure paroi de la vie s'écroule
et du haut des minarets jaillissent
les cris blancs et aigus des sinistrés

du plus rouge au plus noir feu d'artifice
se ferment les plus beaux yeux du monde

rosace les roses les roses et les ronces
et mille et mille épines
dans la main où la perle se pose

une couronne d'épines où l'oiseau se repose
les ailes repliées sur le souvenir d'un nid bien fait

la douceur envolée n'a laissé derrière elle
qu'un long ruban de velours déchiré

rosace rosace les roses
les jours où le feu rampait sous la cendre
pour venir s'éteindre au pied du lit
offrant sa dernière étoile pour une lueur d'amour
le temps de s'étreindre
et la dernière chaleur déjà s'évanouissait
sous nos yeux inutiles

la nuit se raidissait dure jusqu'à l'aube

rosace les roses les roses et les ronces
le cœur bat comme une porte

que plus rien ne retient dans ses gonds
et passent librement tous les malheurs
connus et inconnus
ceux que l'on n'attendait plus
ceux que l'on avait oubliés reviennent
en paquets de petites aiguilles volantes
un court instant de bonheur égaré
des miettes de pain des oiseaux morts de faim
une fine neige comme un gant pour voiler la main
et le vent le vent fou le vent sans fin balaie
balaie tout sauf une mare de boue
qui toujours est là et nous dévisage

c'est la ruine la ruine à notre image

nous n'avons plus de ressemblance
qu'avec ces galets battus ces racines tordues
fracassés par une armée de vagues qui se ruent
la crête blanche et l'écume aux lèvres

rosace les ronces !

rosace les roses les roses et les ronces
les rouges et les noires les roses les roses
les roseaux les rameaux les ronces
les rameaux les roseaux les roses
sous les manteaux sous les marteaux sous les
    barreaux
l'eau bleue l'eau morte l'aurore et le sang des
    garrots

rosace les roses les roses et les ronces
et cent mille épines !

roule mon cœur dans la poussière de minerai
l'étain le cuivre l'acier l'amiante le mica
petits yeux de mica de l'amante d'acier trempé
    jusqu'à l'os
petits yeux de mica cristallisés dans une eau salée
de lame de fond et de larmes de feu
pour un simple regard humain trop humain

rosace les roses les roses et les ronces ROLAND
GIGUERE
il y avait sur cette terre tant de choses fragiles
tant de choses qu'il ne fallait pas briser
pour y croire et pour y boire
fontaine aussi pure aussi claire que l'eau
fontaine maintenant si noire que l'eau est absente

rosace les ronces
ce printemps de glace dans les artères
ce printemps n'en est pas un
et quelle couleur aura donc le court visage de
    l'été?

Histoire naturelle

(I)
La mer est seule ce soir et broie du noir
si seule et si vide qu'elle tiendrait toute entière
dans un miroir de femme du monde

(II)
la lune se couche amoureuse et se lève veuve
dans un lit d'étoiles orphelines

(III)
le paysage souffre au plus profond de sa verdure
l'épée oubliée entre l'arbre et l'écorce
le fruit au centre de la blessure

(IV)
dans les jardins suspendus une parade de feu
l'éclair en tête célèbre l'arrivée de la cendre
on met aux fleurs des couronnes de braise
qu'elles portent comme des reines

(V)
mais c'est le volcan qui s'éveille
et le volcan crache mille soleils
qui retombent dans mille champs déserts

(VI)
au cercle polaire c'est la ronde des banquises
en robes d'hermine et cols à paillettes
autour d'un igloo en flammes
les grands glaciers ont l'œil terne en ce jour de
     fête

(VII)
les îles partent vers de nouveaux archipels
et derrière les îles viennent de jeunes oasis
avec leur eau précieuse et leurs palmiers d'ombre

(VIII)
le désert laissé à lui-même se noie dans ses sables
devenu inutile l'horizon sombre dans une douce
     folie
et multiplie ses mirages :
caravanes d'enfants et villes désuètes
corbeilles d'amants et proches planètes

(IX)
le fleuve majestueux dans la défaite
refait ses vagues et fait l'amour au lit
comme aux plus beaux jours de sa jeunesse
il faut mourir chez soi quand on n'a pas de linceul
dit la rivière en se renversant

(X)
dans le ciel rouge une main bouge.

D. G.
JONES

b. 1929

I Thought There Were Limits

I thought there were limits, Newtonian
Laws of emotion—

I thought there were limits to this falling away,
This emptiness. I was wrong.

The apples, falling, never hit the ground.

So much for grass, and animals—
Nothing remains,
No sure foundation on the rock. The cat

Drifts, or simply dissolves.

L'homme moyen sensuel
had better look out : complete
Deprivation brings

Dreams, hallucinations which reveal
The sound and fury of machines
Working on nothing—which explains

God's creation : *ex nihilo fecit.*

Wrong again. I now suspect
The limit is the sea itself,
The limitless.

So, neither swim nor float. Relax.
The void is not so bleak.

Conclude : desire is but an ache,
An absence. It creates
A dream of limits

And it grows in gravity as that takes shape.

The Perishing Bird

D. G.
JONES

The mind is not
Its own place
Except in Hell.

It must adjust, even
When the place is known.

Only time
Will tell the mind
What to think,

What birds to place
On what boughs :

The catbird
Crying, 'Me, me'
In a dry, hot bush,

At night the owl
Crying, 'Who?'
In a distant wood.

All else
Is an infernal shade

Where family trees
Gather their antique
Nightingales

And the ill will
Flowers in the leaves.

For Hell's the Lord's
Bijouterie,
A Byzantine world

Where the clock-work birds
And the golden bees
Eternally repeat

What the heart once felt,
What the mind conceived.

For the mind in time
Is a perishing bird,
It sings and is still.

It comes and goes like the butterflies
Who visit the hill.

The cries of the children come on the wind
And are gone. The wild bees come,
And the clouds.

And the mind is not
A place at all,
But a harmony of now,

The necessary angel, slapping
Flies in its own sweat.

Cocking its head to the wind
It cries,
'Who me? Who me?'

And whatever the answer,
It forgets.

It is radiant night
Where time begets
The sun, the flowers, Naniboozoo's gift—

Mosquitoes,
Who disturb my sleep—
And everything else.

Soliloquy to Absent Friends

D. G.
JONES

Our best days are now a winter sky
White with coruscations of the clouds,
A mirror of the logos, flared
And cracked across our lives.

(I)

The chimney of my neighbour's house
        stands naked now—the locust,
        only, keeps its withered leaves
        to rust against the stone;
my neighbour's walls look meaner now; his yard
grows ragged as a field of weeds . . .

        The cowherd, summer, is deceased
and all the pasture gates are down—
the fields run empty with the wind.

                      Micheline,
the winds dissolve our towns; the streets
where once we played, bound each to each, even
in solitude to others yet unknown,
        twist like mirrors in the twisting wind
        and are dissolved.

                      Micheline,
the world is a leafless wood; we stare
abruptly upon tundra and the sky—
        soul's frontiers where we meet,
          knowing ourselves only
          capacities for loneliness,
          solitudes wherein the barrens sound.

(II)

It does not take courage, Quixote,
to slaughter windmills in a windy world
or to tilt against entrepreneurs.
        It is waste of breath
to criticize vast corporations.

The difficult thing   D. G.
        is to sit still   JONES
        like a child in the yard
while the whole bleak catastrophe of winter
descends like a glacier into the soul.

        So much depends
        upon
        a red wheel
        barrow
        glazed with rain
        water
        beside the white
        chickens

or a broken basket of clothespins
slowly filling with snow.

(III)
It is to love these hopeless things . . .
                                or not at all.
A world of handy gadgets, of heavy equipment,
puts no weight in the heart; the nerves,
frayed like wiring in the world's exchange,
are replaceable parts. Quixote, only your hands,
their unproductive gestures on the air, *welcome*
or *goodbye*, root us in the vast
silence, the abyss where elsewise all things drift,
a rain of fragments falling into death.
                It is to find
        in a foreign city your peculiar voice
        speaking the earnest, measured lines :

So this world of forms, having no scope for
    eternity,
                is created
In the limitation of what would be complete and
                perfect,
Achieving virtue only
            by the justness of its compromises.

But the abyss is infinite; it can be spanned   D. G.
only by these hopeless things, 'My friend's new   JONES
   poem,'
'these kind letters . . . which have come by post.'

(IV)
The light lowers across the winter hills
In the Duke of Berry's *Book of Hours*,
And the magpies feeding by the fold
Drop sounds like barley in the muted yard.
Beyond the haystack capped with snow,
The little wood where the axeman fells a tree,
A drover trails his donkey with a load
Of firewood, small protection from the cold
Which falls about the distant village roofs
And in the east has cast a greenish glow
On the dissolving hills. No distance, no abyss,
Between the Duke of Berry and his book,
Between the reader and the Duke's last breath,
No individual presentiment of death, yawns
   whiter
Than the stretch of snow that patient ass
Plods beneath the failing light—field and hill,
The land which summer yielded to the plough
Lies alien and naked in the winter light,
Which veils like a translucent film of ice
The cosmic waters in whose depths at last
The stars depart. The sheep huddle in the fold;
A servant huddles in her clothes as after chores
She hurries toward an open door; inside
Three other women sit along a bench,
Skirts hoisted to their thighs, and legs
Spread like lovers' to the open fire.
Behind them in the room stands one great bed.
Above, within an arc of midnight blue,
Half the zodiac takes its lettered way.
There Pisces in the form of two large pike
And Aquarius pouring water from a ewer

Belie the frozen universe below. Grown old,
Helios in his mediaeval van, his horses winged
With light, drives into the ocean foam;
The sun is in his hand and in its light
Two human figures are engaged, Ares
And Aphrodite, it may be, two human gods
Whose clandestine or whose brazen ways betray
Still Hephaestus at his forge, and wage,
Summer or winter, their impassioned war.
And so bound round is the abyss,
The winter void, by battle and by labour and by
     love,
By homely comfort that will warm the thighs,
That in the Duke of Berry's *Book of Hours*
You and I, and old Quixote, Micheline,
And men and women whom we never knew,
And others still whom we will never know,
May find one bed together against cold.

(v)
The last pure leaves
          struggle in the autumn wind;
hosts have fallen, mulching the ground—
would that all the seasons of the soul
expired beneath so rich a shroud.

          Yet more to be admired—the clear
structures of the trees, patient for winter, hold
bleak converse with themselves.
               Let us be bare,
               Let us be poor,
          such poverty makes honest souls,
          and solitude is capital for love.
Out of that silent contemplation of the trees,
          amid the vast candour of the snows,
          rich in loneliness, will come
drenched in sunlight, as from empty seas,
myriad wings and leaves—as though our tongues
grew green with language and informed a world.

Beautiful Creatures Brief as These

D. G.
JONES

FOR JAY MACPHERSON

Like butterflies but lately come
From long cocoons of summer
These little girls start back to school
To swarm the sidewalks, playing-fields,
And litter air with colour.

So slight they look within their clothes,
Their dresses looser than the Sulphur's wings,
It seems that even if the wind alone
Were not to break them in the lofty trees,
They could not bear the weight of *things*.

And yet they cry into the morning air
And hang from railings upside down
And laugh, as though the world were theirs
And all its buildings, trees, and stones
Were toys, were gifts of a benignant sun.

PETER
DALE
SCOTT

b. 1929

Argenteuil County

'Shall horses run upon the rock? Will one plow
   there with oxen?' Amos vi. 12

Freely the dead bracken breaks to your stride
Now that at last the birds and leaves have gone,
Smells of wet granite stay in the mildewed wood,
The tabernacle of the sumac's torch,
Extinct, throws its frail shadow on the
   groundfrost.

Through the thick bush I trace a fieldstone wall   PETER DALE
And line of cedar rails, now rich with lichen,   SCOTT
To a log cabin, smelling of animal,
Scored with the weathered names of the sleeping
    hunters,
A farmhouse once : the dying apple-tree's
Three shrivelled winesaps, cankered and gone wild
But sweet, delay me through the years;
The drop-jawed mailbox with its Biblical name,
Inspired by the wind, discourses like a skull.

The stones these settlers thought to use for fences
Lay in these valleys heavier than their wishes.

And this is Shrewsbury : two dirt roads meet,
A whitewashed church shines in its little parish
Of fenced-in lawn.
I think, *It's Sunday*, and I seem to see
A horse, a buckboard, and a clergyman
Come out of the east —

                    He speaks. *God sent you, boy.*
Here, hitch my horse, you'll find some oats in the
    sack.
City-helpless, holding in my hands
These nervous reins, I feel how strange we all
Become in this land of improbable encounter
Not even the horse belongs to.

He opens his doors out, and will somewhat loudly
Harangue the township : *Brethren, by His love*
A vine was planted in the wilderness
Of human strivings, and the boughs thereof
Were comely, and the voice of praise was heard.
But now, O parents, look to your tender fruit.
The fox is among you, and your sons go down
Into the smoke of Mammon and are lonely.
While we let Papists (here his tired lips purse)
Buy out this land which was our fathers'
    birthright.

Let us pray. It's cold. His anger breaks off oddly   PETER DALE
Spent on one father and his sixty-five-year-old son   SCOTT
Who've driven up from Lachute in their Chevrolet
To keep ceremony.

A rain begins in the marsh. They drive me to town
Through the tall choirs of maples, which have
   witnessed
This old settler tote out when a boy
One hundredweight of potash fifty miles.
His uncle was Bear Morrison, acclaimed
In Palmer's *Tales of Argenteuil County*,
Who with his gun-butt fought and killed a bear.
To farm here took hard liquor. Now they say
That through the streets of Shrewsbury they've
   seen
Stretching from the church to beyond the hill
Three hundred buckboards at an Orange gala
The whole night through.

We progress. The son keeps talking. *Now the*
   Province
Has brought in electricity, keeps the roads open
In winter, more roads than we broke ourselves
In the old days, though there's not six farms left
From here to Morin Heights. My only boy
Sharecrops in California. There's more to be had
On relief there, than ploughing with a team
In this boulderdrift. Nevertheless I tell you
A man was happy scything his own field
Or raising barns for neighbours. Dances, wakes,
We fixed for ourselves, took turns at the reeveship,
And lived by customs we could call our own.
Now we just come up to the farm on Sundays
To see all's well, and maybe in the spring
Cut us a little lilac.

On the way to town   PETER DALE
We passed a dozen cars bringing out deer.   SCOTT
In the gloomy resonance of rain and shooting
I thought of his forebears and their vanished music
And stared at the windshield-wiper's weary sweep
Against the dusky rainlight turning to snow
As our lamps traversed a desolate beaver meadow,
Labrador tea, dead elms, and two scared eyes.

The Loon's Egg

On the eighth day, the rain stopped before dusk
Letting in sun. We canoed again at last.
The trip ruined, we could stop where we liked,
And picked, from the shadow of a tiny island
Like a ship going under, this loon's egg.
Its oval rested in our aching hand,
Turned amid chaos with a strange precision:
An orb, turned inside out, like an astrolabe
Of dimly remembered mists and galaxies
Sepiaed on dull blue. Dull, white within,
It had been broken into. Perhaps a snake
Lubric as night, had wound within its toils
These mottled stars, then with its wily bite
Had let in the catastrophic light,
As if this loon not to be hatched were Time,
And we Time's infants, the grey dust within
This ghostless orrery within our hand.

No trail came near. The jagged waterline
Unchanged in that water since the glaciers,
Rain, snow, wind safely cherishing what we
Could crush in an instant by mistake. O yes
Talk was strange there, letting in contagion;
Yet we listened to it as if we were miles away
Or years. Nor can I tell you, using words

Furbished from savage industry and war,   PETER DALE
Why this inky egg-tint we have no legend for   SCOTT
Rests in my memory as if innate,
Vast, and secular. Is this the universe,
A shell, love's broken O, a voided beauty
The lover dare not look inside? The stones
Were almost worn away; the three short pines
Looked stunted in its formal presence; while the
Berries in the moss and outcrop were
Blue and sweet, as any in Ouareau Township.

> If you cross over from the narrow high
> end of Lake Antostigan (itself
> two days in) where there is some
> maple that was never cut, and wade down
> six miles of creek which is mostly mud and
>   alders
> so dense even the aerial maps have missed
>   them,
> and then, below the cliffs, more like a
> staircase the canoe is handed down
> since the high portages were never cut
> and the rest blown over in the hurricane
> before the war (you could, I suppose,
> come up the other way, with ropes
> around the falls, if you were mad enough)

You will stand above our fireplace and, like us
Seven years ago, perhaps will break off speech,
Kneel, and look down upon
This broken relic of a mottled world
We cannot really know, how hard we try,
Yet carry in the hollow of our heart:
The loon's egg

HENRY
BEISSEL

b. 1929

From *New Wings for Icarus*

PART II

In the one-two domestic goose one-two one-two
   step
of our left-right modern one-two times one-two
we march left-right singing one-two
onward left-right christian soldiers
lift up your one-two hearts and legs
and rifles up up up cocked and down
with the foe we kill for chrissake one-two
hallelujah we're on the move again
left-right one-two New Jerusalem
is just left-right around the corner
we are all brothers big brothers
serving one-two time in battle dress
we must all stick together one-two
god-fearing left-right law-abiding
swelling together our ranks and numbers
swelling our pride swelling our purse
swelling breasts buttocks bellies
one-two one-two one-two swollen privates
pick 'em up, brother, up up up
pride of disney- and mother-
land up to his knees left-right
in bible blood and imperial oil
recruit one-nine-eight-four
defender of the new left-right
faith in international business
machines, brave for the new one-two
world of baptized walkie-talkies
left-right of course there is always
one-two the human one-two element
cream of emotion faith tranquilizer

HENRY
BEISSEL

hope salts charity pills love shots
don't hug that gun like a girl, man
one-two left-right one-two the girl
one-two who loves one-two
a soldier one-two is part one-two
of the grand cavalcade : it all adds up
to nineteenhundredandeightyfour
answers to a single question
what d'hell you think this is —
  a fuckin' funeral parade?
quick march left-right one-two one-two
threeandahalf die every two seconds
ten are born every three seconds
twohundred ejaculations per minute on target
to say nothing of the intercepted ones
over sixthousand burials per hour
ebb and tide of semen and sand
on the bluff shores of time
which way to turn for escape?
abooout face! one-two one-two
nineteenhundredandeightyfour
questions and a single answer
the old man's army is the best goddam
  fightin' machine there is, get it?
triumph of left-right law and one-two order
of the jungle of mathematics—regimental
orders regimental colours regimental
prayers *in nomine patriae*
one-two left-right *et ficti* . . .

And we stand, helmet in hand, wondering
How to pray, waiting for something
To be written on the blank pages of our minds,
Waiting for words to put to the music
We hear faintly in the stillness inside us.
This is no time for prayer or song.
Over the roar of a million machines
Over the blare of a billion explosions

You won't be heard, even assuming
There were anyone to hear. But the birds
On the windswept boughs of their little lives
Know better, know the worm under the grass,
The cold of winter and the duel of love,
And everything is occasion for song.
Pythagoras took the cosmic music-box
To pieces and found all things at intervals
In space and their measure in time music.
Because music declares the design of creation
I would have us sing, words or no words,
Out in the streets of New York, down
By the docks of London, up on the hills
Of Rome, hurl the golden sphere of our song
Into the iron teeth of that ubiquitous monster
With its tongue and eye and brain wired
To the plastic buttons on a million chromium-
    plated breasts—
And that would be prayer enough.

One-two one-two left-right
where d'you think you're goin', buster
we don't know where we're going
until we're there
earthbound astronauts moonbound
prepared to do or die
going left-right in circles
masked and one-two caged
going to visit one-two left-right
Venus Mars Jupiter
dead gods in orbit
going to bury them?
or resurrect them?
No-one's in the know
going because one-two
we must be going left-right
once we are on the go
only who has eyes to be blinded

cannot see left-right one-two
the object is immaterial
we're on the road to anywhere
sicut eritis Christ! a pack of dogs
that's what you are
pick 'em up one-two one-two
or I'll have you on your bloody hands
and knees one-two left-right
onwards upwards downwards
we never say die
though the birds have long known
that we are not at home in the air
the fish have watched us drown often
enough and a child learns about fire
remains the earth
to which all must return
the earth remains

JEAN-
GUY
PILON

b.1930

L'Étranger d'ici

Il était d'un pays de corsaires dévots
Où l'on prenait l'inconscience pour le dogme
L'imbécile pour le maître
Le malade pour le voyant

C'était un pays de luttes inutiles
Et de ruines magnifiques
Un pays rongé par la vermine

Quand il a voulu crier sa rage
On ne le lui a pas permis

C'est à peine si on l'a laissé mourir

Les Cloîtres de l'été . . .

JEAN-GUY
PILON

Refuge de brûlant silence
Présence du vent seul au delà des hauts murs
Au centre de la nuit qui s'attarde
Pour une prière abandonnée
Là grandissent les inquiétants remords
Mais c'est l'été partout
Sur le corps de la bien-aimée
Au principe des jours ouverts
Et des conspirations de bonheur

Mis à nu et pressuré
Et mordu et déchiré
Mon cœur
Trop habile à partager
Écrasé sous la charité de la dernière justice

J'ai refusé le lent acheminement
De la poussière
Pour traverser les jours comme un nageur

O lendemain
C'est le seul désir de mes bras impatients
O cendre de cristal lourde de rester
O cloître

Imaginaires frontières de la transparence
Fortes de ma seule foi
Faibles de toute cette brûlure
Amassée en moi par tant de regards en feu
Sous la nudité de la noire absence

Solitude d'ombres et d'aube
Solitude des villes insouciantes
Des maisons désertes des chambres secrètes
Toujours sans répit sans oubli
L'éclair entre nous de l'invisible négation
Comme une épée encombrante

Cloîtres escales sur la mouvance des jours   JEAN-GUY
Ô patience ô navrance   PILON
Larmes généreuses
Espoirs vides d'espérance

Mais j'entendrai ces mélodies promises
Je passerai ce seuil interdit
Pour dresser contre le ciel reconquis
L'acte nu de ma persistance
Pour élever à bout de souffle
L'offrande lourde du pèlerin
Rouge veine de vie
Dans le sanctuaire du cloître oublié

'Je murmure le nom de mon pays'

Je murmure le nom de mon pays
Comme un secret obscène
Ou une plaie cachée
Sur mon âme
Et je ne sais plus
Le provenance des vents
Le dessin des frontières
Ni l'amorce des villes

Mais je sais le nom des camarades
Je sais la désespérance de leur cœur
Et la lente macération
De leur vengeance accumulée

Nous sommes frères dans l'humiliation
Des années et des sourires
Nous avons été complices
Dans le silence
Dans la peur
Dans la détresse
Mais nous commençons à naître

À nos paroles mutuelles
À nos horizons distincts
À nos greniers
Et nos héritages

Oui
Nous sommes nus
Devant ce pays
Mais il y a en nous
Tant de paroles amères
Qui ont été notre pâture
Qu'au fond de l'humiliation
Nous allons retrouver la joie
Après la haine
Et le goût de laver à notre tour
Notre dure jeunesse
Dans un fleuve ouvert au jour
Dont on ne connaît pas encore
Les rives innombrables

Nous avons eu honte de nous
Nous avons des haut-le-cœur
Nous avons pitié de nous

Mais l'enfer des élégants esclaves
S'achèvera un jour de soleil et de grand vent

Je le dis comme je l'espère
Je le dis parce que j'ai le désir de mon pays
Parce qu'il faut comprendre
La vertu des paroles retenues

Aurions-nous seulement le droit
De serrer dans nos bras
Nos fragiles enfants
Si nous allions les ensevelir
Dans ces dédales sournois
Où la mort est la récompense
Au bout du chemin et de la misère

Aurions-nous seulement le droit
De prétendre aimer ce pays
Si nous n'en assumions pas
Ses aubes et ses crépuscules
Ses lenteurs et ses gaucheries
Ses appels de fleuves et de montagnes

Et la longue patience
Des mots et des morts
Deviendra parole
Deviendra fleur et fleuve
Deviendra salut

Un matin comme un enfant
À la fin d'un trop long voyage
Nous ouvrirons des bras nouveaux
Sur une terre habitable
Sans avoir honte d'en dire le nom
Qui ne sera plus murmuré
Mais proclamé

JEAN-GUY
PILON

FERNAND
OUELLETTE

b. 1930

Femme

Ferme tes yeux
        femme
            en l'éclair de pollen.

Par l'espace déportée
une étoile quitte
          la profondeur triste
et sourd en ton rêve.

S'illumine l'épais de notre chair
comme un pays d'oiseaux
           le long de l'aube.

Ô la forêt de sons sur ton silence. Ô
le talon rouge le genou de lune la cuisse
qu'épurent les flammes de muguet.

Amour fait chant avec l'infini,
amour aux larmes de lilas et de braise.

Notre corps lourd de fruits
                    et d'éclats d'éternité
glisse dans l'horizon en famine.

Géologie

À JEAN

Ô le tremblement du corps,
quand la vie trop vive et blonde
buta contre mort,
                    la mate,
l'espace de glaise.

Peu à peu
            les poreuses,
les paumes noircies à frapper le silence,
se sont remplies de blanc,
de jour à jet de blé.

L'air connut alors
                    ce cri à naître
qui soudain fulmine
                    et fend la pierre
comme un ange.

Le sang doucement
                    aima la chair.

Et les membres montèrent
                        en plein matin,
à perte de feuilles et d'oiselles.

Le soleil se hissait à l'homme.

Langue de l'aile

FERNAND
OUELLETT[

À MARC CHAGALL

Ange ! ange on te songe dans la forte invasion de
l'air sur la mort,

À l'échelle de continents que lent gravit le vent
jusqu'au gîte du miel;

Car l'atterrissage d'un ciel à nos lèvres se prépare.

Et sur terre, par un air de guitare, nos artères
prolongent les gratte-ciel,

Nos alphabets mûrissent sur des toits qui montent.

Attention aux éclats de cœur, aux chansons qui
mordent au cœur de minuit :

L'œil, la main, mille rites de langue exorcisent le
sang.

Attention dans les rues aux sons d'étoile qui
meurt,

Aux glaïeuls debout dans l'incendie du béton :

Car se taisent nos membres à la plainte qui chante
lumière.

SYLVAIN
GARNEAU
1930–1953

Mon École

J'ai quatre bons amis, quatre rois fainéants.
Leurs fronts sont boucliers abritant mille rôles.
Ils dorment, à midi, du sommeil des géants,
Sur le bord des trottoirs, à l'ombre des écoles.

Comme les chats rétifs qui chassent dans les cours,
Ils voient, dans les buissons, des jungles éternelles;
Leurs ongles aiguisés claquent sur les tambours
Et le message va de poubelle en poubelle.

Leurs châteaux, malheureux derrière la cité,
Ont des carreaux brisés; et dans chaque fontaine
Croissent des nénuphars, au soleil de l'été;
Tandis que les gardiens s'en vont avec les reines.

Pendant ce temps, on voit sauter sur les trottoirs
Les enfants du quartier, légers comme des bulles;
Mais demain il pleuvra et, dans leurs yeux trop
     noirs,
Sous leurs fronts obstinés et doux comme le tulle,

Les châteaux d'autrefois, les princes, les géants,
Reviendront, pour danser au son des barcarolles.
Les enfants du quartier sont des rois fainéants
Qui dorment, allongés sur les bancs des écoles.

Le Jeu

SYLVAIN
GARNEAU

J'ai nagé jusqu'à l'autre rive
Pour y chercher des jeux nouveaux.
Je n'ai trouvé qu'un nid de grives
Caché à l'ombre d'un ormeau.

J'ai marché le long de la rive
Pour y chercher des cailloux bleus.
J'ai trouvé quatre sources vives
Et j'ai recommencé le jeu.

J'ai traversé le marécage
Pour faire des tresses d'osier.
Les poissons parmi les herbages
Me prenaient pour un échassier.

Au soleil couchant, quatre grues
Ont essayé de m'entraîner.
J'aimais leurs mines incongrues
Mais je voulais m'en retourner.

Voilà qu'on me prête main-forte.
Ils étaient douze sur le bord.
J'avais les jambes comme mortes.
Ils m'ont ramené vers le nord.

J'ai raconté ce long voyage
Le même soir à mes voisins.
Ils ne m'ont pas cru. C'est dommage.
C'est dommage pour mes cousins

Qui sont si fiers de leur famille
Mais qui ont si peur de leurs fous.
Et tant pis pour la belle fille.
On devait se marier, en août.

Demain matin, sur l'autre rive,
J'irai recommencer le jeu.
Ceux qui n'ont pas peur, qu'ils me suivent
Ça fera moins de malheureux.

La bonne entente

SYLVAIN
GARNEAU

Il fait un temps si triste,
Il fait un temps si gris,
Que Jean, le pauvre artiste,
Et Pierre, qui écrit,
Que Françoise qui chante
Et Jacques, le doreur,
Et Paul, son amante,
Et Paule, peintre d'horreur,
Sont partis sur la route,
Sans parler, sans chanter,
Et sans casser la croûte,
Et sans se consulter.

Ami, si tu rencontres,
Au hasard du chemin,
Ces visages qui montrent
La peur du lendemain,
Ami, si tu les croises,
Pierre et son ami Jean,
Jacques, Jeanne ou Françoise,
Ce sont de braves gens,
Fais-leur un doux sourire.
Ami, si tu les vois,
Dis-leur : je vous admire
Et je suis triste, moi ...

Il fait un temps si triste,
Il fait un temps si gris,
Que Luc, le guitariste,
Et Lou, qui le nourrit,
Et Louis 'la bonne entente'
Et Lucien 'le menteur'
Et Lise que tourmente
Augustin, le relieur,
Sont partis sur la route,
Sans parler, sans chanter,

Et sans casser la croûte,
Et sans se consulter.

Ami, si tu t'ennuies,
Va-t-en sur les chemins.
Si tu aimes la pluie,
N'attends pas à demain.
Ces gens qui se promènent,
Tu les connais, pourtant.
Ne leur fais pas de peine
Et tu seras content.
Si le soleil se lève,
Ils feront des chansons
Qu'ils iront dans tes rêves
Chanter à l'unisson.

**GATIEN
LAPOINTE**

b. 1931

Au Ras de la terre

Assez du ciel du sable et des mots sans défaut
Assez de l'illusion qui me voilait les yeux

Montrez-moi le monde violent et très beau
Montrez-moi l'homme apprenant la souffrance
Et la froideur de la nuit qui l'abrite
Et l'âpreté du soleil sur sa nuque
Et la rude espérance et la haute justice
Et la patiente fidélité de la terre

Montrez-moi l'homme généreux et maladroit
Modelant son visage mot à mot
Mêlant plaisirs et tourments rêve et souvenirs
Les fleurs de son amour et l'honneur de l'aurore

Montrez-moi l'homme apprivoisant son cœur
Rosée après désert repos après fatigue

Et toute l'odeur des racines dans sa bouche
Et toute la sève de l'arbre dans ses veines
Et toutes les saisons et toutes les forêts
Marchant à pas de chevaux dans sa chair

GATIEN
LAPOINTE

Montrez-moi l'homme sur le seuil de sa maison
Faisant monter d'une caresse de la main
La musique puissante et tendre de la terre
L'étoile verte et souple à gauche de la femme

Montrez-moi l'homme baptisant dans l'eau
Allumant dans la plaine un feu familier
Montrez-moi l'homme partageant l'huile et le pain
La lumière du jour et l'outil quotidien

Montrez-moi aussi l'homme en proie au doute
Cherchant une vérité d'homme
Dans les battements de son sang
Cherchant dans l'arbre divisé son cœur jumeau

Montrez-moi une image de l'homme très jeune
Plantant son corps dans l'espace et le temps
Animant un paysage à sa taille
Montrez-moi cet homme de mon pays

Alors je répondrai du destin qui m'habite.

Le Temps premier

Qui terminera ton visage ô terre
Quel mot quel mouvement hors de la chair

Je connais les grilles de mon amour
J'ai nommé les sept jours de ma maison
Ma main rampe sur les rives du feu
Ma main rapatrie la mûre saison

J'imagine les plans de la première route
La mer commence un soir à gauche de mon cœur
Nous avions rêvé un présent immortel
Bateaux renversés désarmés
Quelle neige pourrit le songe dans ma bouche

Quelle aurore attacha l'horizon à mes doigts

GATIEN
LAPOINTE

Je reviens sur le seuil de mon enfance
J'accompagne à pied le retour du soleil
Un souffle pur remplit ma phrase
Je reconnais le salut d'un grand fleuve
Et l'arbre tenant debout toute la forêt

Ô abritez-moi mouvante contradiction
J'apprends la douleur nécessaire
Le feu noue en moi ses algues jumelles
Et les quatre vents germent sur ma tempe

Beauté inachevée terrestre voyage
Brûle mon corps pour que le temps revienne !

From *Ode au Saint-Laurent*

Et je situerai l'homme où naît mon harmonie

Ma langue est d'Amérique
Je suis né de ce paysage
J'ai pris souffle dans le limon du fleuve
Je suis la terre et je suis la parole
Le soleil se lève à la plante de mes pieds
Le soleil s'endort sous ma tête
Mes bras sont deux océans le long de mon corps
Le monde entier vient frapper à mes flancs

J'entends le monde battre dans mon sang

Je creuse des images dans la terre
Je cherche une ressemblance première

Mon enfance est celle d'un arbre
Neiges et pluies pénètrent mes épaules
Humus et germes montent dans mes veines
Je suis mémoire je suis avenir
J'ai arraché au ciel la clarté de mes yeux
J'ai ouvert mes paumes aux quatre vents
Je prends règne sur les saisons
Mes sens sont des lampes perçant la nuit

Je surprendrai debout le jour naissant

GATIEN
LAPOINTE

Une hirondelle s'agrippe à ma tempe gauche
Je pressai dans ma main le clair présage

Ô que je m'embarque sur la mer verte et bleue
Ô que je saisisse les reflets qui m'aveuglent
Le temps dispersé en mille figures
Le mot prisonnier de la chair
L'accord caché au fond du sang
L'infini de l'univers et du cœur
La solitude sans fin de chaque être
Trouverai-je le secret de ma vie

Trouverai-je un jour l'événement qui commence

Être homme est déjà une tragédie
Et j'ai pleuré en découvrant le monde

J'ai allumé un feu sur la haute clairière
Je suis descendu dans l'aine des sources
Le parfum du sol me frappe au visage
La femme aux hanches brillantes d'aurore
L'homme à genoux inventant Dieu
Je suivrai la marche du fleuve
Je connais ensemble hier et demain
Et c'est aujourd'hui qu'il me faut construire

Je découvre ma première blessure
Je plante dans le sol ma première espérance

Espace et temps ô très charnelle phrase

Toutes les routes dans une même figure
L'instant et toute l'année en un pas

Je regarde au plus profond de la terre

C'est de l'homme désormais qu'il s'agit
C'est dans ce pays que j'habiterai

.   .   .

Quelle est cette tige à cinq branches
Jetée en travers de mon corps
Est-ce une main profonde et fluide
Est-ce l'ombre tremblante d'un oiseau
Quels sont ces cinq Grands Lacs
Flottant comme de grandes fleurs sur ma poitrine
Fleuve dont les flots m'entraînent m'enchaînent
J'apprendrai la phrase âpre et belle de tes rives

GATIEN
LAPOINTE

Ta bouche est le début de la mer
J'entrevois une très longue patience

Le cœur plein d'énigmes je rêve d'un ciel pur

Ma langue est une feuille en pleine terre
Je dis tout ce qui éclôt sur la terre
J'inventorie et j'évalue je nomme et j'offre
J'investis la journée de l'homme
J'ouvre des routes je jette des ponts
Je prends des images de chaque événement
J'invente un paysage pour chaque âge
Je taille chaque chose selon sa fonction

Je m'assure d'un souvenir charnel

Donnerai-je visage à tout ce qui existe
Sauverai-je chaque instant de la chair

Solitaire et habité d'amour
J'unis la bouche au flanc qui frissonne
J'unis l'arbre à la terre étonnée
Je mène à leurs noces tous les désirs
Mon pas enflamme chaque saison
Mon souffle agrandit chaque demeure
Et la mer ondule au large de ma main
La mer remplit toute ma main

Je ne laisse rien dans la nuit
Chaque peine chaque plaisir recommencent
    ma vie

Je dresse sur la terre un image de l'homme

GATIEN
LAPOINTE

Ma bouche est une double cicatrice
Un double horizon découpe mes yeux
Vulnérable on m'a jeté parmi les hasards
Mortel on m'a marqué d'éternité
Je ferai une échelle de mon corps
Et j'étendrai mes bras en largeur de la terre
Mon enfance est un sapin plein de neige
Mon enfance est un prisme dans l'espace

Le temps me donnera un visage durable
Aujourd'hui est un sentier à ras de sillons

Je frappe du poing la vivace énigme

La vieille nostalgie soulève mon talon
Je remonte le cours du temps
Je parle d'un commencement du monde
L'ombre et la lumière s'emmêlent sur mon front
Je trace les grandes lignes du cœur
Je refais le premier jour de la vie
Multiple et nouveau dans l'instant
Je cours au cri de ma naissance

J'ai dans mon cœur une grande souffrance

Ô flamme d'un mot dans ma bouche
Éclair au large de mon sang

Je m'enveloppe dans la chaleur de la terre
Je creuse le frisson de chaque chose
Je veux savoir je veux me rappeler
Je donne parole à tout ce qui vit
Je donne confiance je donne élan
Je caresse et j'éveille
Je descends sur la langue chaude et verte du fleuve
Ma face reflète le paysage entier

J'imagine tout ce qui peut être sauvé

Je vis dans le présent   GATIEN
Mes souvenirs m'entraînent   LAPOINTE

Je suis un mot qui fait son chemin dans la terre
Chaque aube me réveille au bord de mon enfance
Un air de printemps me met sur la route
Et la montagne monte au rythme de mon pied
Ma main est une aile guidant le feu
Ma main emporte le vif témoignage
Je trace un signe dans les yeux de la terre
Et c'est le ciel qui vient se blottir dans ma main

J'avance en suivant un reflet sur le fleuve
Je suis dans ma chair le frisson d'un arbre

Mon rêve prend racine dans le temps

Je me reconnaîtrai dans une image de la terre
Je creuse mon berceau et j'élève mon toit
Je dis la force d'une forêt reverdie
Je dis l'extrême faiblesse d'un grain qui germe
Je n'ai plus peur j'énumère mes songes
J'apprends à parler je vous reconnais
L'automne de mon pays est le plus beau de la terre
Octobre est un érable plein de songe et de passion

Ma maison fait face à tous les pays
Et toutes mes tables seront complètes

Je vous nomme et je vous invite

J'ai pris destin dans la marche du fleuve
Ma main s'ouvre comme un miroir
Je me figure le corps de femme d'une moisson
Et je confonds les fleurs avec l'aulne enneigé
Ici le printemps est un bref éclat de rire
Et l'automne un grand fruit qui joint les rives
L'hiver est une bête qui souffre et s'ennuie
Et l'été est un bonheur excessif

Arbres douloureux et pleins d'impatience
Nous faisons du givre et du feu d'un même souffle

Et c'est une même foudre qui nous abat

Le soleil nous cache notre plus grand secret
Et la nuit brûle toutes les étoiles de l'année
Janvier remplit nos premiers pas de neige
Et d'un seul flot avril efface notre enfance
Le jour la vase nous recouvre la figure
Et l'aile du soir souffle en nous toute lumière
Le désespoir s'éteint lentement dans nos mains
Et lentement pourrit la noce dans nos bouches

Mais qui a connu les combats de mon pays

A-t-on vu cet espace immense entre chaque
    maison
A-t-on vu dans nos yeux ce grand exil

Montrez-moi mes compagnons d'espérance
Ô mes mains de neige et de grand vent
Et ce ciel froid qui nous brûle le front
Et cette forêt vaste où s'égarent nos cris
Et ce pas aveugle des bêtes dans l'orage ·
Et ce signe incompréhensible des oiseaux
Comment l'homme pourrait-il vivre ici
Par quel mot prendrait-il possession de ce sol

La distance est trop grande entre chaque homme
Nous n'avons pas le temps de regarder la terre

Le froid nous oblige à courir

Mais a-t-on vu de près l'homme de mon pays
A-t-on vu ces milliers de lacs et de montagnes
Qui s'avancent à pas de bêtes dans ses paumes
A-t-on vu aussi dans ses yeux ce grand désert
Ici chacun marche sur des échasses
Nous existons dans un geste instinctif
Naîtrons-nous dans une parole
Quelles marées nous amèneront aux rives du
    monde

·   ·   ·

'Go take the World'

Go take the world my dearest wish
And blessing, little book.
And should one ask who's in the dish
Or how the beast was took,
Say : Wisdom is a silver fish
And Love a golden hook.

The Martyrs

The sexes waking, now separate and sore,
Enjoy conjunction not feasible before;
But never long enough, never near enough, nor
    yet
Find their death mortal, however deeply met.

Bound to cross purposes, transfixed with desire,
His raw heart unsheltered behind its broken wall,
The first martyr bleeds impaled upon the briar
Whose root is pleasure's spring, whose arms are
    sorrow's fall.

The woman meanwhile sits apart and weaves
Red rosy garlands to dress her joy and fear.
But all to no purpose; for petals and leaves
Fall everlastingly, and the small swords stand
    clear.

Hail Wedded Love!

JAY
MACPHERSON

Oh the many joys of a harlot's wedding,
Countless as the ticks that tumble in the bedding !
All knives are out and slicing fast,
The bread-oven goes with a furnace-blast,
Drink flows like sea-water, cock crows till dawn,
The children of Bedlam riot in the corn.

The nymphs of Bridewell leave their fountains
To come and dance on the blockish mountains,
The meadow shoots cuckoo-pint all over
And Venus-flytrap common as clover,
The goat-shagged fiddler with urgent bow
Drives on the measure of boot and toe,
The bridegroom woos, 'My bird, my cunny,
My jam, my pussy, my little pot of honey—'

Well, delight attend their pillow !
And I'll go seek a bending willow
To hang my silent harp upon
Beside the river of Babylon.

Leviathan

Now show thy joy, frolic in Angels' sight
Like Adam's elephant in fields of light.
There lamb and lion slumber in the shade,
Splendour and innocence together laid.

The Lord that made Leviathan made thee
Not good, not great, not beautiful, not free,
Not whole in love, not able to forget
The coming war, the battle still unmet.

But look : Creation shines, as that first day
When God's Leviathan went forth to play
Delightful from his hand. The brute flesh sleeps,
And speechless mercy all that sleeping keeps.

The Beauty of Job's Daughters

JAY
MACPHERSO

The old, the mad, the blind have fairest daughters.
Take Job: the beasts the accuser sends at evening
Shoulder his house and shake it; he's not there,
Attained in age to inwardness of daughters,
In all the land no women found so fair.

Angels and sons of God are nearest neighbours,
And even the accuser may repair
To walk with Job in pleasures of his daughters:
Wide shining rooms more warmly lit at evening,
Gardens beyond whose secrets scent the air.

Not wiles of men nor envy of the neighbours,
Riches of earth, nor what heaven holds more rare,
Can take from Job the beauty of his daughters,
The gardens in the rock, music at evening,
And cup so full that all who come must share.

Perhaps we passed them? it was late, or evening,
And surely those were desert stumps, not
  daughters,
In fact we doubt that they were ever there.
The old, the mad, the blind have fairest daughters.
In all the land no women found so fair.

The Third Eye

Of three eyes, I would still give two for one.
The third eye clouds: its light is nearly gone.
The two saw green, saw sky, saw people pass:
The third eye saw through order like a glass
To concentrate, refine and rarify
And make a Cosmos of miscellany.
Sight, world and all to save alive that one
Fading so fast! Ah love, its light is done.

342

The Boatman

JAY
MACPHERSON

You might suppose it easy
For a maker not too lazy
To convert the gentle reader to an Ark :
But it takes a willing pupil
To admit both gnat and camel
—Quite an eyeful, all the crew that must embark.

After me when comes the deluge
And you're looking round for refuge
From God's anger pouring down in gush and
    spout,
Then you take the tender creature
—You remember, that's the reader—
And you pull him through his navel inside out.

That's to get his beasts outside him,
For they've got to come aboard him,
As the best directions have it, two by two.
When you've taken all their tickets
And you've marched them through his sockets,
Let the tempest bust Creation : heed not you.

For you're riding high and mighty
In a gale that's pushing ninety
With a solid bottom under you—that's his.
Fellow flesh affords a rampart
And you've got along for comfort
All the world there ever shall be, was, and is.

The Ill Wind

JAY
MACPHERSON

To reply, in face of a bad season,
Pestilential cold, malignity,
To the ill wind weeping on my shoulder,
'Child, what have I to do with thee?'

Is to deny the infant head
And the voice complaining tirelessly:
'Is there room for one only under your cloak,
Mother, may I creep inside and see?
Did you not know my wicked will
When you summoned me?'

ALDEN
NOWLAN

b. 1933

God Sour the Milk of
the Knacking Wench

God sour the milk of the knacking wench;
   with razor and twine she comes,
to stanchion our blond and bucking bull,
   jerk out his lovely plumbs.

God shiver the prunes on her bark of chest
   who capons the prancing young,
let maggots befoul her alive in bed
   and dibble thorns in her tongue.

The Wickedness of Peter Shannon

ALDEN
NOWLAN

Peter had experienced the tight, nauseous desire
to be swallowed up by the earth, to have his blue
eyes plucked out of his fourteen-year-old head,
his arms sliced off, himself dismembered and the
remnants hidden forever, his shame was so
   unanswerable.
Oh, God, God, God, it was so he could take any
   part
of Nancy Lynn O'Mally and lie open-eyed and
   stark
in the darkness with it—her lilting backsides
in the candy-cane shorts—and bring his thighs
   together
like pliers, muttering, and it was like the taste
of peach ice cream and the smoke of leaves
   burning
and the wanton savagery of a pillow over his face,
breaking him, until he swung out over the
   seething
water and the limb went down and down and
   down and
the rain was a thousand horses urinating on the
fireproof shingles and he whispered . . . ohhhhhh,
Jesussss . . . mad as a turpentined colt among the
   rockpiles
in the north pasture; what are your breasts like
Nancy Lynn O'Mally, how is it that no matter
   how much
I'm ashamed I don't blush, except in company . . .
   my cheeks
burning as though Christ slapped them!

The Grove Beyond the Barley

ALDEN
NOWLAN

This grove is too secret: one thinks of murder.
Coming upon your white body (for as yet
I do not know you, therefore have no right
to speak of discovering
you, can address myself
to your body only) seeing the disorder
of your naked limbs, the arms outstretched
like one crucified, the legs bent like a runner's,
it took me less than a second to write a novel:
the husband in the black suit
worn at his wedding, the hired man
in his shirt the colour
of a rooster's comb and, in the end, you
thrown here like an axed colt.
Then I saw your breasts: they are not asleep,
move like the shadows of leaves
stirred by the wind. I hope you do not waken,
before I go; one who chooses
so dark a place
to lie naked
might cry out. The shadows quicken,
I wish you a lover,
dreams of sunlit meadows,
imagine myself a gentle satyr.

Stoney Ridge Dance Hall

ALDEN
NOWLAN

They don't like strangers.
So be careful how you smile.

Eight generations
of Hungerfords, McGards and Staceys
have lived on this ridge
like incestuous kings.
Their blood is so pure
it will not clot.

This is the only
country they know.
There are men here
who have never heard of Canada.

When they tire of dancing
they go down the road
and drink white lightning
out of the bung
of a molasses puncheon.

But they never forget
to strap on the knuckles
they've made from beer bottle
caps and leather

and there are sharp spikes
in their orange logging boots.

JOE
ROSENBLATT

b. 1933

Metamorpho I

Lately I've become religious about atoms
and this is how I've come to dig the element man,
Metamorpho, freak with a 103 personalities

        —the do-it-yourself chemistry set—
like
    ... 'don't get tough with me baby ... or I'll
  explode !'
grrrrr ... I'm hydrogen
        I'm hydrofluoric acid ... hssssss ..
I make pretty bubbles ... I react with zinc
            I'm a real base character
but Christ, NO ! I am not Prince Metamorpho, nor
  was meant to be,
ugly and priceless, working myself into an atomic
  warhead,
a gold brick, a platinum egg ... priceless ...

poets give off so much laughing gas, but not
  Metamorpho
who comes on in metal metaphors : aluminum,
  copper and cobalt;
chases his tail with a tungsten tool, losing atomic
  weight
and burning up like phosphorus
        before he flips his molecules
        into an osmium
           omelette

Saphire (*Metamorpho's Chick*)

JOE
ROSENBLATT

Saphire, you throw more curves
than serpents in a serpentarium;
you slide your sex
            like a snake
from Medusa township
            as you curl the question : matrimony,
before the ugly American . . . Metamorpho !
but he won't marry you
                not in his crazy chemical state . . .
who could love that titanium face ?
not his mother, that's for sure !
why he'd scare a grasshopper out of Kafka.
Lay off this element boy, this chemical creep,
think of the children, the ostracism . .
you're going to get burnt
he's going to turn into a Lucifer
and burn your lovely ass
            watch out baby
            don't push him too hard.
leave the freak alone
leave that gun zippered in his holster
don't play gang busters below the hips,
instead, play with your daddy's Japanese toys
            and not with the voltage.
what perversity !
            copulating with carbon dioxide
you're sick, my little flower, sick
but he's odourless
as he changes from a gas to a sickly skull again
it's enough to make an iodine bottle throw up
                its bones
He ain't human baby and that's a fact !

From *Les Pavés secs*

'Il était là'

Il était là
comme tout bon chat
son œil collé au mien
mon œil fixait le sien dans le mien

il partit boire un peu
il faisait chaud et sec
boire un peu ce qu'il pourrait trouver
il partit
laissa là son œil

mais sans son œil
il ne sut trouver de quoi boire
il faisait très chaud et très sec
il n'avait pas son œil
alors il revint
et ne put me quitter

'Dans le silence parfait'

Dans le silence parfait
des hommes du soir jouent au grillon
et d'un coin à l'autre des rues
se répondent en sifflant
une chansonnette se répercute
d'une bouche au mur et du mur
à une autre bouche
mais tout à coup le dernier vivant
n'a plus que son écho
et la chansonnette prend un air triste
un air de deuil
s'assied

reste là toute la nuit
en bonne chansonnette
elle attend qu'on la reprenne
demain matin
pour recommencer sa vie

JACQUES
GODBOUT

'*Elle est née*'

Elle est née
main dans la main
d'une fleur
Elle est née
fleur du désert
seule comme le pape
l'azur ne léchait pas sa porte
elle craignait l'eau
comme l'enfant le père
ou le loup-garou
Elle est née belle
comme elle-même
sans sève
sans sève sans battements
jusqu'à ce qu'un jardinier
il y a très peu de temps
verse le déluge
un nouveau déluge
une nouvelle arche nécessaire
pour une toute petite fleur
que j'ai mise sous verre

Parce que ton nom

JACQUES
GODBOUT

Les feuilles ne sont plus vertes elles sont or
Tu n'as plus de nom Tu ne t'appelles plus de ton
Nom
Tu es anonyme

Je n'ai plus de nom, anonyme, je suis anonyme

Dans ma main ton coude dort
Sur tes lèvres la sueur du matin
L'odeur des feuilles comme un courroux et
Les arbres comme des échasses tendues vers les
Vents chassés; plantées fichées en terre comme
Les bois de nos corps
L'odeur grise le son bleu des feuilles
Dans le matin tranquille

Les mouches se sont tues
Se taire
Nous venons de quelque part mais
Tout à l'heure nous serons d'ici

Les bagages sont faits
La chaleur ennoblit le lit
Tu n'as plus de nom

Je n'ai plus de nom

L'amour même n'est pas un mot;
Elles sont noires et connaissent   intimement   la
    chaleur
Laisse-les chanter elles sont pures et connaissent
intimement le bonheur   Laisse-les danser elles
sont belles et connaissent intimement la joie

Elles te connaissent aussi rappelle-toi

Rappelle-toi par delà les grilles la gare et la fumée
et les colis si lourds et l'ennui du conducteur qui
avait perdu sa maîtresse qui avait   perdu   ses
tickets qui avait perdu le goût   des   voyages

Rappelle-toi Fernand le barbu qui portait un
chapeau haut-de-forme et un   cœur-de-melon
qui courait dans le bruit
Nous n'aimions pas le bruit
Mais il est aussi difficile d'aimer dans le silence
    des fuites
Rappelle-toi

Je suis anonyme

Malgré les jours les petits-déjeuners mal rasés et
les glaces qui fondent dans le panier du triporteur
Malgré tes tresses noires mal nouées de petite fille
si seule tellement laide croyais-tu tellement triste
aussi affreuse aussi malgré tes cris de femme et tes
pleurs au théâtre je t'aime tu es anonyme

Je suis anonyme

Distincts et semblables
Homme et femme dans notre dignité
Qui ne sera jamais un vain mot relève la tête
Les feuilles aussi se relèveront
Qu'importe l'opéra !
Viens, la vie est rectiligne, une, droite, courte
droite comme le bois de pin

Me faut-il baiser tes yeux?

Derrière les grilles   des   citoyens   grimaçaient
comme poules en cage au son des fanfares;
anonymes non pas dans la foule
    (ce serait trop aisé)

Dans tes bras dans la chambre

Dans notre chambre quand ce ne serait pas nos
    draps
Nous sommes à bout d'espoir à bout de confiance
La vie est une droite si courte

Quand roulaient les wagons à quoi pensions-
    nous?

JACQUES
GODBOUT

Au hasard aux monts aux paysans
Aux prairies modern style   Je criais ton nom

Il faut remonter la pente si douce
À mon bras viens danser
Devant les juke-box
Nous nous salirons la face parce que
La propreté nous sied mal

Et que nous sommes mal à l'aise devant
Tant de glaces
Et d'images propres qui satisfont nos aînés

Dans une rivière harnachée chien jaune
Ventre gonflé
Ce souvenir en remplace d'autres

Ton souvenir ne m'est supportable et c'est toi
Tête nue contre les pierres jambes nues contre
Les murs

Anonyme comme la joie

C'est toi qui enseignera la géographie au soleil
Pour qu'il réchauffe les mers que
Nous avons choisies
Ici là maintenant lors
Après tant de détours pour éviter les sentiers
de la crainte

Ces Racines

JACQUES
GODBOUT

Les racines sont à rez de terre
Je les caresse
Et qui me payera l'impôt d'une tristesse ?
Elles rongent les créneaux bleus

Mousquets arcs canons-par-lesquels-je-vous-
    répondrai
Bleus bleus comme des yeux
Qui regardent sans hésiter le fruit défendu

Les racines sont à rez de terre
Faut-il les couper ?
Faut-il couper ces racines comme si elles étaient
de pissenlit pour en faire une salade amère faut-il
Les nommer sans les connaître
encore
Fermer les yeux et trébucher ?

Dans les rues de nos villes j'ai vu milliers
de racines soulever le pavé; nos villes sont si
neuves, le pavé tellement mince;
Les racines sont à rez de terre et continuent de
pousser

On en fera des pipes des pieds de lampe   des
hésitations du bois vernis des phrases polies à
l'usage d'écoliers distraits

Et ces amis qui disent : debout
Il nous faut marcher
Et puis je me suis assis
À quoi servent les symboles ?
Puis j'ai dormi
À quoi m'a servi le sommeil ?

À l'éveil peut être

Out of the Land of Heaven

FOR MARC CHAGALL

Out of the land of heaven,
Down comes the warm Sabbath sun
Into the spice-box of earth.
The Queen will make every Jew her lover.
    In a white silk coat
Our rabbi dances up the street,
Wearing our lawns like a green prayer-shawl,
Brandishing houses like silver flags.
    Behind him dance his pupils,
Dancing not so high
And chanting the rabbi's prayer,
But not so sweet.
    And who waits for him
On a throne at the end of the street
But the Sabbath Queen.
    Down go his hands
Into the spice-box of earth,
And there he finds the fragrant sun
For a wedding ring,
And draws her wedding-finger through.
    Now back down the street they go,
Dancing higher than the silver flags.
His pupils somewhere have found wives too,
And all are chanting the rabbi's song,
And leaping high in the perfumed air.
    Who calls him Rabbi?
Cart-horse and dogs call him Rabbi,
And he tells them:

The Queen makes every Jew her lover.
And gathering on their green lawns,
The people call him Rabbi,
And fill their mouths with good bread,
And his happy song.

The Genius

For you
I will be a ghetto jew
and dance
and put white stockings
on my twisted limbs
and poison wells
across the town

For you
I will be an apostate jew
and tell the Spanish priest
of the blood vow
in the Talmud
and where the bones
of the child are hid

For you
I will be a banker jew
and bring to ruin
a proud old hunting king
and end his line

For you
I will be a Broadway jew
and cry in theatres
for my mother
and sell bargain goods
beneath the counter

For you
I will be a doctor jew
and search
in all the garbage cans
for foreskins
to sew back again

For you
I will be a Dachau jew
and lie down in lime
with twisted limbs
and bloated pain
no mind can understand

The Only Tourist in Havana
Turns his Thoughts Homeward

Come, my brothers,
let us govern Canada,
let us find our serious heads,
let us dump asbestos on the White House,
let us make the French talk English,
    not only here but everywhere,
let us torture the Senate individually
    until they confess,
let us purge the New Party,
let us encourage the dark races
    so they'll be lenient
    when they take over,
let us make the CBC talk English,
let us all lean in one direction
    and float down
    to the coast of Florida,
let us have tourism,
let us flirt with the enemy,
let us smelt pig-iron in our backyards,
let us sell snow
    to under-developed nations,

(Is it true one of our national leaders LEONARD
COHEN
   was a Roman Catholic?)
let us terrorize Alaska,
let us unite
   Church and State,
let us not take it lying down,
let us have two Governor Generals
   at the same time,
let us have another official language,
let us determine what it will be,
let us give a Canada Council Fellowship
   to the most original suggestion,
let us teach sex in the home
   to parents,
let us threaten to join the U.S.A.
   and pull out at the last moment,
my brothers, come,
our serious heads are waiting for us somewhere
   like Gladstone bags abandoned
   after a coup d'état,
let us put them on very quickly,
let us maintain a stony silence
   on the St. Lawrence Seaway.

GEORGE
BOWERING

b. 1935

The Grass

I must tell you
of the brown grass
that has twenty times
this year, appeared
from under the
melting snow, reared
its version of spring
like a sea lion coming
out of water, a-dazzle
in the sun, this
brave grass the sun
will only burn again
returning like a tiny
season.

Moon Shadow

Last night the rainbow
round the moon

climbed with how sad steps
as I walked home

colour surrounding me
cloud around my head.

I am moon!
Arrows fly at me!

I slide cold & pale
over cold earth
of Alberta winter!

I show one face
to the world,
immaculate still,
inscrutable female
male animal ball
of rock
shining with borrowed light

rolling in that light
the other side of
forgetful space!

I am a shining tear
of the sun

full moon, silver,
who but myself knows
where the sun shall set?

I am able to instruct
the whole universe,

instruct the heart,
the weeping eye
of any single man.

Slide over the moon-
lit earth, a shadow
of a chariot.

      Walk homeward
forgetful where I have been

with how sad steps
my shadow before me

on the earth, moon shadow
rainbow round my heart,
wondering where in the universe I am.

GEORGE
BOWERING

Inside the Tulip

GEORGE
BOWERING

Inside the tulip
we make love
on closer look
seeing faint green lines, new

Let me share this flower
with you, kiss you
press my tongue on pollen
against the roof of my mouth

Look at me long enough
and I will be a flower
or wet blackberries dangling
from a dripping bush

Let me share you
with this flower, look
at anything long enough
and it is water

on a leaf, a petal
where we lie, bare legs together

Está muy caliente

On the highway
near San Juan del Río
we had to stop the car
for a funeral.

The whole town it was
a hundred people or
two hundred
walking slowly along the highway

toward the yellow domed church
on the top of the hill
and we pulled into the shade
of a shaggy tree.

GEORGE
BOWERING

I turned off the engine
and we heard their music
a screeching saxophone
and high broken noted trumpet

alone and sad in the hot afternoon
as they walked slow like sheep
the women with black shawls
the men in flappy trousers.

Every five minutes the men
threw cherry bombs into the air
behind them : loud gun shots
blasting the afternoon

then the saxophone : tin music
odd tortured jazz
in that mysterious Indian Christian march
up the hill : bearing a coffin to the priest.

It was a small coffin
on the shoulder of one man in front
        the father we thought
the cherry bombs were like violence

against us : but we were stopped.
An old rattling truck
nosed thru them : and they closed
together again behind it
            ignoring us.

I walked away from the road
in among the bushes and prickly pear
looking for scorpions on the hot sand
and took a leak beside a thin horse.

An hour later the road was clear   GEORGE
and as I got in the car   BOWERING
a man on a donkey came by
a San Juan lonely in the mountains man.

Good afternoon, I said.
Good afternoon, he said, it is very hot.
Yes it is, I said, especially for us.
It is very hot for us too, he said.

DARYL
HINE

b. 1935

The Double-Goer

All that I do is clumsy and ill timed.
You move quickly, when it must be done,
To spare yourself or save your victim pain.
And then like the light of the sun you move away
While I come face to face with complex crime
Far from the moving of the mellifluous sea.
All that I do is clumsy and ill timed.
When you perform, my errors pantomimed
    Will give an example to the sun
    Of flight, and to shadows how to run.
You will in turn discover in my rhyme
Justifications for your simple crime.

Manifold are the disguises of our love.
We change, our transformations turn about,
Our shadowy forms become the doubles for
Affection or hatred. Yet a kind of growth
Is visible, and may be termed the heart,
Confused by the ambiguities of our art.
Manifold are the disguises of our love.
Contradiction of terms is all we have.

364

To please the self and then the soul
  Is difficult and terrible;   HINE
Impossible to own a single heart
Lost in the double-dealing of our art.

Two-edged is the double-goer's tongue,
Malice and honey, and the prizes in
His logomachy, what lie near the heart :
Money, honour and success in love.
Harmonious ambiguities in a swarm
Burrow at the fulcrum of his speech.
Two-edged is the double-goer's tongue.
One side says, Right, the other side says, Wrong;
    One, Love is red, the other, Black;
    One, Go on, and one, Turn back.
One hopes for heaven, one for earth, and each
To strike a concord through cross-purposed
    speech.

So split and halved and twain is every part,
So like two persons severed by a glass
Which darkens the discerning whose is whose
And gives two arms for love and two for hate,
That they cannot discover what they're at
And sometimes think of killing and embrace.
So split and halved and twain is every part,
Double the loins, the fingers, and the heart,
    Confused in object and in aim,
    That they cannot their pleasure name,
But like two doubles in a darkened place
Make one obscure assault and one embrace.

For they were to duality born and bred.
From their childhood the powers of evil were
No less their familiar than the mirror,
Source of a comfortable terror now and then,
And romantic : What good is a fiend unless
I can think and he, my double, act ?
Thus we were to duality born and bred.

If these two eyes could turn into the one head,   DARYL
    Bright orbs by a brighter sphere enclosed,   HINE
    Mutually blind and self-opposed,
The right supplying what the left one lacked,
Then I can think, and you, my body, act.

In singleness there is no heart or soul
And solitude is scarcely possible.
The one-sailed ship, tossed on a divided sea
As lightly as cork is tossed, as blindly as
The partners toss on their oceanic bed
And rise and fall, is wrecked and lost away.
In singleness there is no heart or soul;
Thus he sees wrong who sees in halves a whole,
    Who searches heaven but for one,
    And not a double of the sun,
Forgets that, being light as cork, the day
Can rise or fall, is wrecked and lost away.

All that I do is careless and sublime.
You walk head-downwards, now your opened
        eyes
Take comfort from the beauty of the site.
What if the vision vary in detail?
What are we but sleepers in a cave,
Our dreams the shades of universal doubt?
All that I do is careless and sublime,
You bore with patience to the heart of time;
    Though your resource of art is small
    And my device yields none at all,
Still this two-handed engine will find out
In us the shape and shadow of our doubt.

Under the Hill

DARYL
HINE

The gates fly open with a pretty sound,
Nor offer opposition to the knight.
A sensual world, remote, extinct, is found.

In walls that like luxurious thorns surround
The exquisite lewdness of the sybarite,
The gates fly open with a pretty sound.

Where venery goes hunting like a hound,
And all the many mouths of pleasure bite,
A sensual world, remote, extinct, is found.

The passionate pilgrim strayed beneath the ground
Meets only death, until, to his delight,
The gates fly open with a pretty sound.

In Venus' clutches, under Venus' mound,
He whiles away the long venereal night.
A sensual world, remote, extinct, is found.

The single function on which Venus frowned
Was birth; and, maybe, life has proved her right.
The gates fly open with a pretty sound.
A sensual world, remote, extinct, is found.

Trompe l'Œil

There is a way of seeing that is not seeing.
Far from the true dimension of our being
Who doubts but there is that we cannot see?
More than the naive employment of the eye
On decorated wall and ceiling,
The spirit's exercise consists in telling
Not right from wrong but rather true from false.
Looking at lies the eye sees something else,
In the pattern of the painted handkerchief
The painted pins that hold it up, and if
They yield, it cannot fall, it is not real.

Reality then is nearly what we feel
The outlines of, even as it dissolves.
Figures with better faces than ourselves
In a glass conduct their brighter lives
In chambers where reality survives
Only as long as it can fool or charm.
There at least we shall not come to harm;
Therein we and our desires belong,
Where lusts like bees perish as they sting.
Accidents that elsewhere fail to happen
Befall us there : doors that do not open,
Drawers that cannot ever be pulled out.
Disenchantment waits until we doubt
Upon the magic words, 'It all is painted.
A queer affair but hardly what we wanted,
A box containing everything but nature,
Not one unpremeditated creature,
A landscape in the manner of our dreams,
Its meaning just, it is not what it seems.'
The shadow of a fly upon the fruit
Whose suspect flesh appears substantial to it,
The deeper, broader shadow on the fly
Of the bird that it is hunted by
In the story of the still life, and
Over both the shadow of a hand
With minatory fingers seems to hover—
Will it move? or will it rest forever
On its work, a part of its creation,
The imitation of an imitation?

Round the ceiling runs a balustrade
In perspective. There the gods portrayed
As painted men and women leaning over
Laugh and kiss and talk, none whatsoever
Bored by their old immortality,
Above their heads a prospect of the sky.
The light declining on their tinted flesh
Colours with ripeness what was lately fresh

Despite the fixed meridian of the sun.   ARYL
They do not seem to know their day is done,   HINE
Themselves perfected out of all ambition,
But lolling in the attitudes of passion
Sumptuously clothed or gloriously nude,
Endymion asleep, Andromeda pursued,
Ageless nymphs and coarse priapic satyrs,
They shew the features that illusion flatters
And throw from the false Olympus of the ceiling
The long, deceptive shadows cast by feeling.

There is a way of seeing that is not sight
Like a candle lit in broad daylight
And darkness too that is not always night.

GEORGE
JONAS

b. 1935

For the Record

I think that I live in a street
Where the evenings are decidedly darker,
A citizen of what is said to be a country,
In the year nineteen-sixty-four.

All the snow melts around April,
In August there is nothing to wait for,
The Fall is established in November,
January is mostly Winter.

A woman claims to be my wife
On the strength of which she lives in my house.
But I am also dangerous to some animals
And have at times been observed to eat them.

369

I have little to say about the structure of society,   GEORGE
There may be certain letters to write occasionally,   JONAS
Certain amounts to pay when they become due,
But it is against the law for some people to hurt
    me.

In view of this I continue to lead
What I am told is an existence
Weeks ending in Sundays
Unasked questions scrupulously unanswered.

Four Stanzas Written in Anxiety

The museums and stockmarkets protect me
Orchestras hold up naked swords in my defence
The steps of a melancholy policeman at midnight
Echo down my quietly segregated street.

My unguarded wealth rests inside the cold walls
Of silent court houses and libraries
Where after seven o'clock the lights are dimmed.
Narrow electric eyes patrol my jewellery stores.

I am fair, peaceful and wise; my smooth voice
Is never raised; I forgive and forget.
My grey navies sit in heavy waters,
My compassionate guns are trained at the world.

But lately the mornings are sudden
Odd noises in my innermost rooms.
They who sidestep my books and bayonets
Worship stones, I hear, and need no beds to sleep in.

DAVID
WEVILL

b. 1935

In Love

She touches me. Her fingers nibble gently.
The whole street leans closer, its doors
Grin open and cluster shut,
Gathering like a fist closing, firmly.
Warm Sunday mornings breathe a way of knowing
God's love, his shuddering mouth to mouth
Vision above the brain's heat,
Beyond leather foot, bible, or prayer book—
Naked, we push their webbed stares out.

Look, bodies that puzzled me no longer love;
Effulgence of grasses cover her body—
I champ and am at sea and drown and feed,
Hurl and kiss, climb and descend,
Lie still with the prickle of ants underneath me.
There was an opening, an opening—
It's gone now. Now there's no question of fire,
Grasses, or drowning; only this first
Dry building of rib above rib, as if
A great house crumbled on its skeleton.

And this is my Sunday lesson she teaches me.
Her texts are pillows, strong wrists and liquid
    ankles.
I could paint her as I fell on her,
And did, with my tongue, lungs and my whole
    heart,
Each breath exploding its hot ether lash
Through our wills to their blind core.
If this is love I grieve for God's
His idolators shuffling by with their scrubbed
    children;
Though her face, with its sky-change coloured
    eyes,
Melts them all one in my privilege.

Snow

DAVID
WEVILL

In the painkilling cold that wrapped
A frozen skin of trousers round his shins,
His ankles in irons, eyelids locked on the air
Barely watching the branches of pines and wind
    gathering
In shifts, snow-socketed and numb as needles,
The sun a pale distraction but never the heart
Of his ice-feast; walking the car-tracks
Woven and crossed like firehoses along
The hospital road, walking, or rather sidling
Frontwards, and thinking, 'Here's this vast white
Revolution, I alone am carrying sex
In our world, something precocious which the sun
Notices moving, of its own will, outwards,
Blemished by motion and by its own unique
Dirt-carrying will, intelligence of squeezed eyes
Against the disembodying white of the land—
Something that parcels the world by walking
    out here
Under an inch of wool, upon rubber feet,
Defying nothing, but touching the limits of cold
Humourless as a locked brook
Or an icicle.' 'I am not alone because I bring
One thread of life into this weave of death,
And each is as whole as the other : sex is warm
In my coat but cold in my shadow, sex
Is broken in the pines and in the bland birch-trees,
The permafrost, of which I am no part,
The rock-hard doormat of grass underneath, the
Scrapping chickadees on the dotted snow,—
All tension, teeth ! I alone am above it, indifferent,
Bestriding this difficult time, watching
A world where everything comes out right if
Left to its own cold course : I, knowing my tracks
Will turn later to meet it, its death unsolved.'

Spiders

DAVID
WEVILL

Muddling up the wooden stairs one night, in my
   socks
Past screens and shuttered bunting-creviced
   wallboards,
My tongue dry, but a cool wind puffing thinly soft
Up my torn shirt-front, the dust hot-thick in my
   hair,
I crossed my sister coming that way in her slip—
The steep way down, half-asleep; her chicken-
   hearted breathing
And toes antennaed for spiders or bits of fluff
That might jiggle and spill a mouse. I tasted my
   own breath
Kekking, milkweed-sour, after the beer—
But not to budge, or her shriek might wake the
   house—
Who is it! I didn't know her face—
Such full pails for eyes; she might have been glass;
The roman nose, pink lips peeled white over salt
While ten years woke up and started . . . I
   thought myself
Back, a loiterer in jeans, hands spittled with oil
From throbbing handlebars. Wind shoulders the
   porch,
Flickers the close trees. . . . I held back then
And jammed my buttocks hard against black
   wood,
My back a prickly heat of rusty nails which
Builders'd slapped in, and left, when the lake was
   young
With all her forests open to the wind, mated
   conifers
Exploding dry cones. I listened in the dark,
And thought, this wife won't wait to be woken
   by me,
But go on down, passing me, always on my left—

Wind clacking the picture-frames through our big DAVID WEVILL
    house—
I wasn't going to wake her. I mightn't have seemed
Her brother, then, but eight legs sprung on her
    dream,
Something she'd sense far worse than spiders, on
    the stair,
That could harm her children. Maybe it wasn't
    just fear,
Or concern, that made me cringe from her.
Two people who cross in the dark walk nearest to
    ghosts,
Her terror might have stuck its mouth in me,
And sealed her against a love she could not cope
    with,
Grinning under heavy sheets, with her heartbeat.

Body of a Rook

God broke upon this upturned field; trees
Wedged tangled and thick as black crotch-hair—
But an eyelid in the field's face flutters,
Winks, blindingly. Whose
Sunrise through that blazing shrub glows
Ram's horns? twin forks of a tree,
Dividing, splitting. And nothing disturbs
These soft tussocks, the woman's one-eyed love.

In the scenery of crushed glass, here,
Among kneading hands of mud, the scoured head
    lies,
A world seized between sunlit clouds,
Spinning with sense, one eye gone black.
I stare out over my roof of towns,
And shiver off my sperm of wet dog-hair—

Night's claw, where cats couple among
The strict soldiering lupins. As afterthoughts,

My manners brush their teeth into the sink;   DAVID
A cloud keeps my bed, the hot patch kept,   WEVILL
Warmth of armpits and incendiary struggles—
I return where my love gloats and swarms to sleep.

Imagine, if our naked bones
Broke up on these same stones, that freed stubble
Mouth jagged as smashed plastic—
Our nakedness breathes and shifts through warm
    holes,
Sighs from pricked gaps (the manners torn);
We know our natures and our flaws
Closer, from such uncharitable hunting . . .

I prise the blue-black feathers back. The beak
    glows,
Soft at the edges, like an urchin's valve—
Mouth. I know my own violence too.
I feel her gnawing, clinging, flesh-stubbed
Teeth in me, my remembrance of her mouth.
It is a killing but who dies?

I killed it slowly with a lump of flint.
Shot down and left to die, what soft thing jerks
Its pulped head, face, body, nerves
Beak-deep in the pasture mud? I watched
Those last sufferings leave her body too,
Twitching black and rook-supple before
I kicked my damaged violence into the wood.

JOHN
ROBERT
COLOMBO

b. 1936

Ideal Angels

They are by nature lonely things,
Immaculate, almost yellow.
Like a reed, brittle and hollow,
Their solitude is filled with psalms.

They stand darkly against the world
And watch the creatures of the one
Common God with indifference.
Their hearts are strangely somewhere else.

Mostly one, occasionally more
Go off at times and stand apart.
They spawn quietly, for their hearts
Seemingly spin on distant cores.

Hypnotized by God, a silent
Rage would so plague them if it could
That now they waste away like food
That goes uneaten at a feast.

These are the angels who would cease
To celebrate when man was made,
For fear that his creation would
Limit their stature and increase.

Like shadows which are everywhere
They stand so near on every side
That, if you place a word beside
Another, you upset them there.

They can feel each other's presence
As one finger feels another.
They sense this with a slight shudder,
Their souls have such fine resonance.

They never appear as they are,
Tubular with wings, until your
Heart's sky is at a noon of faith,
Until the mind's mood too is there.

Often they stand out in paintings
And stained glass windows. Lingering,
They take their place beside you when
They feel the vision in you sings.

JOHN ROBERT
COLOMBO

How They Made the Golem

To the banks of the Moldau River,
  their lanterns light, their scriptures heavy,
    the three men made their way, the three of
      them,
The Holy Rabbi of Prague, Judah Loew,
  his brother-in-law, Isaac ben Samson, Cohen,
    and his pupil, Jacob ben Chayim Sasson,
      Levite.
The night was near midnight. They stopped
  where the banks of the river were of red clay.
    They stood in the darkness, prayed and
      prepared.
Then each sang the prescribed Psalm:
  'My substance was not hid from thee,
    when I was made in secret, and curiously
      wrought
in the lowest parts of the earth.'
  The Rabbi fingered the time-worn pages
    of the Book of Psalms and the Book of
      Formation,

selecting the required passages :   JOHN ROBER
COLOMBO

   'Thine eyes did see my substance,
     yet being imperfect; and in thy book
all my members were written,
   which in continuance were fashioned,
    when as yet there was none of them.
How precious also are thy thoughts
   unto me, O God ! How great is the sum
    of them !' Then, in the earth at his feet,
the bent Rabbi moulded the clay figure
   of my person, making me in length three ells,
    with all the members and measurements of a
     man.
The Rabbi, the Cohen and the Levite
   stood by my feet regarding my clay face.
   'You are fire.' The Cohen walked around me
seven times and sang : 'He hewed, as it were,
   vast columns out of the great intangible air.'
    The charm worked, my clay turned red like
     fire.
'You are water.' The Levite then walked
   around me seven times but the other way,
    singing : 'And He bound the twenty-two
     letters
unto his speech and shewed him all
   the mysteries of them.' Water flowed from me,
    hair sprouted, toes and fingers grew crude
     nails.
'You are air.' The Rabbi bent down to me
   and inserted the parchmented name, the Shem,
    deep into my clay mouth, and together they
     prayed :
'And He breathed into his nostrils
   the breath of life; and the man became
    a living soul.' With that I opened my eyes.
I saw them there, heard the Rabbi's command :
   'Stand up !' And I stood up, a dumb stranger.

They handed me their sexton's dirty
   garments.
'You are Joseph,' the Rabbi said.
   'You will destroy the entire Jew-baiting
      company.' I nodded, for I had no powers of
      speech.
The three of them led me away as a fourth.
   'A dumb creature of magicians,' Isaac said.
      'A creation, like Adam,' Joseph said. But I
         thought:
'How precious also are thy thoughts
   unto me, O God! How great is the sum
      of them!' And they led me into the city of
         Prague.

JOHN ROBERT
COLOMBO

MICHÈLE
LALONDE

b. 1937

Le Silence effrité

le silence effrité
aux rives de mes veines
douces grèves léchées de sang
où s'allongent les corps désunis de nos songes

ô tiédeur initiale des jours
quand l'ocre et le froment
partageaient une même allégresse
au seuil de nos lèvres

l'égalité miraculeuse de chaque désir

j'ai pitié de nos mains disjointes
nos paumes désenchantées et disperses
comme des coquilles crevées

nos regards impairs

l'oubli va nous dissoudre

Le Jour halluciné

MICHÈLE
LALONDE

le jour halluciné s'égrène sur ma tête
et je suis un navire
mes yeux sont des truites
j'ai des limaces
au lieu de mes mains
des crabes roux
sur mes cheveux d'algues

mais je suis morte

j'effleure un mensonger corail
amère et close
comme une huître

je n'accède à nulle clairière d'eau
sous la prunelle hystérique des ciels

je m'agenouille au bord de la terre fiévreuse
rien plus ne rejoint la lointaine illusion
de ma supplique

le geste pernicieux et minéral de l'eau
achève sur moi sa fidèle usure

je n'ai plus à craindre
que mon propre appel
le cri de cette autre qui sommeille encore
peut-être
sous les miroirs

Combien doux

MICHÈLE
LALONDE

combien doux
combien doux l'exil
combien parfaite la solitude

nous hantons les rivages verts
d'une île à la dérive
un seul horizon nous garde
impassible et fixe

nous projetons notre ombre gigantesque
sur toute la mer
nous sommes démesurés
vastes de tout nous-mêmes
nos jours sont sans mesure
à la merci du seul désir

nous cueillons les petits poignards
semés au jardin de notre être

la clameur obstinée des anciens continents
nous atteint
comme un large éclat de rire

les mains chargées des derniers débris d'un fol
    orgueil
nous nous tenons debout droits et défiant les
    mondes

par ce geste vertical
de notre présence

La Fiancée

MICHÈLE
LALONDE

Et soudain il y eut une grande déchirure, comme
une scission en deux de tout le paysage
et le monde chavirait tout d'un coup devant ma
     face,
et soudain, tu n'étais plus là.

Et je t'appelais je l'appelais je t'appelais avec mon
     cri
de métal incisif qui lacérait la nuit de grandes
     entailles sonores.

Mais déjà tu étais loin, bien au devant de moi, et
     je devinais
encore ta silhouette hâtive et solitaire dans le
     sillage
fluorescent de la musique,

ta haute stature d'homme avançant selon le gré
     des alouettes
magnétiques, les épaules voûtées, les coudes raidis
     et collés
aux flancs sous le large camail de la brume . . .

Ah redites-moi le nom du bien-aimé, que je
     l'interpelle,
que je l'appelle par son nom et par sa désignation
     propre,

car la seule sollicitation familière de mon cri
     dénudé de
paroles ne suffit plus ! Et la sourde invitation de
     mon cœur
battant, (ah mon cœur s'exaspère et s'épuise
     comme un fruit
trop mur sur la tige des artères !) le langage étouffé
     de mon
cœur excédé n'a plus de pouvoir sur lui.

Quel est le nom du fiancé? que je lui parle!

MICHÈLE
LALONDE

Ah qu'il se retourne seulement une fois, et je lui
    ferai de
larges signes désespérés avec mes bras déployés et
    anxieux!

Le refuge ogival de mes bras l'attend et le réclame!

Redites-moi le nom du fiancé, car je l'avais oublié,
    ayant
perdu l'accoutumance de lui parler avec des mots,
    mais
seulement avec les syllabes de mon cœur
    véhément...

Confiez-moi le nom du fiancé, que je l'ajoute
    comme une
flèche à l'arc bandé de mon appel!

SUZANNE
PARADIS

b. 1937

Dépouillements

Quand nous allumerons en bonne saison, ces
feux que le soleil clot sur des cendres complètes,
        agenouillés dans les choses prêtes
        comme au milieu des chemins tracés,
je veux qu'un vent chargé d'horizons voyageurs
éclabousse nos mains et souille nos rivages,
que le sable tournoie jusqu'à enfouir nos bagues
        et l'ancien anneau qui pèse au cœur.

Je veux que nous soyons libres à cet instant,
d'une force sauvage obligés de sourire,
et que soit effacé ce qu'il fallut écrire,
et que soit arrachée cette preuve du temps!

Nous danserons alors, autour d'un feu de fous SUZANNE
—écoulés comme une eau dans nos dénuements   PARADIS
   pâles,
         marqués au front par de brusques hâles—
         sur les lambeaux de nos deux genoux.

Enfin purifiés et grandis malgré nous
dans ce soulèvement de sable et de fleur rare,
sous ce vent déchaîné prêt à tordre les gares
         j'écouterai mourir nos amours.

Nul ne recueillera nos débris d'univers.
Ce que nous livrerons au vent, sans faire grâce
         même de la plus légère trace,
         s'égaillera vers les quatre mers.

Allez, merles blessés, ailes de rêves clos,
parfums de jardins morts et de serres livides,
         la terre d'un seul être se vide
on dirait que la mort a touché jusqu'à l'os. . . .

Roulez, fumées de joie, complices dans l'azur
de la veille légère où j'espaçais les songes
         à la merci du temps qui ronge
         au flanc des vignes le raisin sûr;
roulez dans les anneaux du feu qui gravira
le bois vivant ou mort et nos mains exposées,
la suie retombera en dernières rosées,
         la terre noire nous mangera.

Et nous ne serons plus, bientôt à bout de bras,
que le débris de geste aux doigts des vents de
   palmes;
l'aube dissipera, perdue au soleil calme
         la trace passée de notre pas.

Les Naissances secondes

SUZANNE
PARADIS

Les autres avant moi, sur mes pas existèrent,
mais j'avance sans bruit, aube de jeune accueil,
mon désir infini recommence la terre
je mets la mort du monde en son constant cercueil.

J'étreins la mort croissante de paralysie
avec mon pas de danse jailli d'autrefois
de planète promise et de rose choisie.
Je mets la vie en marche, au pas, derrière moi.

La terre boit aux sources sûres de mes veines
et mord à pleines dents ma chair d'âpre saison;
elle se nourrira en vain de ma chair vaine
et mourra lentement de son subtil poison.

Mais j'aurai eu le temps d'espacer un silence
vieux de siècles venus obstinés jusqu'à moi,
en un geste léger de multiple balance
et d'alourdir d'un jour son millénaire poids.

J'aurai eu le pouvoir d'éveiller l'innocence,
stigmate refermé au fond du mal profond,
mes deux mains explosant de mortelle puissance
auront ouvert la plaie et ravivé l'affront.

J'aurai eu la douceur immobile des choses
et le baiser de l'homme où verser tout mon sang;
je recule la mort encore d'une rose
et l'oubli, d'un parfum. Je suis le jour naissant.

Je suis le nouveau jour, l'innombrable dimanche
bondi de la dernière étoile du ciel clos;
je retarde la mort d'une feuille à la branche
je mets la mort du monde en échec d'un oiseau.

La vie à mon poignet rive son pouls sonore,
épouse sans regard, mêle son œil blessé
à mes yeux qui verront pour l'émouvoir encore
la fraîche imagerie du soleil annoncé.

Je mêlerai mon pas dans la lumière franche
au vol du papillon, j'établirai l'oiseau
et l'écureuil jaillis du frisson d'une branche,
je distance la mort à peine d'un ruisseau.

SUZANNE
PARADIS

Pour garder le péril et devancer le risque
de rouler en pleine ombre au seuil d'un peu de
    nuit
—sous la mort qui poursuit au pas de précipice
le jeune jour levé dans un soleil qui fuit—

j'aurai eu la clarté d'une immense promesse
la couleur de son fruit à ma lèvre donné.
Je suis le jour suivant, recommencé sans cesse . . .
Je diffère la mort du désir que j'en ai.

Le Coup de grâce

Obéis, je suis maître à bord de mon verger,
ô soleil chien couché aux portes de la terre !
Au galvaudeur de fruits, aboie, à l'étranger,
plante tes crocs brûlés dans ses paumes de verre.

Arrache à son bras mort la dernière vigueur
s'il corrompt dans les fruits l'humble chair
    entamée
et corrige sa bouche à la lèvre des fleurs
qu'elle saigne le sang des blessures fermées.

Délivre ses poignets du pouls de la fureur,
une hache de vent rompt la tête des saules,
étouffe au mors des dents son souffle de tueur.
Je veux son cadavre pour le mordre à l'épaule.

Obéis, sans pitié, chien noir de ma colère,
soleil de nuit couché dans la montagne au loin,
soleil du jour juché sur l'escabelle claire
d'une plaine d'avoine ou d'un champ vert de foin.

Chasse aux rayons—dix doigts de mortelle
    lumière—
l'ombre à ses pores clos, à ses paupières froides,
sèche son torse au sang, bois-le jusqu'à la pierre,
je le veux voir rongé et roulé dans ta gueule.

Obéis ! j'ai surpris l'étranger dans mes arbres,
son poison dans mes fruits éclate aux dents
    d'enfants.
Grand chien nourri de feu, ligote-le à l'arbre
et tords-lui la cheville, ô soleil piaffant !

Je suis maître, obéis ! lève-toi de ta niche
et n'attends pas qu'à l'aube la montagne ploie
que le voleur de fruits s'en aille en des mains
    riches
vendre mes vergers nus contre bijoux et soies,

qu'il s'en aille, d'amours que j'ai vives, chargé
ainsi qu'un mort ancien dans son tombeau de
    pierre
à qui l'on fournissait le pain l'or et le vin. . . .

Dévore-le, soleil, soleil chien de berger,
puis va le vomir nu à la proche rivière.

SUZANN
PARADIS

LIONEL
KEARNS

b. 1937

Stuntman

This time
in the darkness
a twelve-foot
pleasure-launch
sleek
and gleaming white.

The crew
(both male
and female)
in bikinis,
laughing

LIONEL
KEARNS

And in tow
two water-skiers
doing acrobatics.

At the back of the boat
instead of an out-board engine
a man
has been bolted into place.

He kicks his feet
in frantic
propulsion.

His arms
are fastened
to the steering cables.

Blood
trickles
into the water.

His neck
seems broken
too.

But now
there is scarcely
any noise

For the boat
is moving faster
than the speed of sound.

JOHN
NEWLOVE

b. 1938

The Double-Headed Snake

Not to lose the feel of the mountains
while still retaining the prairies
is a difficult thing. What's lovely
is whatever makes the adrenalin run;
therefore I count terror and fear among
the greatest beauty. The greatest
beauty is to be alive, forgetting nothing,
although remembrance hurts
like a foolish act, is a foolish act.

Beauty's whatever
makes the adrenalin run. Fear
in the mountains at night-time's
not tenuous, it is not the cold
that makes me shiver, civilized man,
white, I remember
the stories of the Indians,
Sis-i-utl, the double-headed snake.

Beauty's what makes
the adrenalin run. Fear at night
on the level plains, with no horizon
and the stars too bright, wind bitter
even in June, in winter
the snow harsh and blowing
is what makes me
shiver, not the cold air alone.

And one beauty cancels another. The plains
seem secure and comfortable
at Crow's Nest Pass; in Saskatchewan
the mountains are comforting
to think of; among

the eastwardly diminishing hills
both the flatland and the ridge
seem easy to endure.

As one beauty
cancels another, remembrance
is a foolish act, a double-headed snake
striking in both directions, but I
remember plains and mountains, places
I come from, places I adhere and live in.

The Pride

(I)
The image/   the pawnees
in their earth-lodge villages,
the clear image
of teton sioux, wild
fickle people the chronicler says,

the crazy dogs, men
tethered with leather dog-thongs
to a stake, fighting until dead,

image : arikaras
with traded spanish sabre blades
mounted on the long
heavy buffalo lances,
riding the sioux
down, the centaurs, the horsemen
scouring the level plains
in war or hunt
until smallpox got them,
4000 warriors,

image—of a desolate country,
a long way between fires,
unfound lakes, mirages, cold rocks,
and lone men going through it,
cree with good guns
creating terror in athabaska
among the inhabitants, frightened
stone-age people, 'so that
they fled at the mere sight
of a strange smoke miles away.'

JOHN
NEWLOVE

(II)
This western country crammed
with the ghosts of indians,
haunting the coastal stones and shores,
the forested pacific islands,
mountains, hills and plains;

beside the ocean ethlinga,
man in the moon, empties
his bucket, on
a sign from Spirit
of the Wind ethlinga
empties his bucket, refreshing
the earth, and it rains
on the white cities;

that black joker, broken-
jawed raven, most prominent
among haida and tsimshyan tribes,
is in the kwakiutl
dance masks too—
it was he who brought fire,
food and water to man,
the trickster;

and thunderbird hilunga,
little thought of
by haida for lack of thunderstorms

in their district, goes
by many names, exquisite disguises
carved in the painted wood,

he is nootka tootooch, the wings
causing thunder and the tongue
or flashing eyes engendering
rabid white lightning,
whose food was whales,

called kwunusela by the kwakiutl,
it was he who laid down the house-logs
for the people at Place
Where Kwunusela Alighted;

in full force and virtue
and terror of the law, eagle—
he is authority, the sun
assumed his form once,
the sun which used to be
a flicker's egg, success-
fully transformed;

and malevolence comes to the land,
the wild woman of the woods;
grinning, she wears
a hummingbird in her hair,
d'sonoqua, the furious one—

they are all ready
to be found, the legends
and the people, or
all their ghosts and memories,
whatever is strong enough
to be remembered.

(III)
But what image, bewildered
son of all men
under the hot sun,

GÉRALD
GODIN*

b. 1938

Pour Maria (I)

il y a une étoile de plâtre au plafond de notre
    chambre blanche
'when I die I want the smell of Whisky all over
    the place
and I wanna sit on the knees of the finest
    female-angel of them all'
je m'ennuie du français parle-moi français maria
dans central-park un vieil homme aux cheveux
    blancs
songe-t-il comme moi maria comme je songerai à
    toi dans mille ans
à une jeune fille que jadis il a aimée
maria
je jetterai en toi l'ancre de mes lèvres
à jamais ivre à jamais immobile et mes bras
    comme des racines
une ancre d'anciennes amours rouillée
la ramènerai quand morte éventrée ma mer n'aura
    plus besoin
que des froids éclairs du soleil absent maria
mes bras se souvenant mieux que moi de la plage
    rêche
et du navire que je fus neuf et de loin venu
comme un cri d'orage et la rocaille du vent
se souvenant du ressac de l'amour se brisant à la
    jointure
de la croix que nous sommes nous voyagerons à
    jamais unis

AUTHOR'S NOTE: *Gérald Godin ne se considère pas
comme poète canadien, mais comme poète québécois
et s'il a accepté de figurer dans cette anthologie c'est
uniquement parce qu'on lui a permis de faire cette
distinction et qu'il importe qu'elle soit connue.*

maria
ma jeune fille aux seintelets
les seintelets maria c'est des seins de jeune fille
oui c'est un mot nouveau oui c'est moi qui l'ai
    trouvé
il était dans ta blouse
maria mon épouse
amidonnée
dévidoir de mes beaux jours
ô seul dévidoir carrefour
de nos quatre volontés
mon voyage redouté
ma nuit mon cœur
ô ma mythologie
maria ma douce ma noire
ô mes mensonges
ô les clés de mes songes mon église d'images grises
mon île là-bas mon faux acacia mon voyage en pot
maria dans la nuit noire
maria mon épouse inventée
de toutes mes amantes composée
ferme les rideaux sur nos cœurs
mon doigt marche sur ton bras tu prends ma main
une gerbe de désir déliée court dans nos veines
maria mon âme je t'oublierai ma noire
tu fermeras les rideaux sur ta mémoire
à la porte me laissant je t'oublierai
prendre ces nuages par le cou
dans leur image renversée
avant de m'y noyer
l'on ne verra plus maria l'on ne verra plus au fond
    du temps
que briller mon rire au soleil
mais les mots dans ma gorge dénoués
les mots maria
même sans moi prononcés les mots t'appelleront.

GÉRALD
GODIN

Cantouque d'amour

GÉRALD
GODIN

C'est sans bagages sans armes
qu'on partira mon steamer à seins
ô migrations ô voyages
ne resteront à mes épouses
que les ripes de mon cœur
par mes amours gossé

je viendrai chez vous un soir tu ne m'attendras pas
je serai dressé dans la porte comme une armure
haletant je soulèverai tes jupes pour te voir avec
    mes mains
tu pleureras comme jamais
ton cœur retontira sur la table comme un intrus
on passera comme des icebergs dans le vin de
    gadelle et de mûre
pour aller mourir à jamais packtés
dans des affaires catchop de cœur et de foin

quand la mort viendra
entre deux brasses de cœur
à l'heure
du contrôle on trichera comme des sourds
ta dernière carte sera la reine de pique
que tu me donneras comme un baiser dans le cou
et c'est tiré par mille spanes de sacres
que je partirai retrouver mes pères et mères
à l'éternelle
chasse aux snelles

quand je prendrai la quille de l'air
un soir d'automne ou d'ailleurs
j'aurai laissé dans ton cou à l'heure du carcan
un plein casso de baisers blancs moutons
quand je caillerai comme du vieux lait
à gauche du poèle à bois
à l'heure où la messe a vidé la maison
allant d'venant dans ma barçante en merisier

c'est pour toi seule ma petite noire
que ma barçante criera encore
comme un cœur

GÉRALD
GODIN

quand de longtemps j'aurai rejoint mes pères et
    mères
à l'éternelle
chasse aux snelles.

mon casso de moutons te roulera dans le cou
comme une gamme
tous les soirs après souper
à l'heure où d'ordinaire chez vous j'ai ressoud
comme un jaloux

chnaille chnaille que la mort me dira
une dernière fois j'aurai vu ta vie
comme un oiseau enfermé mes yeux courant
    fous du cygne
au poêle
voyageur pressé par le fin je te ramasserai partout
à pleines poignées
et c'est dans mille spanes de sacres que je partirai
trop tôt crevé trop tard venu
mais heureux comme le bleu de ma vareuse les
    soirs de soleil

c'est entre les pages de mon seaman's handbook
que tu me reverras fleur noire et séchée
qu'on soupera encore ensemble
au vin de gadelle et de mûre
entre deux cassos de baisers fins comme ton châle
les soirs de bonne veillée

MARGARET
ATWOOD
b. 1939

The Explorers

The explorers will come
in several minutes
and find this island.

(It is a stunted island,
rocky, with room
for only a few trees, a thin
layer of soil; hardly
bigger than a bed.
That is how
they've missed it
until now)

Already their boats draw near,
their flags flutter,
their oars push at the water.

They will be jubilant
and shout, at finding
that there was something
they had not found before,

although this island will afford
not much more than a foothold :
little to explore;

but they will be surprised

(we can't see them yet;
we know they must be
coming, because they always come
several minutes too late)

(they won't be able
to tell how long
we were cast away, or why,
or, from these
gnawed bones,
which was the survivor)

at the two skeletons

The Settlers

A second after
the first boat touched the shore,
there was a quick skirmish
brief as a twinge
and then the land was settled

(of course there was really
no shore : the water turned
to land by having
objects in it : caught and kept
from surge, made
less than immense
by networks of
roads and grids of fences)

and as for us, who drifted
picked by the sharks
during so many bluegreen
centuries before they came :
they found us
inland, stranded
on a ridge of bedrock,
defining our own island.

From our inarticulate
skeleton (so

intermixed, one
carcass),
they postulated wolves.

They dug us down
into the solid granite
where our bones grew flesh again,
came up trees and
grass.

Still
we are the salt
seas that uphold these lands.

Now horses graze
inside this fence of ribs, and

children run, with green
smiles, (not knowing
where) across
the fields of our open hands.

Eventual Proteus

I held you
through all your shifts
of structure : while your bones turned
from caved rock back to marrow,
the dangerous
fur faded to hair
the bird's cry died in your throat
the treebark paled from your skin
the leaves from your eyes

till you limped back again
to daily man :
a lounger on streetcorners
in iron-shiny gabardine
a leaner on stale tables;

at night a twitching sleeper
dreaming of crumbs and rinds and a sagging
    woman,
caged by a sour bed.

The early
languages are obsolete.

These days we keep
our weary distances :
sparring in the vacant spaces
of peeling rooms
and rented minutes, climbing
all the expected stairs, our voices
abraded with fatigue,
our bodies wary.

Shrunk by my disbelief
you cannot raise
the green gigantic skies, resume
the legends of your disguises :
this shape is final.

Now, when you come near
attempting towards me across
these sheer cavernous
inches of air

your flesh has no more stories
or surprises;

my face flinches
under the sarcastic
tongues of your estranging
fingers,
the caustic remark of your kiss.

Against Still Life

MARGARET
ATWOOD

Orange in the middle of a table :

It isn't enough
to walk around it
at a distance, saying
it's an orange :
nothing to do
with us, nothing
else : leave it alone

I want to pick it up
in my hand
I want to peel the
skin off; I want
more to be said to me
than just Orange :
want to be told
everything it has to say

And you, sitting across
the table, at a distance, with
your smile contained, and like the orange
in the sun : silent :

Your silence
isn't enough for me
now, no matter with what
contentment you fold
your hands together; I want
anything you can say
in the sunlight :

stories of your various
childhoods, aimless journeyings,
your loves; your articulate
skeleton; your posturings; your lies.

405

These orange silences MARGARET
ATWOOD
(sunlight and hidden smile)
make me want to
wrench you into saying :
now I'd crack your skull
like a walnut, split it like a pumpkin
to make you talk, or get
a look inside

But quietly :
if I take the orange
with care enough and hold it
gently

I may find
an egg
a sun
an orange moon
perhaps a skull; centre
of all energy
resting in my hand

can change it to
whatever I desire
it to be

and you, man, orange afternoon
lover, wherever
you sit across from me
(tables, trains, buses)

if I watch
quietly enough
and long enough

at last, you will say
(maybe without speaking)

(there are mountains
inside your skull
garden and chaos, ocean

and hurricane; certain
corners of rooms, portraits
of great-grandmothers, curtains
of a particular shade;
your deserts; your private
dinosaurs; the first
woman)

MARGARET
ATWOOD

all I need to know :
tell me
everything
just as it was
from the beginning.

From 'The Circle Game'

(II)
Being with you
here, in this room

is like groping through a mirror
whose glass has melted
to the consistency
of gelatin

You refuse to be
(and I)
an exact reflection, yet
will not walk from the glass,
be separate.

Anyway, it is right
that they have put
so many mirrors here
(chipped, hung crooked)
in this room with its high transom
and empty wardrobe; even
the back of the door
has one.

There are people in the next room
arguing, opening and closing drawers
(the walls are thin)

MARGARET
ATWOOD

You look past me, listening
to them, perhaps, or
watching
your own reflection somewhere
behind my head,
over my shoulder

You shift, and the bed
sags under us, losing its focus

There is someone in the next room

There is always

(your face
remote, listening)

someone in the next room.

.   .   .

(IV)
Returning to the room :
I notice how
all your word-
plays, calculated ploys
of the body, the witticisms
of touch, are now
attempts to keep me
at a certain distance
and (at length) avoid
admitting I am here

I watch you
watching my face
indifferently
yet with the same taut curiosity
with which you might regard

a suddenly discovered part
of your own body :
a wart perhaps,

and I remember that
you said
in childhood you were
a tracer of maps
(not making but) moving
a pen or a forefinger
over the courses of the rivers,
the different colours
that mark the rise of mountains;
a memorizer
of names (to hold
these places
in their proper places)

So now you trace me
like a country's boundary
or a strange new wrinkle in
your own wellknown skin
and I am fixed, stuck
down on the outspread map
of this room, of your mind's continent
        (here and yet not here, like
        the wardrobe and the mirrors
        the voices through the wall
        your body ignored on the bed),

transfixed
by your eyes'
cold blue thumbtacks

.   .   .

MARGARET
ATWOOD

Summer again;
in the mirrors of this room
the children wheel, singing
the same song;

This casual bed
scruffy as dry turf,
the counterpane
rumpled with small burrows, is
their grassy lawn

and these scuffed walls
contain their circling trees,
that low clogged sink
their lake

(a wasp comes,
drawn by the piece of sandwich
left on the nearby beach
        (how carefully you do
        such details);
one of the children flinches
but won't let go)

You make them
turn and turn, according to
the closed rules of your games,
but there is no joy in it

and as we lie
arm in arm, neither
joined nor separate
        (your observations change me
        to a spineless woman in
        a cage of bones, obsolete fort
        pulled inside out),
our lips moving
almost in time to their singing,

listening to the opening
and closing of the drawers
in the next room

MARGARET
ATWOOD

(of course there is always
danger but where
would you locate it)

(the children spin
a round cage of glass
from the warm air
with their thread-thin
insect voices)

and as we lie
here, caught
in the monotony of wandering
from room to room, shifting
the place of our defences,

I want to break
these bones, your prisoning rhythms
        (winter,
        summer)
all the glass cases,

erase all maps,
crack the protecting
eggshell of your turning
singing children :

I want the circle
broken.

WILLIAM
HAWKINS

b. 1940

The Wall

I'm up against the wall,
up to the coarseness,
surrounded by it.

I have imagined the wall,
am responsible—

you'd think
it is reasonable
to assume
I know what it's for,
but I don't.

I'm painting the wall,
green & blue
predominates,
figures shimmer elusive
& I name them.

I'm up against the wall,
I'm part of it
almost, in it
almost, a figure shimmering;
but I don't belong, I don't fit,
for it but not of it
I'll stick around
to see what happens.

A New Light

WILLIAM
HAWKINS

For seeing, a
brightness within,
a luminous centre

for knowing
where to see
where seeing is—

the movement
beyond the darkened window,
beyond the yard,
is seized;
it returns
knowing all along
that's me, yes,
there I am
there too.

Spring Rain

This black life
this conversing with shadows

& what about reality
or economic aspects, restricting movement,
halting growth
or the children in a room apart
torturing themselves?

are we not mutations
reconciling diverse things?

is not water
a symbol of life
& life of death?

is not that haze
before my eyes
spring rain?

Arcanum One

and in the morning the king loved you most
and wrote your name with a sun and a beetle
and a crooked ankh, and in the morning
you wore gold mainly, and the king adorned you
with many more names

beside fountains, both of you slender
as women, circled and walked together
like bracelets circling water, both of you
slender as women, wrote your names with
beetles and with suns, and spoke together
in the golden mornings

and the king entered your body
into the bracelet of his name
and you became a living syllable
in his golden script, and your body
escaped from me like founting water
all the daylong

but in the evenings you wrote my name
with a beetle and a moon, and lay upon me
like a long broken necklace which had fallen
from my throat, and the king loved you
most in the morning, and his glamorous love
lay lengthwise along us all the evening

The Caravan

GWENDOLYN
MACEWEN

precede me into this elusive country,
travel the tracks of my old laughter,
tame this landscape, and I will follow after—
yet do not let this desert inherit you,
absorb your caravan into sand—
(which is your body, which is the land?)
O love elude me, this recurring journey
darkens my speech, disorients me
forever from my natural country,
while the orient eye decides geography.

bandar abbes, el minya, el gatrun,
taif, dongola, beni abbes . . .
(once, during an eclipse
the polarities of my body argued me out
from an arctic dream
and I journeyed east, and south,
to enter the final africa of your mouth)

my caravan falters, stops and starts,
its tracks upon the sand are arabesque;
this night is a dream of jackals
and disorient, I cannot decide which turn is best,
and so I circle, so I dance—
(precede me into this elusive country)
always this place, this latitude escapes me

The Thing is Violent

GWENDOLYN
MACEWEN

Self, I want you now to be
violent and without history
for we've rehearsed too long our ceremonial ballet
and I fear my calm against your exquisite rage.

I do not fear that I will go mad
but that I may not, and the shadows of my sanity
blacken out your burning; act once
and you need not act again—
give me no ceremony, scars are not pain.

The thing is violent, nothing precedes it,
it has no meaning before or after—
sweet wounds which burn like stars,
stigmata of the self's own holiness,
appear and plot new zodiacs upon the flesh.

ANDRÉ
MAJOR
b. 1942

Verte ma parole

nous disions malades
'c'est la mer qui dicte aux rivages leurs visages
et si l'hiver vient nous nous établirons sans colère
dans sa saison'

—esclaves nous fermions les yeux sur nos
    chaînes—

le mal de ce pays m'arrachait à ma verdure
(je parle d'une terre froide à nourrir de brûlures
 je parle pour les pauvres qui la maudissent
 je parle pour qui les passe innocent dans la
    machine à épuisement)

ni orgueil ni peur
le sang libéré de sa solitude
ne craint pas les démentis de tous les vents

ANDRÉ
MAJOR

mon pays plus seul que nos frissons
ravagé par le froid la croix et le silence
mon pays cœur de ma haine
nous avons survécu à la déroute des glaces
nous avons survécu à la mort

(je reprends plaisir aux feuillages
aux vents des plages
et aux baisers)

je suis le chant la courbe brisée de la semaine
l'œuf chaque matin et le café
me réjouir du seul plaisir d'être aimé du soleil
voilà l'homme que je suis
quand ne me bouscule plus le souffle de mes frères

je suis franc comme la tornade
comme l'oiseau blessé
pourtant je suis taureau parmi les insectes
quand libre comme le feu j'aime ce qui passe
—l'épaisseur des rêves en mes yeux
je m'arrache le cœur dans un baiser—

toi mon amie qui habites le doux rire de l'érable
mes mains te donnent plus de lumière que le
jour   l'été la santé des sapinages le parfum de
ton sourire tu rends mon amour à la chaleur du
midi pour que j'y reprenne sève
voici le temps des seins
mousse à nourrir de baisers
voici le temps des régions où brûle la rumeur de
    la caresse

le paysage m'habite cruel
et verte verte ma parole
—blessure donnée à mon pays—

Toute douceur d'une fille

ANDRÉ
MAJOR

une fille douce m'aime
que je gonfle de chaleur

une fille douce ruine ma solitude
une fille et sa douceur
je l'aime pour la nuit qu'elle écarte de mes yeux
je l'aime   baiser ininterrompu des cœurs
lourdeur de mon regard sur la fragilité de sa joie

je l'aime dans la révolte de mes muscles et de son
    sang
je l'aime dans la perte des choses
je l'aime pour recommencer le monde selon sa loi

une fille douce en ce pays de froid
rachète le silence
et je m'instaure cratère au cœur du pôle
hanches et joues ma miséricorde
je visite un brasier et j'y romps mon accablement

une fille douce mon flanc comblé
je lui dis la seule parole qui naisse
du mystère de l'arbre et de la fleur
—ciel ouvert à la course des mains—

l'amour seul rêve justifiable
en nos yeux frontières indéracinables

une fille douce
ce pays me la rend divine

b. 1942

Indicatif présent

Ville dans le bitume Feu de bengale et de plaisir
Élégie électrique
La chair crue des néons ensorcelle la nuit
Avec des cris de jazz
Au fond des ruelles de grands nègres lessivent
    l'amour

Ils ont des mains d'acier
Des sexes de bambou
Ils violent les blanches et sont le désespoir
C'est la rhapsodie du malheur
Avec les phares des autos les incendies de la
    lumière
Qui se réverbèrent aux mille vitres des buildings
Icebergs échoués aux trottoirs

Et moi je marche sous la pluie
Je rêve de filles et de merveilles
Et de musiques désolées
J'ai aux lèvres le goût de pleurer et d'aimer

Un Enfant du pays

(I)

J'ai désappris le chant

Jusqu'à hier je chante—dès l'aube—il n'y a pas si
              loin de la mère au poème
Du poème au pays
Mais fausse était ma joie
Faux le pays
Si l'amour est en berne

Fausse était cette mère aux ongles biseautés ANDRÉ
J'étais rivé BROCHU
À mille doigts à mille absences
'Mère tu m'as livré cru aux ronces
Mère tu as versé le kérosène et l'abandon sur mes
    bûchers
Mère tu as forcé un à un les retranchements de
    mon âme plaie bée . . .'
J'étais rivé à la terreur de mes clapiers
Mon chant était absence dans la plénitude du jour
Ne jouait que d'absence

J'ai désappris le chant l'enchantement

(II)

Que chanterais-je les moissons qui me sont
    interdites
Les paradis couleur de clair de lune de l'amour
Nulle amour ne m'attend je suis couleur de terre
J'ai la cendre aux fesses et au cœur
J'ai plein d'injures contre Dieu
Nulle amour ne m'attend au détour de mes ans
Mon pays a vendu son honneur et son pain
Je n'ai pas d'âme à perdre et le ciel est trop loin
Je n'ai que la terreur d'être trop vain
Chaque cri m'est compté
Chaque silence
Je n'ai que mon espoir à jeter aux chiens
J'ai tué ma mère un soir de juin
Je n'ai que mon pays à aimer   renier

Ô mon pays ô mon opprobe

(III)

Par contre   or   cependant
Là-bas s'insurge l'héritage
Par contre   or   cependant
Là-bas tonnent les bombes des enfants.

L'Espoir pays sauvé

ANDRÉ
BROCHU

Je me disais Je ne suis pas poète
Je n'ai pas cœur aux larmes aux chansons
Et je m'ennuyais très malin

Je me mirais aux vitres du silence
J'aimais aussi et j'étais bête
J'aimais moi-même en cheveux longs

Regards vains perdus traqués oubliés
Sentinelles de mes rêves
Regards hautes vigies de ma terreur

Je me disais Je ne suis pas poète
Et je marchais sans lendemains
Quand soudain
L'ESPOIR
L'espoir en coup de feu
L'espoir comme un éclat de bombe au ventre de la
     peur
Comme la peur tant il est neuf
L'espoir d'étreindre l'aube dans mes bras une fois
     l'aube délivrée
L'espoir pays sauvé

Regards vaines terreurs dans les vignes du songe
Je vous ai consignés dans les vitrines du passé
Et aveugle je marche et aveugle je crie
L'amour en bandoulière et le fusil au poing
J'ai lassé ma tendresse où je l'avais trahie
J'ai trahi confiance bonheur et pardon
Et je m'avance au pas de la colère
Vers l'homme qui se lève au bout de l'horizon
Homme de mon pays frère de ma colère
Homme ma seule déraison

Et je criais je crie à toutes sentinelles
VIVE LA RÉVOLUTION

Little Falls

And the voice said : Walk
upriver then
you will find her
at Little Falls

where I had
left her, ankles
amid flow
walking the precipice

brazen, she was
not afraid to fall
or that she would fall
down

as the water as
I did once fall
years later, walking
upriver, the rifle

clattered & fell
gouged by the rock
and I hurt my knee
while hunting

I had meant to
speak of an old woman
whose hair . . .

and of a bend in the river where . . .

and of a tree whose leaves hang over · · ·

It was all
mirrored there

Poem

ROBERT
HOGG

In its going down, the moon
has slipped through my fingers

I am left with the memory
the embarrassment
of reaching

In this darkness
is there nothing but myself
and the heaviness of night
as it weighs upon me?

How I have denied your nearness
the weight of your arm on my waist
your warmth up against my back

I am turned away
as always
reaching for the moon
and calling on the night
to take me

Love does not brook such division
is born of itself
out of nothing
is the act of itself
as Dawn is
not of the sun
but of its own rising

Eros and Eos have joined hands this morning
and we, who are less familiar
awake in ourselves
the distance that belies our bed

O Love
let us get out of our separate heads this morning

It is late in the year
and the leaves have begun to fall

MICHAEL
ONDAATJE

b. 1943

A House Divided

This midnight breathing
heaves with no sensible rhythm
is fashioned by no metronome.
Your body
eager for an extra yard of bed
reconnoitres and outflanks;
I bend in peculiar angles.

This nightly battle is fought with subtleties:
you get pregnant I'm sure
just for extra ground
—immune from kicks now.

Inside you now's another
thrashing like a fish
swinging, fighting
for its inch already.

INDEX OF AUTHORS

Acorn, Milton   262–4
Anderson, Patrick   167–73
Atwood, Margaret
  401–11
Avison, Margaret   207–19

Beissel, Henry   319–22
Birney, Earle   59–70
Bowering, George   360–4
Brochu, André   419–21

Choquette, Robert   71–7
Cohen, Leonard   356–9
Colombo, John Robert
  376–9

Daniells, Roy   46–8
DesRochers, Alfred
  39–46
Dudek, Louis   219–27

Everson, Ronald   55–6

Filion, Jean-Paul   288–90
Finch, Robert   28–30
Ford, R. A. D.   174–6

Garneau, Saint-Denys
  138–47
Garneau, Sylvain   329–32
Giguère, Roland   299–306
Glassco, John   104–13

Godbout, Jacques   350–5
Godin, Gérald   397–400
Gotlieb, Phyllis   277–9
Grandbois, Alain   30–9
Grandmont, Éloi de
  251–4
Grier, Eldon   194–7
Gustafson, Ralph   121–4

Hawkins, William
  412–13
Hébert, Anne   185–94
Hénault, Gilles   240–50
Hertel, François   78–85
Hine, Daryl   364–9
Hogg, Robert   422–3

Johnston, George   160–2
Jonas, George   369–70
Jones, D. G.   307–14

Kearns, Lionel   387–8
Klein, A. M.   90–104
Knight, David   280–5

Lalonde, Michèle   379–83
Lapointe, Gatien   332–9
Lapointe, Paul-Marie
  293–9
Lasnier, Rina   178–85
Layton, Irving   149–59
Le Pan, Douglas   162–7

INDEX OF AUTHORS

Livesay, Dorothy   114–20
Lowry, Malcolm   85–9

MacEwen, Gwendolyn
   414–16
Macpherson, Jay   340–4
Major, André   416–18
Mandel, Eli   259–62
Miller, Peter   236–9
Morin, Paul   12–18

Newlove, John   389–96
Nowlan, Alden   344–7

Ondaatje, Michael   424
Ouellette, Fernand   326–8

Page, P.K.   197–204
Paradis, Suzanne   383–7
Pilon, Jean-Guy   322–6
Pratt, E. J.   1–12
Purdy, Alfred   228–36

Reaney, James   271–7

Rosenblatt, Joe   348–9
Ross, W. W. E.   18–21
Routier, Simone   56–9

Scott, F. R.   21–7
Scott, Peter Dale   314–18
Smith, A. J. M.   48–54
Souster, Raymond   254–8
Sparshott, Francis   268–71

Trottier, Pierre   264–8

Vigneault, Gilles   291–3

Waddington, Miriam
   204–7
Watson, Wilfred   134–7
Webb, Phyllis   285–7
Wevill, David   371–5
Whalley, George   176–8
Wilkinson, Anne   124–33
Woodcock, George
   147–9